Labrador Retrievers For Dummies®

P9-ELT-570

Finding a Good Dog Trainer or Canine Behavioral Consultant

- ✔ Ask for recommendations from friends, neighbors, and relatives who have friendly, well-behaved dogs.
- ✔ Ask the opinion of pet professionals, such as veterinarians, vet techs, groomers, boarding kennel managers, humane societies, and rescue groups.
- ✔ Call the Association of Pet Dog Trainers at 1-800-PET-DOGS to ask for the names of dog trainers and canine behavior consultants who use positive training methods, such as lure-and-reward and clicker training (see Chapter 10).
- ✔ Join one of the doggy e-mail lists listed in the Appendix.
- ✔ Expect a good dog trainer/canine behavior consultant to understand how dogs learn and to communicate with you — in terms you understand — about how to manage and train your Lab.
- ✔ Ask about experience and ask for references. And check them! A good dog trainer/canine behavior consultant will have extensive experience educating owners and their pets.
- ✔ Ask about correction styles. A good dog trainer/canine behavior consultant doesn't advocate or use physical punishment (shock collars, choke chains, prong collars, leash jerks, or hitting).
- ✔ Expect fun! A good dog trainer/canine behavior consultant gives you the feeling that training will be fun for you and your Labrador!

Healthy Foods Your Lab Will Love

Your Lab loves to eat! It's your job to keep her at the proper weight for optimum health. The following five foods are excellent occasional additions to a bowl of high-quality dog food. (Reserve the eggs and oil for very active Labs who aren't overweight and don't offer these higher fat choices more often than once per week.)

- ✔ Small pieces of raw or cooked carrots
- ✔ Small pieces of raw apples
- ✔ One or two tablespoons of plain, nonfat yogurt
- ✔ Half of a cooked egg
- ✔ One teaspoon of canola oil

For Dummies: Bestselling Book Series for Beginners

Labrador Retrievers For Dummies®

Understanding the Anatomy of a Lab

Use the following figure to understand the terminology of the breed standard.

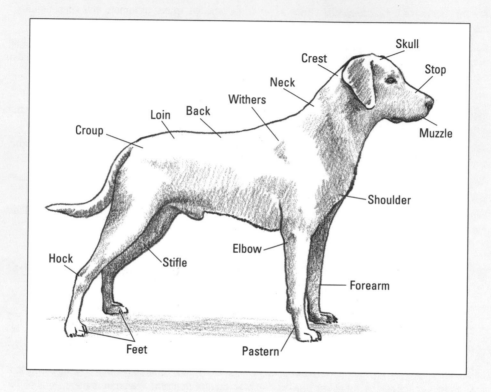

Wiley, the Wiley Publishing logo, For Dummies, the Dummies Man logo, the For Dummies Bestselling Book Series logo and all related trade dress are trademarks or registered trademarks of Wiley Publishing, Inc. All other trademarks are property of their respective owners.

For Dummies: Bestselling Book Series for Beginners

TM

References for the Rest of Us!®

BESTSELLING BOOK SERIES

Do you find that traditional reference books are overloaded with technical details and advice you'll never use? Do you postpone important life decisions because you just don't want to deal with them? Then our *For Dummies*® business and general reference book series is for you.

For Dummies business and general reference books are written for those frustrated and hard-working souls who know they aren't dumb, but find that the myriad of personal and business issues and the accompanying horror stories make them feel helpless. *For Dummies* books use a lighthearted approach, a down-to-earth style, and even cartoons and humorous icons to dispel fears and build confidence. Lighthearted but not lightweight, these books are perfect survival guides to solve your everyday personal and business problems.

Already, millions of satisfied readers agree. They have made For Dummies the #1 introductory level computer book series and a best-selling business book series. They have written asking for more. So, if you're looking for the best and easiest way to learn about business and other general reference topics, look to For Dummies to give you a helping hand.

Wiley Publishing, Inc.

5/09

Labrador Retrievers FOR DUMMIES®

by Joel Walton and Eve Adamson

Wiley Publishing, Inc.

Labrador Retrievers For Dummies®

Published by
Wiley Publishing, Inc.
909 Third Avenue
New York, NY 10022
www.wiley.com

Copyright © 2000 by Wiley Publishing, Inc., Indianapolis, Indiana

Published simultaneously in Canada

For general information on our other products and services or to obtain technical support, please contact our Customer Care Department within the U.S. at 800-762-2974, outside the U.S. at 317-572-3993, or fax 317-572-4002.

Wiley also publishes its books in a variety of electronic formats. Some content that appears in print may not be available in electronic books.

Library of Congress Cataloging-in-Publication Data:

Library of Congress Control Number: 00-106338

ISBN: 0-7645-5281-3

Manufactured in the United States of America

10 9

1B/QT/QZ/QS/IN

About the Authors

Joel Walton, his wife, Janet, and their two boys, David and Jimmy, got their first Labrador Retriever, Bart, in September 1969. Bart crossed the Rainbow Bridge in 1981. The Waltons had their first Labrador litter in 1983. Although some Walton Family Labradors have excelled in obedience, drug detection, hunting and hunt tests, and other doggy activities, the Waltons continue to focus on breeding the best possible family pets. Joel has been a member of the Labrador Retriever Club of the Potomac for many years and helped found Lab Rescue of LRCP, Inc., serving as their first secretary.

Karen Pryor opened Joel's mind to the science of positive dog training when she passed through the Washington, D.C., area giving her famous "Don't Shoot the Dog" seminars based on her classic book of the same title. In June of 1987, Joel and Janet took Cocoa and her two pups, Bear and Ginger, to Dr. Ian Dunbar's first ever Puppy Training Workshop. Joel immediately adopted lure-and-reward training and stopped using the old-fashioned methods involving punishing dogs by giving them a leash correction with a choke collar when they made a mistake. Joel says it is much more fun to reward dogs when they get it right!

Walton Family Dog Training LLC was founded in 1986. Joel trains families in the Washington, D.C., area to train their puppies and dogs. Joel provides classes for aspiring positive dog trainers and operates five Internet e-mail lists for pet dog trainers and pet dog owners. Joel and Janet continue to breed a few Labrador litters each year. They share their home with over 25 Labradors and one Rottweiler.

Eve Adamson is a freelance writer in Iowa City, Iowa, who specializes in pet and holistic health subjects. She is a frequent contributor to *Dog Fancy* magazine and many other pet-related publications and a member of the Dog Writer's Association of America. She holds an MFA in creative writing from the University of Florida and has authored and co-authored many books.

About Howell Book House
Committed to the Human/Companion Animal Bond

Thank you for choosing a book brought to you by the pet experts at Howell Book House, a division of Wiley Publishing, Inc. And welcome to the family of pet owners who've put their trust in Howell books for nearly 40 years!

Pet ownership is about relationships — the bonds people form with their dogs, cats, horses, birds, fish, small mammals, reptiles, and other animals. Howell Book House/Wiley understands that these are some of the most important relationships in life, and that it's vital to nurture them through enjoyment and education. The happiest pet owners are those who know they're taking the best care of their pets — and with Howell books owners have this satisfaction. They're happy, educated owners, and as a result, they have happy pets, and that enriches the bond they share.

Howell Book House was established in 1961 by Mr. Elsworth S. Howell, an active and proactive dog fancier who showed English Setters and judged at the prestigious Westminster Kennel Club show in New York. Mr. Howell based his publishing program on strength of content, and his passion for books written by experienced and knowledgeable owners defined Howell Book House and has remained true over the years. Howell's reputation as the premier pet book publisher is supported by the distinction of having won more awards from the Dog Writers Association of America than any other publisher. Howell Book House/Wiley has over 400 titles in publication, including such classics as The American Kennel Club's *Complete Dog Book,* the *Dog Owner's Home Veterinary Handbook, Blessed Are the Brood Mares,* and *Mother Knows Best: The Natural Way to Train Your Dog.*

When you need answers to questions you have about any aspect of raising or training your companion animals, trust that Howell Book House/Wiley has the answers. We welcome your comments and suggestions, and we look forward to helping you maximize your relationships with your pets throughout the years.

The Howell Book House Staff

Dedication

To you, kind reader, who will be a better Lab owner because you read this book.

Authors' Acknowledgments

Many people and dogs helped to make this book a reality, so we would like to thank them all generally and a few special individuals in particular.

Thanks to Janet, my wife, the hardest working person I have ever known. Untold people and dogs are happy because of her efforts. And she has put up with me for over 33 years! I also thank Cocoa, who taught me that you cannot train all dogs by jerking them around; Ian Dunbar, who taught me how to train dogs without jerking them around; and Gus Viergutz, my father-in-law, who taught me that you have to be smarter than the dog. This book would not have been possible without Dominique De Vito's faith and Eve Adamson's skill.

Joel Walton

Thanks to my kiddos, Angus and Emmett, who demonstrate on a daily basis how much training children has in common with training dogs. To my parents, Richard and Penny Watson, whose grandparenting skills allowed me to finish this book — I could not possibly have done it without them! Thanks to Joel for his good nature and great knowledge and to Madelyn Larsen, Dominique De Vito, and Scott Prentzas for their support and patience. Thanks to Marylou Zarbock for always taking time out of an impossible schedule to answer my questions, and for always having an answer. And, thanks to my dog Sally, who sits under my desk when I work and in my bed when I sleep. She may not be a Lab, but she is all dog, and a continual inspiration. Last of all, I send out my heartfelt thanks and love to the Chewdog, Whiskey, Bart, Valis, Ed and Zeke, all gone, but never, ever forgotten.

Eve Adamson

Publisher's Acknowledgments

We're proud of this book; please send us your comments through our online registration form located at www.dummies.com/register.

Some of the people who helped bring this book to market include the following:

Acquisitions, Editorial, and Media Development

Project Editors: Tere Drenth, Kelly Ewing

Senior Acquisitions Editor: Scott Prentzas

General Reviewer: Pat Miller

Editorial Manager: Pamela Mourouzis

Editorial Administrator: Michelle Hacker

Production

Project Coordinator: Nancee Reeves

Layout and Graphics: Jason Guy, Angela F. Hunckler, Tracy K. Oliver, Jill Piscitelli, Rashell Smith, Erin Zeltner

Special Art: Barbara Frake

Proofreaders: Laura Albert, Susan Moritz, Nancy L. Reinhardt, Marianne Santy, Jeannie Smith, Ethel M. Winslow

Indexer: Sherry Massey

Special Help
Dominique C. De Vito

Publishing and Editorial for Consumer Dummies
Diane Graves Steele, Vice President and Publisher, Consumer Dummies
Joyce Pepple, Acquisitions Director, Consumer Dummies
Kristin A. Cocks, Product Development Director, Consumer Dummies
Michael Spring, Vice President and Publisher, Travel
Brice Gosnell, Publishing Director, Travel
Suzanne Jannetta, Editorial Director, Travel

Publishing for Technology Dummies
Richard Swadley, Vice President and Executive Group Publisher
Andy Cummings, Vice President and Publisher

Composition Services
Gerry Fahey, Vice President of Production Services
Debbie Stailey, Director of Composition Services

Contents at a Glance

Cartoons at a Glance

By Rich Tennant

page 5

page 115

page 31

page 195

page 171

page 223

Fax: 978-546-7747
E-mail: richtennant@the5thwave.com
World Wide Web: www.the5thwave.com

Table of Contents

Introduction

● ●

*W*e love dogs in general and Labrador Retrievers in particular, and we're guessing that you do, too! Our love for this remarkable (and remarkably popular) breed compels us to share our knowledge with you. We hope to help ensure the happiness and health of your Lab, and to benefit future generations of Labs and Lab owners.

About This Book

Whether you're a Labrador Retriever owner, a Labrador Retriever owner-to-be, or someone just beginning to get curious about this wonderful breed, we congratulate you on finding this book. You're buying a book written by an old father and a young mother. Neither one of us was born with total knowledge about dogs in general or Labs in particular, and we continue to learn from every dog and every dog lover we meet, experts and "regular" owners alike. But we've learned a fair amount over the years and hope to pass on some of this knowledge to you.

We may do other things with our dogs — breeding, training, showing, playing — but we are first and foremost proud pet owners. What better task for humans and dogs than to be great companions for each other? And what better dog for humans than a Labrador Retriever? Labrador Retrievers are truly a dog-lover's dog. They are gentle, joyful, and above all, eager to please you. Who could ask for a sweeter package? And who could resist that friendly Labrador Retriever grin? Not us!

As you read this book, you may notice that we're very much in favor of preventing problems through good planning and management, rather than fixing problems after they occur. You don't like to punish your Lab, and you'd rather not punish him, especially for failing to do something you never taught him to do! We don't like punishing dogs for the mistakes of their owners, either.

We also feel that you and your Lab should have as much fun as possible together, and we want you to develop a warm, friendly, rewarding relationship that will grow and endure for years to come. So get comfortable, kick back, relax, and enjoy this book. We provide you with the knowledge and the skills you need to help your canine member of the family become the best dog he can be and the best friend you've ever had.

Foolish Assumptions

We don't assume much about you in this book. If you're looking for your very first dog, this book is for you. If you've owned — or even bred or trained — dogs for years, this book is also for you.

We do assume, however, that you aren't hoping to find miracle cures to produce instant, perfect behavior; that you realize that dogs aren't humans and can't possibly know what you want until you make it clear to them; and that you're open to training and management suggestions that don't involve jerking, yanking, or smacking dogs around. (Nobody deserves to be treated that way.)

How This Book Is Organized

We've organized this book into six distinct parts to help you find what you need as easily as possible.

Part I: Just the Facts, Ma'am

In this part, we give you all the basics in one easy-to-read-in-one-sitting summary. If, after reading this part, you want to explore any of the subjects explained here in depth, flip to the Table of Contents or the Index for more information.

Part II: Finding and Living with a Labrador Retriever

In this part, we help you to find the dog who will best match your household and give you some practical hands-on hints for how to live happily with a Labrador Retriever.

Part III: Training Your Lab with the MRE System

If you haven't heard of the MRE system, you're missing out on a great way to manage (M), relate (R) to, and educate (E) your Lab. This part goes through each of the three steps, with easy-to-follow steps and real-life advice on how to bring out the best in your Lab.

Part IV: Your Lab: A Member of the Family!

Your Lab is part of your family! This part shows you how to involve your Lab in your life, travel with your dog, and exercise with your Lab.

Part V: Showing Off and Having Fun

Labs aren't just for sitting around and looking pretty. You can show or work your Lab and have fun in the process. Labs love to keep busy, and this part shows you how to give your Lab (and you) something fun to do.

Part VI: The Part of Tens

Ten is such a satisfying number, so we decided to give you ten great training tips, ten ways to connect with your Lab on a daily basis, and ten ways your Lab can make a difference in the world. We could probably have listed 50 of each, but we didn't think our editor would let us.

Icons Used in This Book

While you're reading the book, keep an eye out for these icons that highlight helpful tips, interesting facts, important cautions, and useful activities.

These are tips, tricks, techniques, and other helpful tidbits.

These are notables that you'll want to tape to your 'fridge because remembering them and putting them into practice means building a better Lab-human relationship.

These warnings caution you about pitfalls to watch for as you live, play, and learn with your Lab.

With these icons, you'll find checklists, helpful questions, step-by-step instructions, and other fun activities to try with your Lab.

Where to Go from Here

Not everybody likes to read a book from start to finish, and you needn't approach this book in such a strict and linear fashion, either. (It was hardly written that way!) You can start anywhere, although we do suggest you read Part II before buying a Lab (if you haven't already bought one), and Part I is always a good overview to help you decide if this breed is for you. We also hope you'll "bone up" on the MRE system in Part III before you begin training your Lab, just to keep your technique consistent. Other than that, go for it, back to front if you like. (Oh, and if you're an orderly type, reading from beginning to end works nicely, too.)

Part I
Just the Facts, Ma'am

The 5th Wave   By Rich Tennant

"Careful Herb – this breed's good at sensing irony."

In this part . . .

So you think a Lab is the dog for you? Well, in this part, we help you make sure that you're the right kind of companion for a Labrador Retriever.

We also fill you in on what to expect from your Lab and what not to expect and also talk about your Lab options (types, colors, ages). Finally, we give you a brief overview of how to care for, train, and compete with a Lab.

Chapter 1

A Match Made in Heaven: You and a Lab?

In This Chapter

▶ Understanding the pros and cons of owning a Lab

▶ Figuring out if you're Lab-owner material

▶ Assessing whether you have the time, energy, money, and space for a Lab

*Y*ou have a picture in your head. A picture of you with your practically perfect dog. You've always preferred big dogs, and the practically perfect dog in your head is sturdy, strong, and energetic, yet gentle and completely in tune to your needs, your whims, and your every move. Maybe you imagine the two of you jogging in the park, your dog in a perfect heel, watching out for your safety and enjoying your company. Perhaps you imagine curling up on the sofa with your cozy, beautiful dog as a soft pillow and trustworthy confidante. Maybe you picture teaching your dog the ins and outs of obedience, agility, flyball, and Frisbee or simply "Sit," "Stay," and "Fetch the Sunday paper, please."

Whatever your dream of the practically perfect dog, we're guessing that if you're flipping through the pages of this book, you have a Labrador Retriever in mind. After all, the Labrador Retriever is the most popular dog in the United States according to American Kennel Club registrations. Labs are beautiful, friendly, adaptable, easygoing, brave, loyal, dependable, and intelligent. What could be better?

What's the AKC?

The *American Kennel Club (AKC)* is a not-for-profit organization, established in 1884, devoted to the advancement of purebred dogs. The AKC maintains a record of all registered dogs; publishes ideal standards for each recognized breed; sponsors a variety of dog events including dog shows, obedience and field trials, agility and the Canine Good Citizen program; and publishes educational information.

What a Lab Can Bring to Your Life

Because Labrador Retrievers were bred to work with and take directions from humans, your pup can grow to be a wonderful companion, more reliable than most people! If you keep him out of trouble, teach him the basics of what you want him to do, and make his good behavior rewarding for him, he will compensate you with years of devoted friendship.

What a Lab Can't Do

Some people dream of getting a dog for all the wrong reasons. If you're looking for a way to get dates, look cool, or have an animal to guard your yard, or if you're hoping for a clone of a previous pet, you may want to rethink whether you are ready for the immense responsibility of pet ownership. Every dog and every Lab is different. Labs need training, attention, exercise, veterinary care, and a regular routine. They are active, boisterous, large, and sometimes overly affectionate animals.

A Lab won't fix your life. But if you're willing to engage in some serious give-and-take, we admit that a Lab may make you a whole lot happier. You probably know a lot of reasons why that practically perfect picture in your head looks an awful lot like a Labrador Retriever. Are your reasons good ones? Perhaps you need to spend a little time examining your motives.

Examine the following statements and circle all those that sound like what you've been thinking when considering bringing a Labrador Retriever into your home. Be honest now!

- ✔ I want a Lab because I used to have a Lab in the past, and I want another one just like her.
- ✔ I want a Lab because my friend/neighbor/coworker/boss has one, and I want one just like her.
- ✔ Everyone likes Labs, so if I get a Lab, everyone will like me!
- ✔ I want a big dog for protection.
- ✔ I want a good hunting dog.
- ✔ Labs are easy. I won't have to spend time on training because they quickly pick up on what to do.
- ✔ I think they're so cute!
- ✔ I feel a kinship with the breed and feel ready to spend the time and energy necessary to raise and train my dog so that she can become a companion and friend for life.

Do any of the above sound like you? Well, guess what? Only one of the items on the above list is a good reason to bring a Labrador Retriever into your life. You guessed it, the last one. If you're interested in a Lab for any of the other reasons, the following sections can help you debunk these myths.

One Lab isn't like another Lab

No matter how many Labs you've known, admired, or loved in the past, the Lab you bring home won't be the same. Dogs, like people, are individuals, and although breeds have certain consistent characteristics, personalities can be as different as black and white (or black, yellow, and chocolate). You probably wouldn't make the mistake of saying that, for example, everyone from Minnesota is easygoing or everyone from Idaho loves to go running. Why should all Labrador Retrievers be the same? They shouldn't, and they aren't.

It's unfair to expect any dog to conform to some idea you have of how some other dog once behaved. You have to get to know your own dog and love her for who she is.

A Lab won't make you popular

As far as a Lab being your ticket to popularity, although many people like Labrador Retrievers, not everyone does. Besides, your dog won't influence people's opinion of you. If you're a good person and a good dog owner, people might think better of you because of it. But if you're generally irritable, impatient, or unkind (or worse, an animal-hater), getting a dog won't fool anyone, especially if they sense that your dog fears or distrusts you.

A Lab isn't the best guard dog

Although some dogs are better protectors than others, getting any dog solely for protection is a bad reason to get a dog. Dogs are thinking, feeling, responsive beings who deserve more than a job as a security guard. They deserve to be members of the family, and they need your commitment of time, energy, and love. Besides, Labs have less of a guard-dog instinct than do some other breeds.

However, if you want a Lab for all the right reasons and you also want some protection, get a dark-colored (black or chocolate) Lab. For some reason, dark-colored dogs seem to serve as a better deterrent than yellow dogs. People tend to ask, "Is she friendly?" when they meet a black or chocolate Lab, whereas people tend to assume yellow Labs are always friendly. Don't ask us why!

Labrador Retrievers come in three colors: black, yellow and chocolate. Apart from a permissible white chest spot, the American Kennel Club (AKC) breed standard allows solid colors only.

A Lab isn't a cinch to train

Labs are intelligent and ready to please, but no dog is easy to train. All dogs require time, energy, and consistency if they are to become well-trained, and Labs are no exception. If you don't train your Lab, chances are she will end up behaving in ways you don't appreciate. You may even end up feeling that you have to give up the dog.

A Lab is more than a hunter

We can't deny that Labs are excellent retrievers for hunting purposes, but if they aren't also beloved family members, you won't be making the most of your Lab.

Labs are cute — but they need your devotion

Sure, Labs are cute. Heck, we'd even say adorable. But that's no reason to buy a dog. But you say you feel a kinship with the breed and are ready to spend the time and energy necessary to raise and train your Labrador Retriever so that she can become a companion and friend for life? Now we're talking!

Determining Whether a Lab Wants You!

You may be sure that you are ready for a dog, but is a Lab the dog for you? Sure, they're popular. Lots of people have them. But few people should have them and are able to bring out the best in them. You could be one of those precious few, the God's-gift-to-Labrador-Retrievers kind of human companion. Or maybe you at least have the potential. (Humans usually need some training, too!)

Asking hard questions

Take our test and see if you're meant for a Lab:

1. How would you describe your lifestyle?

    a. Weekend warrior

    b. Home body

    c. Desk jockey

    d. Party animal

    e. Couch potato

2. How would you describe your energy level?

    a. Volleyball league? Office softball? Running club? You're there!

    b. Pretty high, as long as the activity is pleasant and enjoyable, such as long walks around the neighborhood or in a park on a nice day.

    c. You exercise to stay healthy, but you don't enjoy it. You may wonder whether exercise would be more fun with a dog in tow.

    d. Football? Basketball? Hockey? What channel is it on? Better yet, what sports bar is showing the game?

    e. You read this book, and every book, about two pages at a time because you keep falling asleep.

3. How do you feel about getting periodically slapped with a huge, wagging tail or having your knees buckled by a rambunctious dog body barreling by?

    a. Bring it on! Sounds like a dog that would be great at jogging or catching a Frisbee.

    b. The more tail wagging and enthusiasm, the better. It means my dog is happy!

    c. I guess I could put up with it for a few months, until my dog matures and can be trained.

    d. *My* Lab would never do that.

    e. Hmm, I'm not sure something like that wouldn't knock me right off my feet. Can I order a Lab that just sleeps most of the time?

4. How often is someone home at your house?

   a. You work at home and are there most of the day.

   b. You work but could come home for lunch, and your evenings and weekends are usually free or filled with some dog-friendly activity.

   c. You're away for about ten hours per weekday, and then when you get home, you have a quick dinner and collapse in front of the TV to unwind.

   d. You often go out after work with coworkers for drinks, a few rounds of pool, or office gossip over nachos and pretzels. Weekends are the time for a social life.

   e. You work long hours and are at home so seldom that you wonder why you bother to pay for electricity! When you do get home, you usually go straight to bed.

5. Where do you live?

   a. Out in the country on several fenced acres — dog heaven!

   b. In a house in town with a large fenced yard.

   c. In an apartment or townhouse with a small, enclosed yard.

   d. In an apartment or condo in the city with no yard.

   e. In a place where they don't allow dogs, but you're thinking you could sneak one in.

6. What do you see happening in your life in the next ten years?

   a. You've got a good job, lots of friends, and many commitments. You're not going anywhere.

   b. You may move, get married, or change jobs, but you couldn't see your life without a dog and wouldn't live somewhere that wasn't dog-friendly.

   c. You hope to meet someone, maybe get married, maybe have kids and certainly advance in your career. If a dog doesn't fit in later, you'll cross that bridge when you come to it.

   d. Your job is your life. Wherever it takes you, you're willing to go.

   e. You don't like to make a habit of thinking beyond tomorrow. You're a go-with-the-flow sort of person.

7. How is your financial situation?

   a. No problems. You make plenty to support yourself and your family. If your dog needs medical care, you're willing to do whatever it takes.

   b. You spend pretty much what you make, but you save a little, and in emergencies, you always find a way to meet the bills.

   c. Pretty tight, but dogs aren't expensive, are they?

   d. You certainly wouldn't spend more than $40 or $50 dollars at a veterinarian. After all, it's just a dog.

   e. You think you'll be able to convince the phone company to turn the phone back on sometime in the next month. Meanwhile, no phone means the creditors can't keep bugging you!

8. How do you spend your leisure time?

   a. You're as active as possible: hiking, camping, biking, swimming, jogging, or just being outside in the fresh air.

   b. You like to go new places and try new things: relaxing on a beach, exploring a new town, going on car trips, and so on.

   c. You get things done around the house or simply catch up on your sleep or the soaps. You pretty much prefer to stick close to home.

   d. When you're not at work, you like to go out and party with your friends.

   e. Leisure time? What leisure time?

9. How do you imagine a dog fitting into your life?

   a. Companion and pal on your many adventures.

   b. Confidante, best friend, and family member, always with you whether you're taking a walk or taking a nap.

   c. A pet to keep you company, make you feel safe, and generally add to the atmosphere of your home.

   d. Home security system or backyard guard.

   e. A dog is a dog. They hang out in the backyard and eat dog food. What more is there to say?

10. What is the most important thing to know before getting a dog?

   a. What their physical and emotional needs will be.

   b. The characteristics and tendencies of the particular breed.

   c. What to feed them and what medical care they'll need.

   d. What kind of dog will take the least effort.

   e. Where to get a free one.

Evaluating the answers

What kind of a potential Labrador Retriever companion are you? Tally up your answers and check your profile.

✔ If you had mostly As and/or Bs, congratulations. You'll probably make a great Labrador Retriever companion. You have a reasonably high energy level and can provide your dog with the activity she requires. You also value dogs as family members, are willing to find out what their needs are, and are willing to meet those needs. Whether you're an athlete extraordinaire or the stay-at-home type, you understand that dogs aren't impulse purchases but long-term commitments, and you're ready to take the plunge. Of course, that doesn't mean you know it all, so don't chuck this book aside just yet. There's always more to discover about your canine companion, so keep reading.

✔ If you had mostly Cs, you have potential, but you have some misconceptions about Labrador Retrievers and/or pet ownership. You may not be quite active enough or home often enough to be the ideal dog owner. You also may not be fully aware of the commitment involved. Maybe you grew up with a dog but your Mom or Dad was responsible for her care and maintenance. You see a dog as a pet that would be nice to have around, but shouldn't be too much trouble. You like dogs, however, and if you're willing to make some changes in your life, a dog may become a valuable and beloved family member. Perhaps adopting an older dog that doesn't require the rigorous attention and training of a puppy is best for you, but you still need to do some research about Labs and be sure you're ready for an active, exuberant dog that requires your love and constant attention.

✔ If you had mostly Ds and Es, think twice about bringing home a Labrador Retriever. We're not saying you absolutely shouldn't have one, but your lifestyle isn't ideal for a dog, and your ideas about dog ownership could use some revamping. Of course, that's what this book is for.

Got the time?

You may feel ready to take on the responsibility of a dog, but you may not realize how much time a Lab — or any social animal — requires. Your Lab will need daily training sessions, lots of purposeful socialization as a puppy, and time to simply hang around with you. You and your Lab need to form a relationship, and any successful relationship takes time. If you aren't home very often or have too much on your plate when you are home, enjoy a friend's Labrador Retriever now and then. Don't take on your own until you can pencil in lots of time for your new family member. You wouldn't have a child if you didn't have the time to raise it well, would you? Give your Lab the same courtesy.

Got the energy?

Labs, unlike some other dogs, require as much energy as time. If you're a certified couch potato, your Lab may adjust, but inactive dogs (like inactive people) are less healthy, and Labs that aren't provided outlets for their energy (like catching a ball, shown in Figure 1-1) may become destructive. Labs aren't small dogs and can't get sufficient activity running back and forth across the living room like a Chihuahua. (If your Lab did get its exercise this way, you'd probably soon be in need of some new furniture!)

Figure 1-1:
Labs can play fetch much longer than most humans can.

©Ron Kimball Photography, Inc.

Well-trained Labs that get sufficient exercise shouldn't be hyperactive and can certainly adapt to different levels of activity, but your Lab will need to be walked at least once a day, taken for occasional swims, and given the opportunity to do lots of retrieving, the thing they love best. If you aren't up to the physical challenge, consider a less active or smaller dog — or perhaps, a cat.

Although active, Labrador Retrievers can easily become overweight. Overfeeding and feeding table scraps can quickly lead to obesity, which is the most common nutritional health problem in dogs, according to many vets. Try using halved baby carrots or small broccoli florets as treats rather than dog biscuits, which are often too caloric to be used daily.

Got the space?

If you don't have the living space for a large dog, don't bring home a Labrador Retriever. The ideal situation is a single-family, detached house with a fenced yard and dog-friendly neighbors or a country home with lots of fenced land. Other situations can work, too, especially if you walk your Lab religiously and train her well. However, if your living space doesn't allow dogs or your apartment walls are paper thin, if you live in a tiny apartment with no yard and can't walk your dog every day, or if you like your home immaculate and value your collection of ceramic figurines or glassware or antique china above all else, please consider another type of dog. Labs need lots of exercise, puppies can sometimes be loud in the middle of the night, and those Lab tails can be downright destructive if your house isn't Lab-proofed.

Got the money?

Purchasing a Labrador Retriever through a breeder can cost anywhere from $300 to $1,000 (more if you want a quality show or field-trial dog). And if you do adopt a Lab from an animal shelter or through a rescue group, you may think that the dog will be cheap — even free. But the cost of acquiring a dog is insignificant compared to the cost of keeping a dog healthy and well-behaved throughout its life.

The cost of health maintenance, including vaccinations, heartworm preventive, parasite control, and regular check-ups, plus the cost of good food, a quality kennel or other enclosure, a supply of chew toys, obedience classes, trainers and/or behaviorists, and any emergency medical costs or treatment for serious health problems or accidents can add up to quite a sum. Can you say "college fund?" If you can barely afford groceries or medical bills for yourself and your own family, don't bring any dog, Lab or otherwise, into your home until you're on a firmer financial footing.

Chapter 2

Finding a Lab to Fit Your Life

● ●

In This Chapter

▶ Understanding two types of Labs: English and field

▶ Taking a look at the three colors: black, chocolate and yellow

▶ Noting differences between the two sexes and the five age groups

● ●

So a Lab is the breed for you. You've decided. You're sure. Congratulations! But wait — slow down — don't race off to get your Labrador Retriever just yet. You still have a few more decisions to make. Not all Labs are the same. You should consider what type of Lab you want, what color, what sex, and what age of dog to bring into your home. This chapter helps you determine those details.

Two Types of Labs

You can find two general types of Labs: the English type and the field type. While these aren't official differences, they are distinct differences when it comes to breeding.

✔ The *English types* are active pups who tend to settle down with good, positive training and can make great family companions. They are the dogs bred for the show ring, with *conformation* (physical appearance) and temperament as first priorities.

✔ The *field types* have lots of field titles in their pedigree and are usually much more active. While just as much Labs as English types, field types have been specifically bred to have the qualities necessary for a successful hunting dog: boundless energy and more endurance than most families want in a pet dog. Remember, field trial champions are like Olympic athletes. Too high an activity level in a family pet isn't desirable unless you plan to put the dog to work doing an extremely active task, such as (as the name suggests) training for field trials.

A *pedigree* is the written record of a dog's ancestry and must go back at least three generations. A *show champion pedigree* means a dog is descended from dogs that have earned champion titles in dog shows. See Chapter 17 for more on showing your Lab.

You want to consider which type of Lab will fit into your life. Check all of the qualities in the following list that appeal to you or are important to you in a dog:

- ✔ I want a dog with a show champion pedigree for showing and breeding.

- ✔ I want a dog with a show champion pedigree so that I can brag about it!

- ✔ I want a dog who won't be more active than I can manage.

- ✔ I want a dog whom I can train to become a well-behaved companion.

- ✔ I want a heavy-duty hunting dog.

- ✔ I want a dog to compete in *field trials* (which test a dog's ability to retrieve — see Chapter 15).

- ✔ I want a dog that I can train to be a good companion, but with whom I can also compete in the higher levels of AKC *obedience trials* (which test dog and owner in performing certain exercises — see Chapter 11).

If you checked any of the first four items, you'll probably want an English Lab. If you checked any of the last three items, look at field Labs, although English Labs also do quite well at obedience trials.

If you're looking for a mellow, pleasant family dog to accompany you on leisurely walks around the block, don't go for the puppy with a pedigree rife with field and utility titles. If your dog is bred to be an ultra-achiever and you aren't willing to do the work it takes to channel that drive, you'll probably end up with a problem on your hands. Instead, consider a dog in good health who has been bred to be an excellent pet.

The English Lab

Although the term *English Lab* doesn't designate an actual sub-breed of Labrador Retriever, it does have meaning to dog people. It refers to a Lab with show dogs in his pedigree. If a dog has earned championship status in the show ring for conformation (being the closest specimen to the breed standard or ideal), he gets a *Ch.* before his name. Lots of Chs in the pedigree indicate that a dog had a lot of ancestors that were also judged to be closest to the ideal of the breed.

To title or not to title

Entering your Lab, whether an English or a field Lab, in obedience trials is a great way to bond with your dog while training him to use his energy constructively and to be well-behaved, useful, and fun. Most dogs can earn an obedience title with a little work. If the obedience bug bites you and you have a particularly high-energy dog, keep up the training and see how much the two of you can achieve. Active dogs need something to do, and training them for such events gives them a purpose as well as an all-important outlet for their energy. Plus, they love to spend their days with you. See Chapter 11 for more information.

And of course, don't forget that Labrador Retrievers are excellent hunting companions. Labs can participate in hunting tests that evaluate aspects of a dog's hunting ability. Check out Chapter 16 for the lowdown on hunting tests.

If showing in conformation and/or breeding Labs is your passion (see Chapter 17), you'll probably want to consider an English Lab. Consider joining your local or regional Labrador Retriever Club (check the Appendix for ways to find local and regional AKC-affiliated clubs or an independent club.) After doing your research, get on a waiting list for that special puppy that will have the potential to earn his Show Championship. If you want to breed your Labrador (and please be sure you're really ready for what is involved — see Chapter 6), get to know one or more excellent breeders and find out as much as you can from them. In every case, make sure your dog comes from a breeder who tests for the common problems that Labs have (more on that in Chapter 4). Then get ready to find out how to handle a show dog, or consider hiring a *professional handler* — someone you hire to handle your dog in the show ring. Handlers are trained to bring out the best in a dog in the ring and can sometimes make the difference between winning and not even placing. Doing your own handling requires some education. Go to dog shows and research the subject to find out more (the Appendix has a list of resources).

Of course, a good family pet needn't have a championship title and needn't even be particularly close to the breed standard in appearance (though he should match the breed standard in personality and temperament). If you're looking for a Lab to join your family, a dog with obedience titles will probably be at least as important as a dog with conformation titles. If you just like the idea of having a dog with a champion pedigree, that's certainly okay (it's your money), but just be sure that isn't the only reason you want a dog. Dogs aren't status symbols — they're living beings who need care and love.

The field Lab

The field Lab (not an official sub-breed, but a description of what purpose the dog was primarily bred to serve) is a great choice for someone who wants to participate actively with his or her dog in field trials and who has money and time to spare. Successful field trial dogs take a lot of training, and you need to learn the ropes, too. Attend some field trial events to see what it's all about. If you love the idea, look for a breeder who has demonstrated success at producing dogs that have done well in field trials. Then start researching, learning, and practicing.

Deciding among Labs of a Different Color (And Gender)

Beyond the type of Lab you choose, you also get to make some more minor decisions. Color and gender are two issues people tend to overemphasize, as far as we're concerned. Better to focus on the individual puppy's or dog's personality and energy level. But if these issues are important to you (or even if they aren't), read on.

Pick a color, any color!

Labrador Retrievers come in three colors: yellow (from light cream to fox red), chocolate, and black — see Figure 2-1, but please keep in mind that the photo is in black and white! (The color photo section, near the center of this book, has pictures of Labs of every color.) According to the breed standard, a small white spot on the chest is permissible. You may prefer a certain color, but don't believe anyone who tells you that any temperament or health differences are related to coat color. Let us repeat: No temperament or health differences are related to coat color in the Labrador Retriever!

Black Labs aren't meaner. Yellow Labs aren't nicer. None of those other things you may have heard are true. Of course, that doesn't mean people won't think your black Lab is more protective or your yellow Lab is the friendliest dog on earth. They probably will; considering that, if you're looking for a dog who will intimidate people, you need to choose a dark-colored Lab. If you want a dog who won't intimidate people and you plan to properly socialize your dog to accept strangers patting him on the head, you may want to go for the lighter color. But that's up to you. As far as how your dog behaves, color doesn't make any difference at all. You're better off basing your decision on a dog's health, temperament, energy level, and other factors (for more on how to choose the right puppy, see Chapter 4).

Figure 2-1:
What color Lab you choose is strictly a matter of personal preference. Whether black, yellow, or chocolate, Labrador Retrievers share the same physical and temperament characteristics.

© *Close Encounters of the Furry Kind*

What makes the Lab unique?

You probably know that Labrador Retrievers aren't the only retrieving dogs: Golden Retrievers, Chesapeake Bay Retrievers, Curly-Coated Retrievers, and Flat-Coated Retrievers are other AKC-approved retriever breeds. What distinguishes the Lab from these other retrievers?

Many retrievers have Newfoundland and spaniels in their backgrounds, and all were bred to aid hunters in retrieving game. Labrador Retrievers, however, are unique in that they were first discovered in Newfoundland, a chillier and icier climate than the British Isles, where most other retrievers were probably developed

(except for the Chesapeake Bay Retriever, an American original). Labs have a shorter coat than some other retrievers, which prevents ice from clinging to the coat when the dog exits the water.

All retrievers should be friendly, intuitive, and willing helpers that learn quickly and are eager to please, but the Labrador Retriever isn't the most popular dog in the United States by accident. Particularly agreeable, trainable, outgoing, and ready to go to any lengths to please his owner, the Lab is a definite charmer and, in many ways, the ideal medium-to-large dog (when properly trained, of course).

Think you've found something exotic and wonderful when a breeder offers you a "rare" white, silver, or golden Lab? Think again. Golden Labs are just another name for yellow Labs (and an incorrect name, at that). The word is sometimes also used to describe a yellow Lab/Golden Retriever mix, which is not a purebred dog. So-called white Labs are very light yellow Labs, and "silver Labs" are purely a scam — probably just diluted chocolate Labs, very light chocolate Labs, or crosses with a Weimeraner. Silver Labs are not an accepted color variation in the breed standard (see Chapter 17). If someone tries to charge you a lot for any of these color variations, beware. A good, well-bred Lab should cost between $300 to $1,000 and not much more or less.

Male or female?

People have a lot of funny ideas about the differences between male and female dogs. Have you fallen prey to the misconceptions? Take this quiz to find out. Answer true or false to each statement:

- ✔ Male dogs roam more than females.
- ✔ Female dogs are more affectionate than male dogs.
- ✔ Male dogs are harder to house-train than female dogs.
- ✔ Female dogs are better family dogs than male dogs.
- ✔ Male dogs are more aggressive than female dogs.
- ✔ Female dogs are more protective than male dogs.

If you answered any these questions as true, you may have known a dog who happened to fit one of the stereotypes, but in just as many cases, the stereotypes aren't true. A female in heat is just as likely to roam as a male looking for a female in heat. Male dogs can be incredibly affectionate, easy to house-train, and unaggressive. Female dogs can be standoffish, difficult to house-train, and as aggressive as any male dog. Likewise, males may be extremely protective.

Take note, however, that unneutered male dogs *are* more likely to roam, according to shelter statistics.

Dog behavior, in other words, is a product of many interrelated factors, including breeding, socialization (or lack of it), training, environment, and health. Gender isn't one of those factors.

Spaying (for female dogs) is far more complicated than *neutering* (for male dogs). If you worry about subjecting your dog to major surgery or accidentally ending up with an unwanted litter of puppies, consider a male. Of course, just because male dogs can't physically bear the puppies doesn't mean they can't make puppies, so help curb the epidemic of unwanted dogs and have your male neutered.

From St. Johns Water Dog to Labrador Retriever

In 1949, Newfoundland and Labrador together became Canada's easternmost province, and the province is known collectively as "Newfoundland and Labrador" (as their license plates say). Newfoundland proper is an island off the coast of Labrador; Labrador is part of the Canadian mainland. Yet both areas share similar geography, wildlife, and climate. Both also share many rivers, lakes, and a rugged, irregular coastline. Until the twentieth century, both relied almost solely on fishing as an export.

The probable ancestor of the Labrador Retriever was first observed on the island of Newfoundland rather than the mainland of Labrador. In any case, the climate was cold; life was harsh; and working hours for man, woman, and dog alike were long and unforgiving.

The settlers of Newfoundland, mostly fishermen, needed dogs for hunting (you can only eat fish so many days in a row!) and to help on the fishing boats. It took awhile before the smaller, short-coated, utilitarian dog so eager to please

and so adept at retrieving was given a name that stuck. Called the Lesser Newfoundland (reflecting a previous belief that the Labrador Retriever was a descendant of the Newfoundland dog), the St. John's Water Dog (St. John's is the largest city in Newfoundland), or just plain Retriever, these dogs were excellent hunters and could also fit in small fishing boats. (In fact, one of Joel's favorite Labs used to love to retrieve fish from rivers and ponds — evidence of her ancestry, perhaps?)

In 1662, the "small water dog" was described in the journal of W.E. Cormack, a St. John's native trekking across Newfoundland. Englishmen exploring the area took note of the breed's many abilities and soon began to revamp their hunting parties by replacing their pointers and setters with Labs. By the 19th century, the dog found her way to England and graced the hunting parties of the English gentry. By the 20th century, Labrador Retrievers had made their mark in the United States.

Looking at a Lab's Age and Stages

Far more significant than color or gender is the age of the dog you choose to bring home. A world of difference exists between a young puppy and an adult dog, for example, or an adolescent dog and an aging dog. The age of your dog largely determines the amount of time you have to spend in training and socializing (although other factors, such as a dog's previous history, also contribute to the time commitment factor).

The young puppy

House-training, house-training, house-training! You'll think of little else when you first bring your tiny little Lab home with you. Sure, she's cute. Sure, you can cuddle her, teach her to walk on a leash, and romp with her in the backyard. But you know what happens when you bring her back in? And again after every meal? And in the middle of the night?

House-training and lure-and-reward training take up a lot of your time when you bring home a new puppy, and you may begin to believe that you can't handle the rigors of puppy care. But if you stay consistent and keep at it (see Chapter 10), your puppy will soon be trained, and you'll be on to obedience training, walks in the park, and long evenings curled up on the sofa without a single accident.

The older puppy

Older puppies (3 to 6 months) tend to be a little easier to house-train because they are physically more mature and more able to control their bodily functions. To make up for missing those early weeks or months, the most important thing to remember with an older puppy, shown in Figure 2-2, is that you'll need to do lots of training (using positive reinforcement) and give lots of socialization.

Figure 2-2:
Older puppies are still plenty of work.

© Close Encounters of the Furry Kind

The adolescent Lab

Adopting an adolescent dog (6 months to 2 years) can be misleading. They look so grown-up, but inside, they still feel like puppies. (Remember your teenage years? You know the feeling!) Adolescents are at an awkward stage. Not quite comfortable in their large bodies, they are often less than graceful. They are also energetic, even frisky. Of course, a frisky 75-pound dog that's also clumsy can be quite a challenge to handle. Adolescent dogs need to be consistently trained with positive reinforcement, and that takes patience. But you can do it! The payoff will be well worth the effort. And house-training usually isn't something you'll have to worry about, although an adopted adolescent Lab may need house-training just as a puppy would.

The grown Lab

With an adult Lab (2 to 8 years), what you see is what you get. Genetic health problems that wouldn't be obvious in a puppy may be showing at this age, as are the effects of how the dog was raised. If he wasn't properly socialized, for example, an adult Lab may be overly shy or nervous around strangers. If he was well-trained, though, he'll be friendly, obedient, and compliant.

Bringing home an adult dog can be a gamble unless you spend sufficient time getting to know the dog. Even then, you may be in for a few surprises. But never fear! Most behavioral obstacles can be overcome with some good, consistent, positive-reinforcement-based training and lots of love. And often, by adopting a grown Lab, you bring a well-mannered, fully house-trained, non-chewing pet into your family.

If an adult dog has been abused or otherwise mistreated, the previous owner may not reveal that fact, and the resulting behavioral problems may not be obvious at first. Don't let that scare you away from adopting an adult dog from a reputable source, however. They are much easier to bring into your home than a new puppy is.

The aging Lab

The older Lab (over 8 years old) is a choice many people don't even consider. Why get to know and love a dog when you only have a few years left? Yet older Labs can be the most wonderful Labs of all. Already trained, nicely mellowed by time, and wise with experience, an older Lab can be a wonderful pet and can still understand your house rules, even if they were different than the rules by which he used to live.

Chapter 3

Getting the Lowdown on Labs

· ·

In This Chapter

▶ Giving a little grooming and a lot of caring

▶ Understanding management tips and fun training techniques to help your Lab become a great companion

▶ Bringing your Lab along on everyday activities and fun, dog-only activities

· ·

*A*fter you find your Lab, what do you do with her? How do you take care of, manage, train, and have fun with your Lab? What can you and your Lab do for fun? This chapter gives you the basics. (The rest of the book fills in the details — check out the Table of Contents or Index to find what you need.)

Because Labs are so social and love to be around people, the Lab left to his own devices all day every day is likely to become destructive or try to escape just to alleviate boredom. Don't get a Lab if you don't plan to give him a lot of attention.

Basic Grooming and Care

If you don't want to spend hours brushing and grooming your dog, you picked the right breed! Here's the maintenance you'll need to perform on your Lab:

✔ A once-a-week brushing is all your Lab's coat needs to say shiny and clean.

✔ If your Lab doesn't keep his nails worn down, you will need to clip them. Get your Lab used to nail clipping as a puppy, if possible.

✔ Keep his ears cleaned with a moist cottonball (don't go into the ear canal).

✔ Brush his teeth (use a toothpaste made for dogs) once a week.

✔ Take your Lab for an annual check-up, keep his vaccines and other tests such as heartworm tests up-to-date, and if fleas and ticks are a problem in your area, use a handy monthly spot-on treatment.

✔ Feed your Lab a quality food. Your vet may have suggestions.

✔ Give your Lab plenty of exercise to keep in good shape.

And that's all there is to it! But if you'd like more details, see Chapter 5.

Training Basics

Training is simple with the MRE system, but absolutely necessary if you want your Lab to be a good human companion. MRE stands for management, relationship, and education. Managing your Lab means keeping her out of trouble: the ol' "prevention is the best medicine" theory at work. Improve your relationship with your Lab by spending lots of time together and by remembering that your Lab doesn't know what you want her to do unless you make it clear, through teaching. Educate your Lab by teaching her what you want her to do and, most importantly, rewarding her lavishly when she does it. You'll find lots more information on the MRE system in Part III.

Luring and rewarding

Lure-and-reward training is a method of training that has been used for many years by progressive trainers to teach puppies and dogs the meaning of simple requests (what we call "commands"). If you have any difficulty in using this method, you can likely find a trainer in your area who can teach you how to do it. If you can't find a trainer, call the Association of Pet Dog Trainers at 1-800-PETDOGS and ask them to refer you to a lure-and-reward trainer.

Breeders who practice lure-and-reward training tend to have very responsive pups. The method uses positive reinforcement, which many trainers believe is the most effective method of training, far exceeding harsher punishment or negative reinforcement methods that use choke chains or prong collars to force a dog to comply.

Your Family Lab

A good family dog doesn't just happen. You can help your Lab be a great family companion by including your Lab in any family activities that allow dogs. Take your dog with you to run errands (never leave your dog in the car in hot weather, though!), to the park with the kids, to soccer and baseball games, to the lake, when camping, even when on vacation. And don't forget to work on training for a few minutes every day.

Showing, Working, and Competing

Depending on where you live, you may have access to all kinds of doggy activities, from formal obedience trials to fun Frisbee games and flyball competitions. Obedience trials help you continue to train your Lab to be a great companion (read more about those in Chapter 11). Agility trials (like an obstacle course for dogs), flyball (a relay race), and freestyle (a creative dance/obedience contest) are other fun dog activities. These dog activities take a lot of energy on the part of both Lab and handler, so they're good for you, too!

For working Labs, hunt tests and field trials may interest you, especially if you have a dog that loves to retrieve. Chapter 16 tells you more about these activities and how to get involved. You can also teach your Lab to be a therapy dog in nursing homes or hospitals, help the disabled (some Labs are formally trained as assistance dogs), or even do search and rescue and law enforcement. Chapter 20 tells you more about these activities and the training and work involved.

Part II

Finding and Living with a Labrador Retriever

The 5th Wave   By Rich Tennant

In this part . . .

*I*n this part, we give you some tips on finding a good breeder and keeping your lab puppy healthy. (We also share some alternatives to purchasing a puppy, including rescuing a grown Lab.)

That little puppy may be the picture of health, but keeping your Lab healthy takes some care, including preventive measures and plenty of preparation. We help you choose a practically perfect veterinarian and even make suggestions for other professionals to include on your Lab's health care team. Although choosing a great vet involves more than just flipping through the Yellow Pages, it's an effort that will pay off time and again over the course of your Lab's life. In addition, we recommend some preventive approaches to health care, from an appropriate vaccination schedule to a great diet and plenty of exercise. We also help you to prepare for any emergencies by assembling your own canine first-aid kit.

And if your life changes drastically, as many lives do, we help you to ease the transition for your pet, whether that transition involves the introduction of a new baby, a new pet, a divorce, or the death of a family member. If you're there for your Lab, he'll be there for you.

Chapter 4

Choosing Your New Best Friend

*Y*ou probably have a pretty good idea about the type of Lab you would like. What's left to do but go out and buy one? Plenty! Finding that practically perfect Lab isn't as easy as looking up "Labrador Retriever" in the Yellow Pages. You have a lot of options and a lot of limitations, too, if you want to find the right dog for you.

The Breeder Option

Purchasing a dog from a reputable and responsible breeder is a good way to assure that your puppy will be healthy, have a good temperament, and have an appearance close to the breed standard. Finding your practically perfect puppy from a breeder is probably the safest route as far as knowing what you're getting.

The trick is finding a good breeder. "Good" by some standards may not be good for you. Chapters 1 and 2 give you a much better idea of the qualities you prefer in a Lab. But how do you find the breeder who is breeding for those qualities?

Finding a good breeder

Time to do a little research! Different breeders have different priorities. Some breeders may strive to produce puppies that will excel in *conformation* (physical characteristics) or in field trials. You want to make sure these breeders are also very interested in breeding puppies who will excel at being great family pets.

Networking with breeders

The Internet can be a great place to make first contact with any number of breeders. Go to `www.k9web.com/breeders_directory/` for a list of Labrador Retriever breeders. If you can't find a breeder within driving distance, search on **Labrador Retriever breeders,** and you'll get a big list. Add your city or state to the search to find breeders in your area.

You can look for some clues that will help you separate the good from the less-than-good breeders. A good breeder will want to show you the dogs behind the puppies (in other words, the parents) and the puppies themselves, but only after conveying lots of important information. A good breeder will also want to interview you to make sure you're good enough for one of his or her puppies! Pay attention and take notes. Bring along a pen and the breeder checklist covered in the following section. The checklist will help you with what to look for. You can tell a lot about the breeder by observing both the adult dogs and the place where the puppies are being raised.

Ask the breeders you visit what their priorities are for their lines. If they are breeding for field champions, for example, their dogs may be too energetic and driven to be satisfied with a life as a family pet. The ideal breeder for someone looking for a family pet is one who breeds with good health and temperament as the top priorities.

Using a breeder checklist

Use the following checklist when interviewing a breeder:

- ✔ **Where are the puppies?** If they're raised in the house with the family, that's a good sign. If they're raised in clean, well-maintained kennels, that could be okay as long as the puppies are being socialized properly. If the kennels are broken down and dirty (a few "piles" here and there aren't evidence of a dirty kennel — puppies shoot those out night and day) or if the dogs look like they rarely see a human being and are skittish around you, that's a red flag.

- ✔ **How do the puppies look?** Are their coats clean or caked with dirt? Do they have feces around the rectum? Are they bright-eyed and energetic, or do they look sick or fatigued? Are their coats in good condition or are they missing patches of hair? Are their nails clipped or too long? Do they have fleas or ticks?

✔ **Does the breeder seem interested in how you're going to manage and raise the puppy, instead of just trying to put the puppy in your lap and have you take her home?** Does he or she seem like someone you can trust, both in taking care of dogs and in business dealings? Does the breeder emphasize that he or she will be there to answer questions on the phone after you take the puppy home?

✔ **How do the dogs act around the breeder?** Are they jumping with joy to see their beloved caretaker, or do they shy away or act indifferent? The latter two are red flags.

✔ **Is at least one of the parents available for you to see?** Figure 4-1 shows a yellow Lab with her yellow and black puppies. If you can't see either parent, you have to wonder if you really know what you're getting.

Figure 4-1:
A yellow Lab with her yellow and black puppies.

© *Close Encounters of the Furry Kind*

When you visit a breeder, bring the whole family. A good breeder will want to see everyone in the family and observe how they interact with each other and with the puppies to make sure the puppies have the best possible home.

Conducting an interview

After you take a look around the premises, spend a little time asking some smart questions. Good breeders expect this interview, and one of the best signs that you're talking to a good breeder is that you find yourself getting interviewed right back! Responsible breeders care just as much about placing their beloved charges into good homes as you care about bringing the right dog home with you.

Buying a dog isn't a decision to be taken lightly. Never rush through it or buy a dog on impulse! Most importantly, don't let a breeder rush you into any decision that doesn't feel quite right. The puppy may be the eventual victim if you can't keep her because she wasn't a good match.

What should you ask about? Well, we tell you in the following bullet list! (Keep in mind that many good breeders will tell you this information before you ask, which makes your job a whole lot easier.) We also tell you what answers you want to hear, and which answers should raise red flags.

- **What can you tell me about the breed and about your particular Labs?** Good breeders really know their breed. They should be able to tell you what the standard characteristics are, both in conformation and in temperament, and should also know the specific qualities and tendencies of their particular lines, which will be more specific than the breed standard. For example, does the breeder breed for field champions? These dogs are probably super-energetic and may be more than an average pet owner wants to handle. Does the breeder breed for conformation and are there show champions in the pedigrees of the puppies? Does the breeder consider his or her pet-quality dogs to be the dogs that didn't quite make the conformation standards, or does the breeder breed primarily for the kind of temperament and health in all the dogs that make for an excellent pet?

   Any breeder who cares about his or her puppies is also going to emphasize the downsides of the breed (every breed has downsides). A breeder who only raves about and praises the breed and his or her own lines isn't giving you the whole truth. The breeder should also give you the downsides of owning a dog in general to make sure you know what you're getting into.

- **How long have you been breeding and how many litters have you bred?** Although a breeder just starting out isn't necessarily a bad breeder, breeders with years of experience are oftentimes a better gamble. Experienced breeders have developed lines of dogs and have been able to really get to know and refine their dogs for the better. Breeders who are irresponsible, either in the breeding itself or the business end (or both), often don't last too long, so if a breeder has been breeding Labs successfully for twenty-five years, you can, to some extent, trust the test of time.

Number of litters is significant, too. If a breeder has been breeding Labs for twenty-five years but has only bred a few litters, that breeder will have far less experience. On the other hand, if a breeder has only been breeding Labs for a few years and has bred twenty-five litters, that's a red flag, too. That breeder is probably just trying to turn out as many puppies as possible to make a quick buck without taking the time to breed for health and temperament and without making any attempt to breed dogs that are free of genetic problems.

✔ **May I talk to your veterinarian and can you give me any referrals?**
Ask the breeder if you can talk to his or her veterinarian. Why wouldn't a breeder want you to talk to his or her veterinarian? If his or her dogs have a lot of health problems, or if the breeder rarely sees the vet unless the dogs have a health emergency, the breeder may not be eager to let you in on that information. But a good breeder who routinely takes puppies in to his or her vet and has healthy dogs should be happy to let you give the vet a call. A breeder's veterinarian should be able to give you a different perspective on the puppies you're considering. The vet probably has an idea of the longevity of dogs from that breeder, whether genetic abnormalities or other health problems tend to occur more often than should be expected, and good knowledge of any other medical problems or concerns.

As far as referrals go, sure, your breeder will probably give you only the names of people who are happy with his or her dogs, not the names of any who have complained. But what's wrong with that? The red flag should go up if your breeder won't give you any names. Chances are, that means few if any are happy with his dogs, or the breeder is afraid you may find out about something he or she doesn't want you to know. It can be hard to pinpoint a breeder with a bad reputation if you aren't in the dog community, but getting a few referrals is one way to get the skinny.

✔ **Do you offer any guarantees?** Some breeders offer written guarantees that allow you to return the puppy if she develops any genetic problems, and she will be replaced by a puppy of equal value. This guarantee may give you some peace of mind that the breeder is doing a good job and is fairly confident the dog won't develop a genetic problem. But sometimes problems occur despite a breeder's best efforts. And think about this: Are you going to want to return a family member because she didn't turn out to be perfect? (What family member is?)

All living beings have defective genes. Some of them are visible; some are not. You're looking for a breeder who is doing everything reasonable to produce pups who will have a full and healthy life. (It's a good sign if the breeder has very old dogs.) Longevity is very important. Some people have bred a litter and haven't done any of the health checks (such as OFA for hip dysplasia and CERF for eye problems), yet they'll offer a written guarantee! If they don't know what they're doing, will they be around when your pup grows up? Probably not. Your guarantee may not be worth the paper it was written on.

Good breeders openly discuss the possible genetic problems that may appear and how they can be dealt with. Such breeders may offer to help you if your dog does develop problems. A reputable breeder will want to know if one of his or her puppies has a genetic problem because that information helps determine future breeding strategies. Good breeders sell puppies who aren't going to be shown in conformation under an AKC limited registration. An *AKC limited registration* means that a dog is registered with the AKC as a purebred dog, but that no litters produced by that dog will be eligible for registration. Dogs with limited registrations are ineligible to compete in conformation, but they are eligible to compete in obedience and other types of competition, such as tracking and hunting.

Having an open dialogue with the breeder and taking the time to make sure your choice of breeder and choice of puppy are good ones are probably worth more than any health guarantee.

That being said, however, any good breeder should be willing to take a puppy back and refund your money if a veterinarian says the puppy has a significant health problem; some breeders offer even more extensive guarantees. Take your puppy to the vet, preferably straight from the breeder, before you've had a chance to get too attached. The breeder may require that you take the puppy to a veterinarian sometime within the first seventy-two hours. (A leisurely vet inquiry three months after you've bought the puppy shows you aren't taking your puppy's health seriously.) A vet is the only person who can tell you whether you've purchased a healthy puppy.

Make sure you don't use the excuse of a written guarantee and/or falling in love with a cute puppy to avoid doing your job. What's your job, again? To identify a good breeder who is doing the proper health checks, raising the puppies in a family surrounding, and screening *you* to make the best match.

✔ **How soon can I take the dog home?** In many states, the law requires that dogs can't be sold until they are a particular age, often 7 weeks old. But even that is a little young. According to many breeders, 8 weeks is the earliest a puppy should be taken from her mother. Puppies need the chance to learn from their mothers and littermates, which is one of the first steps towards socialization. If a breeder says you can take home that tiny, sickly-looking 4-week-old puppy, run! Yes, the other way! (Before you look too closely and get too attached. You'll just be asking for heartbreak.)

Also beware of the *bait and switch con.* If a breeder tells you over the phone that he or she has exactly what you're looking for and promises to reserve her, then when you arrive, says, "I'm so, so sorry! I just sold that puppy to someone, but I have this other puppy I know you'll just love. She may look small, but . . . ." That breeder is probably trying to get you on the premises (even though he or she never had what you're looking for, in the hope that once you see the dog he or she is trying to pawn off on you (because the dog has some problem), you'll fall in love and won't be able to say no.

✔ **What do you do to keep your dogs healthy and happy?** Ask the breeder what he or she does to keep the dogs happy and healthy. This general question gives the breeder a chance to volunteer additional information about what he or she does to care for the dogs. Good breeders can feel free to brag about the quality of food they use, the degree of socialization they employ, how their dogs are a part of the family, extensive veterinary and/or preventive care, and so on. Let the breeder brag. It's an education on what you can do to continue your puppy's good health in the future. A red flag answer to this question is "Huh?"

Questions for you

Wait just a minute — the interview is far from over. In fact, before you have a chance to ask the breeder all of your questions, chances are the breeder will (and should) ask a few questions, too. If a breeder doesn't ask you any questions about where you plan to keep the dog, why you want a dog, how much you know about Labs, and other questions designed to determine whether that breeder's puppies will fit into your particular situation and home (and even match your personality), you should be hesitant to continue the deal. A breeder who isn't concerned about where the puppies are going probably won't be too likely to take them back if there is a health problem and probably isn't as conscientious as other breeders who put the welfare of their dogs before profits.

The breeder will probably ask you some of the following questions (if you're a breeder reading this book, take note):

✔ **What are you looking for in a dog?** This is a breeder's chance to make sure you want a Lab for all the right reasons. For example, a good breeder wants to weed out people just looking for a guard dog to patrol the backyard. The breeder wants to know that you're in it for the long haul and are looking for a dog to bring into your family. If you're interested in breeding and/or showing, the breeder wants to make sure you know what you're doing and, especially in the case of breeding, that you plan to proceed responsibly and in the best interest of the breed.

✔ **Do you plan to spay or neuter this puppy?** Some breeders require you to sign a spay-neuter agreement, depending on the puppy you're taking home. (A *spay-neuter agreement* is a contract you sign stating that you agree to have your dog spayed or neutered and that you won't breed that dog. Many breeders require these agreements for dogs they don't think should be bred, either because they don't meet the breed standard or because they have some genetic problem.)

Other breeders rely on you to consult with your vet to determine the right time to spay or neuter your pup. If your dog is registered under an AKC limited registration, don't breed your pup! The puppies can't be registered, not even under a limited registration. Even if your puppy isn't registered under a limited registration, you will still want to spay or neuter it if you aren't prepared to enter into the complex, expensive, and difficult task of breeding quality dogs. A veterinarian can tell you all of the health benefits of spaying or neutering (check out Chapter 6). Of course, if you're buying a puppy for showing or breeding, the breeder should know so that he or she can advise you. In this case, spaying or neutering doesn't apply.

✔ **Where do you plan to keep this puppy?** Breeders want to know if their beloved puppies will end up backyard denizens, locked in a kennel for ten hours every day while you're at work, or snuggled on the couch with someone who works at home or stays home much of the time. Of course, just because you have a job and have to work (most people do) doesn't mean a breeder will refuse to let you take home that practically perfect puppy. The breeder will want to know your plan, however. And you should have one!

   • Will you come home for lunch to walk your puppy?

   • Will someone else be there most of the time who is willing to take care of your new pet?

   • Have you considered hiring a pet sitter or dog walker to do middle-of-the-day duty? If you live in a big city, you may even be close to a doggy daycare center; more and more are popping up all the time.

✔ **Can you afford a dog?** We aren't just talking the cost of the dog, you understand. Dogs are an ongoing, continual expense that you must be ready to take on. What if your dog gets sick? What if she gets hurt? And don't forget vaccinations, rabies shots, heartworm pills, flea and tick control, a good quality food, training costs, and supplies — the list goes on and on. A responsible breeder will think twice about selling a dog to someone who can just barely pay for the dog herself, keeps asking about price and trying to wrangle a deal, or who gives the impression that he or she wouldn't be able to afford any unexpected veterinary care.

✔ **How committed are you to being a good dog owner?** Some people visiting breeders are obviously dog people. They've owned and loved dogs before, or they just seem to have a natural rapport with the puppies. These people will get down on the floor, call the puppies to them, and revel in puppy play. Inexperienced dog owners or people who aren't particularly comfortable with dogs may sit and wait for a dog to come to them. A breeder will be watching you and the way you interact with the puppies just as closely as you should be watching him or her. The breeder will also want to know that you understand the time commitment, financial commitment, and even the emotional commitment involved in owning a dog.

> ✔ **Do you and the puppy have a good rapport?** Even with dog people, certain human-dog combinations just don't click. Others are matches made in heaven. A breeder knows how to recognize those wonderful matches. You may have in mind that you absolutely have to have that female yellow Lab, but that chocolate male trying so hard to get your attention may think you're just about the greatest human being he's ever met in his life. Don't overlook him!

After you and a breeder have passed each other's interview, business can proceed. You're not through yet!

Health tests and guarantees

Good breeders guarantee the health of their puppies and should take a puppy back and refund your money if something is wrong with the puppy. The best way to tell if something is wrong is to take your puppy from the breeder's place immediately to the veterinarian, and some breeders require that you do this within seventy-two hours of purchasing the puppy. Ask the vet if you should be watching for other problems that may show themselves later in your puppy's life.

To maintain the best odds for future health, you also want included in the health guarantee or other evidence that both parents of the litter have had their hips x-rayed and are certified free of hip dysplasia by the Orthopedic Foundation for Animals (OFA). You also want proof that both parents have had their eyes examined by a board-certified veterinary ophthalmologist to minimize the chance your puppy will develop inherited eye problems such as *progressive retinal atrophy (PRA)*, a degenerative disorder that eventually causes blindness. Many breeders register their dogs with an organization called the Canine Eye Registration Foundation (CERF) to certify that their dogs are free from genetic eye problems. This foundation works in conjunction with the American College of Veterinary Ophthalmologists (ACVO) to maintain a registry of purebred dogs who have been examined and found to be unaffected by any major inheritable eye disease such as PRA.

Make sure you also have a record of how many vaccinations the breeder has given your puppy (she should have had at least one round). The breeder should also already have the puppy on a worming program.

The health of your puppy isn't all up to the breeder, of course. After your puppy comes home with you, it is your job to keep her healthy. Although many breeders will take a puppy back if you neglect her and she gets sick (for example, your puppy could easily get heartworm if you neglect to give her heartworm pills), if the problem isn't genetic, don't expect to get your money back. If you aren't willing to pay for your puppy's medical care, many breeders would rather take the puppy back than have you take her to a shelter or worse (some breeders may actually require in writing that you return the dog to them). But breeders in the business for the love of Labs will certainly try to avoid selling puppies to people who would neglect them.

If your puppy does develop a genetic problem later in life, however (such as hip dysplasia or any other problem that may be inherited), the breeder will want to know about it.

Whatever the breeder is or isn't willing to do should definitely be set down in writing before any puppies or money change hands. After the guarantee is agreed upon, don't expect the breeder to do more than promised. A deal is a deal; make sure it's a good one and a fair one for both of you right from the start.

Even if all precautions have been taken, genetic disorders do sometimes occur unexpectedly in puppies (as in people). Some of the more common genetic disorders in dogs are canine hip dysplasia (more common in larger dogs, like Labs), some kinds of heart disease, *entropian* (a condition in which the eyelid rolls inward), *ectropian* (a condition in which the eyelid rolls outward), glaucoma, progressive retinal atrophy (PRA), central progressive retinal atrophy (CPRA), deafness, and renal defects.

Letting your breeder help you choose

But what if all the puppies in your breeder's litter look like textbook examples of healthy pups? What if they all dote on you? How on earth do you choose?

Ask the breeder! A good breeder does more than engineer the creation of those adorable little puppies. He or she also pays attention to each puppy and tries to determine inborn tendencies, energy level, personality, and health. The breeder knows those puppies much better than you can know them all in a visit or two, so take advantage of that knowledge. Tell the breeder everything you can about your personality, situation, and preferences in a dog. The breeder will then be able to help you choose the puppy that will best suit you (and you, her).

The breeder will be looking for a puppy who seems to have that special rapport with you. Trust the breeder to help you find your perfect match if you just aren't sure which one is best. (For more information on how to choose the perfect puppy from a practically perfect litter, see the following section.)

Choosing Your Puppy

You're at the breeder's or the shelter, or you're getting ready to meet with a rescue representative. You'll probably meet several Labs, whether puppies or adult dogs. How do you pick which one is your Lab? Choosing your particular puppy involves a combination of factors: research, testing, and good old-fashioned chemistry.

Refining your expectations

The first step in choosing your particular puppy is to have a clear idea of what you want. Chapters 1 and 2 can help you figure out your personal requirements for a puppy; now, you can refine your Labrador Retriever wish list a little. We'll help! Write out your answers to the following questions, as completely as possible:

- Do you think you want a young puppy, an older puppy, a young adult dog, or an older dog?

- What positive behaviors are priorities for you in your new dog?

- What negative behaviors are you particularly concerned about avoiding?

- Describe the type of relationship you would like to have with your dog.

- Explain your training plan. Will you train your dog yourself? Take him to obedience classes? Hire a professional trainer? A combination of all of these (the option we recommend)? A training plan is essential before you bring home your dog. Know how you will manage and educate your dog, so he knows how to behave. (We give you extra space to answer this most important of all questions.)

Have you considered a pet rock?

If your one requirement for a puppy is "I want a dog who doesn't require any work," we strongly suggest you peruse your local department store's wide selection of stuffed toy dogs. Or consider a pet rock. Every real live dog requires and deserves good management, training, time, and lots of love.

Look over your answers. You want a puppy who's house-trained, doesn't play-bite, doesn't chew the furniture, listens to you, and does what you ask? Be ready to spend some time managing and training your pup.

Do you want a great family pet? What does that mean to you? A dog who lies on the couch and watches television with you, a dog who goes running with you every morning, or a dog who accompanies you on your hunting trips?

You want a very trainable puppy? Find a breeder who practices the Start Puppy Training Procedure (see the following section) or something like it. You want a hunter or an obedience champ? Find a breeder who has had success producing dogs skilled in these areas, but also make sure the breeder breeds for the qualities necessary in a good family pet.

Do you have a clearer, more realistic picture in mind than you did when you first picked up this book? Perhaps the picture looks about the same. Either way, defining your expectations is important, and making them realistic is only fair to you and your dog.

Testing and selecting your puppy

There they are — a bunch of adorable little Labrador Retriever puppies rolling around and playing or sleeping in the whelping box in front of you (see Figure 4-2). They're all so cute! They all look healthy! However will you choose?

The first thing to do is to ask the breeder what kind of training they're doing with the pups. If the answer is "None," ask to be able to see the pups when they are relatively hungry, so you can try what Joel has dubbed the Start Puppy Training Procedure. If the breeder has already begun this practice or something similar, ask to see a demonstration.

Figure 4-2: These roly-poly puppies are the picture of health.

The Start Puppy Training Procedure

Joel developed the Start Puppy Training Procedure (SPTP) as an alternative to some of the methods that many breeders, trainers, and behaviorists currently use to determine a puppy's personality. When a breeder begins to work with pups as soon as they're able to eat solid food, the puppies grow up already accustomed to this gentle lure-and-reward training method. But if your puppy hasn't been oriented yet, it isn't too late. Try the SPTP right at the breeder's and see how the puppies respond. One puppy may stand out as being especially responsive to your efforts, and that he may be the one for you.

Set aside a small handful of kibble, and then take one piece in your hand. Bring the puppy to an area slightly away from his brothers and sisters (but not to an unfamiliar area — you want the pup to be comfortable and unafraid). Stand him in front of you and then slowly raise the piece of food in an arc so that when the puppy follows the food with his nose, his rear end winds up on the ground. Did this eight-week-old puppy just perform a "sit"? Sure looks like it! Reward your puppy by giving him the food.

With the pup in the sit position, take another piece of food, and while the puppy is still sitting, slowly move the piece of food away from the puppy at nose level until the puppy has to stand to get it. Did the puppy just perform a "stand"? Sure looks like it! Reward your puppy again by giving him the food.

Staying away from impulse buys

Everyone has great expectations for a new pet, but too often, those expectations soon turn to disappointment. Why? Because bringing a new dog into the family isn't easy. It's work. Anyone who has brought a new baby home knows that babies don't come fed, burped, diapered, and potty-trained; in fact, new babies don't come with very many skills at all. Don't expect much more from your new puppy. Even if you bring home an older dog that has mastered some basics, she may also have mastered some behaviors you aren't at all happy to tolerate.

Before you bring home a Labrador Retriever — or any dog — think long and hard about what's involved. You have to be ready to make a serious commitment to the care, training, and development of a relationship. Otherwise, you'll have a dog that's more trouble than fun, and the poor dog will probably end up either banished to the solitude of the backyard for life or at the local animal shelter, where she may then become someone else's problem or worse.

So don't buy a Lab on impulse. Labs are big, energetic, and sometimes boisterous dogs (especially as puppies), and they don't take care of themselves. They need you. Don't let them need you unless you're ready to be needed.

When you've repeated the sit-stand exercise for awhile, take another piece of food and slowly move it straight down from the puppy's nose to the floor. When the puppy follows the food, he will be performing a "down." Good dog! This is probably plenty for session one. When you bring your puppy home, you can begin to say, "Sit" before you lure the puppy with the food and then say, "Yes" after he is sitting and before you offer the reward. Your puppy will learn to sit with one sweet request and a simple hand signal. The same applies for "stand" and "down."

Try this method with several of the puppies, and each may react in a different way. Some may ignore you. The test may not work if a puppy isn't hungry. After all, he's just a baby and may take a bit of time getting used to what you're asking of him. Some puppies may follow you for a minute or two and then lose interest and go back to their siblings for another romp. But then, one puppy looks you in the eye and does exactly what you want. A-ha! Could it be you've found your perfect pup?

The personality test

Trying out the SPTP on different puppies is a great way to get a glimpse of each puppy's personality potential, including his energy level and his general interest in you personally. On the other hand, a puppy who doesn't quite get it the very first time may be exceptionally bright, just exceptionally busy at the moment. The dog who does hone in on you and seems particularly eager to get it right and understand what you say may have just the personality you want.

As you test for personality using the SPTP, remember your refined list of expectations and use it to judge the actions and reactions of the puppies. Does that one seem as though he may make a great hunter? Does this one seem particularly interested in learning tricks? Is this one a little less active? In particular, evaluate the following puppy qualities:

- Activity level
- Shyness or boldness
- Interest in you
- Interest in the SPTP
- Appetite (dependent on when he had his last meal)
- Tendency to play-bite (normal behavior in most pups)
- Distractibility (a quality in all puppies, but in some more than others)
- Overall appearance of health

Take notes if it will help you to remember: "The black one wouldn't sit still long enough to see that I had food in my hand. The yellow one slept the whole time. The chocolate one loved me!" Now you have some idea about who you're dealing with.

The healthy puppy test

You want to determine, to the best of your ability, how healthy the puppies are in your pool of potential pups. You probably aren't a vet so you must have a vet check out your puppy as soon as possible. You can look for a few obvious signs of good or poor health, however. Take the following checklist along with you:

- **Look at the puppy's eyes.** Are they clear, bright, and clean or are they runny, weepy-looking, or caked with goo?
- **Look at the puppy's ears.** Are they clean both inside and out, free of ticks and bald patches?
- **Look at the puppy's mouth.** Are his gums and teeth (he may not have many teeth yet) clean; the proper color; and free of sores, plaque, and food? Check the roof of his mouth — is it clean and without sores? Is the tongue clean? Does his breath have that sweet-milk puppy smell, or does it smell rotten?
- **Look at the puppy's coat.** Is it free from mats, dirt, and feces, especially around the rectum? Is it clean and very soft? Or is it patchy with bald spots (possible sign of a skin infection)? Is there any evidence of ticks or fleas? (Small black spots and/or raised red bumps are evidence of fleas. Ticks are easier to spot, but they may range from the size of a pinhead to the size of a big marble.) Does his coat smell bad?

✔ **Look at the puppy's paws.** Are they clean with clipped nails and nothing lodged between the pads? Are the pads clean and intact or scraped up? Does the puppy walk easily or does he limp?

✔ **Look at how the puppy acts.** Is he energetic, curious, interested in you, and eating well? Or does he seem to be lethargic, to not want to eat, to have trouble defecating, or to not notice you even when you try to get his attention?

If the puppy you're beginning to fall in love with is clean, pest-free, odor-free, and free from any evidence of skin infections, and if he acts energetic, curious, hungry, and fascinated by your very presence, you have a winner!

Good breeders take the entire litter of pups to their vet for a complete physical before you pick up your puppy.

Basic chemistry

Even though we advocate choosing your puppy carefully by considering many factors about the breeder (or other source), we certainly wouldn't discount the power of chemistry. Sometimes, a match is right. All the other factors are, ideally, right as well. But when you're looking at a litter of healthy, active, interested pups who all pick up your training suggestions and seem to think you hung the moon, chemistry may be all you have to select one over the others.

Which dog keeps drawing your attention? Which one seems particularly fascinated in you? Which one looks you right in the eyes as if to say, "I know you! You're the one I've been waiting for!" This is where love at first sight kicks in. Try not to let it kick in before you've objectively eliminated certain puppies who wouldn't be good choices for other reasons. But when it does kick in at the appropriate time, go with it. This is what dog ownership is all about. This is the fun part, the rewarding part, and the part that makes you feel good.

"But he picked me!"

Avoiding puppy-picking pitfalls is just as important as remembering all the right things to do. One of the biggest mistakes potential owners make is letting the dog do all the choosing. Whether actively or passively, puppies can sway you. Did that adorable yellow Lab run right up to you as soon as you entered the room? And even though his eyes were a little runny, did he just want to curl up in your arms and sleep? Thinking that a dog is asking you to save him or that he picked you, even when other signs indicate he may not be healthy or well-bred, is asking for heartbreak. Be realistic about the dog you choose.

"But my friend told me never to . . ."

The world is full of people who think they know all and are happy to impart their vast knowledge to you. Sure, sometimes people give good advice, but other times, they're simply repeating what they've heard from some other advice-giver. Don't let anyone influence you besides the members of your own family and the breeder or trainer you trust, especially if you've heard anything like the following:

✔ **Myth:** Big dogs are nothing but trouble.

Truth: A larger dog that's well trained is a joy!

✔ **Myth:** You should never get a dog if you have to work all day.

Truth: You can always make arrangements to come home for lunch or hire someone to check on your dog during the day. Larger cities even have doggy daycare.

✔ **Myth:** Purebred dogs are bound to have major health problems.

Truth: If a dog is bred responsibly with health as a priority, chances are good that your dog will be the picture of health.

✔ **Myth:** An older dog will never bond to you because he already bonded to somebody else.

Truth: Ridiculous! Older dogs can be excellent companions that are forever grateful to you for loving them. Labs are especially adaptable.

✔ **Myth:** You'll end up giving that puppy away. They're too much work.

Truth: Puppies are a lot of work, but a dedicated and loving owner can quickly guide the puppy to good behavior.

✔ **Myth:** Now you'll be tied down for life!

Truth: Having a dog does mean you'll need to plan for vacations and long periods away from home, but it certainly doesn't mean you can't ever leave home. Take your dog along, hire a pet sitter, or board your dog at a good kennel. See Chapter 13 for more on traveling with your dog.

In other words, every dog is an individual, and every family is unique. No one knows you like you, and no one knows your dog like the breeder. Working together, you can ensure the perfect match. No outside advice required (although we're glad you're reading our book)!

Debunking Lab myths

Here are a few more pieces of advice you may hear when choosing your Labrador Retriever that you should feel free to ignore:

✔ Yellow Labs are dumber. (Nope.)

✔ Black Labs are more aggressive. (Not true.)

✔ Chocolate Labs are smarter. (Nuh-uh.)

✔ Yellow Labs are more active or hyper. (Afraid not.)

✔ Black Labs have more health problems. (No way.)

✔ Chocolate Labs don't listen. (No siree.)

All three coat colors can come out of the same litter, and no study has demonstrated any difference in behavior or health related to normal coat color in Labs.

Avoiding second thoughts

Planning and preparation are the keys for avoiding second thoughts. If you know exactly what you're getting into and what degree of time, effort, and financial commitment to expect, you won't experience any rude awakenings. You'll have realistic expectations, and you'll be able to provide a consistently loving environment for your new friend.

That doesn't mean you won't get frustrated once in awhile. Puppies can be trying, and when you're standing in the middle of your front yard at 3:00 a.m. for the fourth night in a row as your puppy joyfully romps through the grass as if he has no intention of relieving himself for quite some time, you may think, "What was I thinking?" Just remind yourself what you were thinking: That you will make an excellent dog companion, and that you're committed to making your new Labrador Retriever the best dog he can be. Before you know it, your puppy will be able to make it through the night without having to go outside, so why not enjoy it while it lasts? How often do you get to enjoy the night at 3:00 a.m.?

The Rescue Adoption Option

Maybe something is gnawing at the back of your mind. Could it be that you can't quite forget how many dogs are abandoned and euthanized each year? And could it be that you suspect lots of these dogs are Labrador Retrievers or Lab mixes? Could be.

For some people, purchasing a dog from a breeder, although a better risk as far as knowing what you're getting, just isn't the right way to go. Maybe you want to do your part to help at least one of the hundreds of thousands of dogs who are abandoned every year. Many of those dogs are euthanized. A few lucky ones are given a second chance, rescued by breed rescue groups and placed into good homes. Could a down-on-her-luck Lab be the perfect pet for you?

Maybe you have your heart set on a puppy, but keep in mind that an older Lab can be the ideal dog. Older Labs generally require far less work than puppies and are likely already trained in good behavior. Sure, an older Lab may not have the lifespan ahead of her that a puppy would, but the years she does have left can be filled with joy for both of you. Please consider adopting an older Lab who has lost her home.

Adopting a rescue dog could well be the best dog-related decision you ever make. On the other hand, it could also result in disaster. It all depends on how well you prepare (and on a little bit of luck). Many wonderful, friendly, well-trained, loyal dogs are given up to rescue groups because of circumstances having nothing to do with the dog, such as a divorce or a job that requires a move to a place where dogs aren't allowed. A family may be heartbroken to give up their beloved pet but may hope that a good rescue organization can place her with a new family where she will be just as loved.

On the other hand, some dogs are put into shelters because of behavioral problems or health problems, or because the owners just didn't want to spend the time or the money to take care of the pet they never should have acquired. Such people are often less than straight with rescue organizations. Rescue workers do their best to evaluate a dog's temperament and health, but the effects of past abuse or neglect may not always be immediately obvious. Even these dogs can eventually make wonderful pets, however. If you're willing to put some time, energy, and money into these dogs, they'll know they owe you a huge debt, and they'll probably show you their gratitude every day for the rest of their lives.

Many rescued dogs are adolescent or adult dogs. These dogs can be excellent choices for someone who doesn't want to take on housetraining and all the other necessary duties of puppy raising. If you're patient, loving, understanding, gentle, and consistent, a rescued Lab may well be your practically perfect Labrador Retriever.

Before you take on a rescued Lab, spend some serious time getting to know the dog. Work with the rescue group to determine whether you and your potential pet are a good match. If the dog seems to have serious problems, enlist the help of a good canine behavior consultant. Be persistent. A good rapport can be an important step in overcoming problems, and many problem dogs have quickly become practically perfect dogs when they find the right human companion.

Don't overlook Lab mixes

Because the Lab is the most popular dog in America, because many dog owners don't control their dogs, and because many dog owners don't spay or neuter their dogs, there are a lot of Lab mixes out there. Lab/Shepherd mixes, Lab/Rottweiler mixes, Lab/Hound mixes, and Lab/Pit Bull mixes are all common (we've even seen a Lab/Dachshund mix — a full-sized Lab on short little legs), not to mention Labs mixed with other retrievers such as Golden Retrievers and Chesapeake Bay Retrievers. Unfortunately, many Lab mixes are unwanted "accidents" and end up in animal shelters. Lab mixes can be wonderful, intelligent, practically perfect pets and certainly can't be blamed for the indiscretion of the owners of their parents. If you're considering rescuing a Lab, don't overlook the Lab mixes. One may be perfect for you. And you can compete with your Lab mix in a number of sports and obedience competitions.

Labrador Retriever rescue organizations

Labrador Retriever rescue organizations are run by people who love the breed and are committed to finding appropriate homes for dogs who have been abandoned. But breed rescue work can become overwhelming. Breed rescue workers describe receiving several hundred e-mails a day and hundreds of phone calls every week from people who need to give up their dogs. Although a few saints out there have devoted their lives to rescue and have been doing it for years (without pay), many rescuers start with good intentions and soon burn out. As a result, any list of rescue organizations we could provide in this book would probably soon be out of date.

To find a good rescue organization currently in operation near you, call the American Kennel Club or the Labrador Retriever Club, Inc. (See contact information in the Appendix.) Or search the Internet for the keywords **Labrador Retriever rescue.** You'll get up-to-the-minute information on who is doing Labrador Retriever rescue right now.

Don't be surprised if rescue organizations return your message collect — that's common procedure for rescue due to the vast number of calls breed rescue organizations typically receive. Remember, these people do the work for free and purely for the love of Labs. The least you can do is pay your part of the phone bill.

Other rescue groups

Even if you don't have a Labrador Retriever rescue organization near you, you may have an all-breed rescue group. Search on **dog rescue** on the Internet, or talk to local veterinarians, dog trainers, animal shelter, or pet stores (those that don't sell dogs). Local breeders may even have good information.

Animal Shelters

Finding a Lab (or a Lab mix) at an animal shelter is another option. Animal shelters vary widely in quality, but an increasing number are either private adoption centers or shelters that do euthanize but make every possible effort to place the more adoptable dogs into good homes. Shelters may have stiff requirements for adoption (they want to make sure the dogs don't end up right back in the shelter!). Some don't allow college students (who are notoriously transient) to adopt dogs under any circumstances. Some require written proof from renters that the landlord accepts dogs. Some interview prospective adopters to find a good match, and many require spaying or neutering (many also have the procedure done before you can adopt or give adopters discount coupons for the procedure).

Adopting a shelter dog carries many of the same risks as adopting a rescue dog (see "The Rescue Adoption Option" section, earlier in this chapter). Although shelter workers make every effort to evaluate the personalities of different dogs, they are often overburdened, overworked, and understaffed, and barraged with more animals than they can keep track of. But, again, with some time, effort, and financial resources, including classes with a good trainer and sessions with a canine-behavior consultant, many shelter dogs, even with troubled pasts, can be successfully and lovingly rehabilitated into the ideal family pet.

Labs from Neighbors or Friends

Maybe your neighbor is a breeder. Maybe you're lucky, and she's a good breeder. But a lot of people (though certainly not all) breeding dogs in their backyards aren't doing it with specific goals such as health and temperament in mind. Dogs from breeders like these will often have more than their fair share of genetic and behavioral problems, and although they may be cheaper up front, they may be far more expensive in the long run. "But Mrs. Smith is such a nice lady!" you may protest. Go ahead and have coffee with her every Wednesday afternoon. Feel free to gossip over the fence together or swap recipes or power tools or whatever. But we suggest you get your dog from a more reliable source.

If, on the other hand, your neighbor's Lab had an unwanted litter, you may be tempted to take one of the puppies off her hands so they don't end up euthanized. You're running a risk if you don't know the health, temperament, or even the appearance or breed of the *sire* (the father of a litter of puppies; the *dam* is the mother). Yet if you raise the dog well from puppyhood, don't care what she will look like, and don't mind what size she will be, you very well may end up with a great pet. Plus, you can rest easy knowing you have rescued a Lab or Lab mix from possible destruction. But be ready for surprises, especially in the way of unexpected health problems.

Classified Labs: The Newspaper

A lot of breeders advertise in the classified section of the newspaper, so this is one way to find breeders in your area. However, a classified ad in no way proves that the breeder is a good one. Go ahead and call a breeder listed in the newspaper, but screen the breeder over the phone, asking the same questions you will ask in person (see the "Conducting an interview" section, earlier in this chapter). If they can't give you the right answers, save yourself the trip. The breeder should also screen you on the phone; if they don't, he or she must not be too concerned about where their pups wind up.

The newspaper is also the place to find dogs whose owners can no longer keep them. Maybe the dog is a gem, and the owner wants to avoid taking her to the animal shelter. On the other hand, maybe the dog is a big problem, and the owner has no intention of telling you that his 95-pound Lab, Skippy, has to find a new home because she has chewed her way through all the neighbors and is working on a serious criminal record. That "free to good home" dog may end up costing you a fortune. Spend adequate time with the dog and the owner to get a sense of the true situation before making a decision.

That Doggy in the Window: Pet Stores

Pet stores are the first place many people look when they consider buying a dog, and lots of people have purchased great pets from pet stores. We feel, though, that if you're going to pay a lot of money for a dog, you should be able to talk to the breeder and see the dog's parents. When you purchase a dog from a pet store, you have no access to the breeder, so you can't ask any questions or see the premises.

However, some pet store employees know a lot about Labs and some make a serious effort to sell dogs only to those who appear as though they will provide a good home. While we don't highly recommend it, we'll admit that lots of people have purchased great pets from pet stores.

Chapter 5

Taking Care of Your Lab

• •

In This Chapter

▶ Naming your dog's parts

▶ Knowing your Lab's genetic tendencies

▶ Deciding what to feed your dog (and how much and how often)

▶ Exercising and grooming your Lab

• •

*A*fter you bring home your practically perfect pet, you want to keep her healthy. Maintaining a healthy Labrador Retriever is a relatively easy task, especially if you focus on preventive maintenance. Health problems, just like behavior problems, are a lot easier to prevent than to fix!

Labrador Retrievers are a particularly healthy and robust breed with few genetic abnormalities (although genetic problems do occasionally crop up in any breed). They are the prototypical medium-sized dogs and are often the breed used to illustrate a typical dog in all kinds of books, magazines, and other publications. Of course, your Lab is anything but typical — she's special! And you want to know everything about her.

It is important to find a breeder who makes health a breeding priority. How do you know whether a breeder has healthy stock? Get a veterinary reference. If the vet confirms that the breeder tends to have healthy puppies that only need to see the vet for preventive maintenance (such as vaccinations and worming), you'll feel much better about your puppy's chances for good health. See Chapter 4 for more on finding a breeder.

Lab at a Glance

When you look at your Lab, what do you see? You see those loving eyes and that playful demeanor, but do you know the signs of good health? Are you familiar with basic canine anatomy? And do you know what your dog's genetic tendencies are in terms of health? You'll be better able to maintain and preserve your dog's health if you know what to expect, what looks and feels normal, and what signs to watch for that may indicate a potential problem.

Each day during your dog's grooming session, move your hands over her coat. Get to know how your Lab feels. If you're familiar with your Lab's normal condition, you'll recognize any changes, such as lumps, bumps, dry skin patches, hair loss, weight loss, weight gain, or sores. The sooner you alert your vet to problems such as these, the better they can be resolved.

Anatomy of a Labrador Retriever

As you get to know your dog, you may wonder what all of her body parts are called. Knowing a little bit about canine anatomy helps you to know your dog better and also to be able to talk to your vet in a more specific and informative way.

Do you know a hock from a stifle? The withers from the croup? Check out Figure 5-1 for a complete rundown of the body parts of your Labrador Retriever:

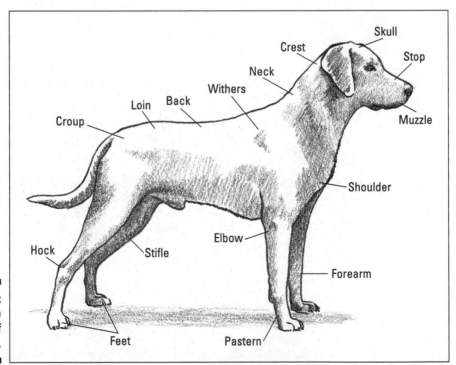

Figure 5-1:
The anatomy of a Lab.

- The *skull* consists of the bone components of the head.

- The *crest* is the upper rear arched portion of the neck, just below the *occiput* (base of the skull).

- The *neck* is the area between the head and the shoulders.

- The *withers* are the highest points of the shoulder blades.

- The *back* is the long plane between shoulder blades and hips.

- The *loin* is the area between the back and end of the ribcage and the croup or pelvic girdle.

- The *croup* is that portion of the body above the hind legs and extending from the loin to the base of the tail and the buttock area.

- The *hock* joint is the lower joint on the rear leg between the lower thigh and the rear pastern.

- The *stifle* is the knee joint located between the upper and lower thigh.

- The *elbow* is the joint between the upper arm and forearm.

- The *dewclaw* is a vestigial claw on the pastern of the front legs; it's often removed on puppies.

- The *pastern* is the region between the wrist and forefoot.

- The *wrist* is the joint connecting the forearm and the pastern.

- The *forearm* is the region between the elbow and the wrist.

- The *shoulder* is the shoulder blade or scapula and associated muscles.

- The *muzzle* is the foreface or forward portion of the upper and lower jaw and the nose portion of the head; in other words, the portion of the head in front of the eyes.

- The *stop* is the dividing point between the muzzle and the skull. It marks a change in the profile line between the muzzle and skull.

Size doesn't matter

Labrador Retrievers come in all sizes, from very small (around 35 pounds) to very large (over 100 pounds). Although the breed standard (the standard used to judge purebred show dogs) calls for a dog between 21½ and 24½ inches and weighing between 55 and 80 pounds, that doesn't mean your practically perfect Lab will necessarily fall into that standard. Most breeders would agree that form follows function and because Labs do so many diverse jobs, it only makes sense that they come in many different sizes. A friendly, eager, and intelligent character is a more consistent quality of the Labrador Retriever than size.

Labrador Retriever health in brief

Because there are so many Labrador Retrievers, breeders have a large gene pool to draw from. That translates into healthier dogs. Knowledgeable breeders do health checks and everything else they can to avoid genetic disorders. However, because breeding is not only a relatively new science but also an art, it isn't possible to completely avoid all genetic problems. Science is continually developing better tests to pinpoint genetic diseases, sometimes before the dog shows any symptoms. Yet there still is much work in this area to be done.

While Labs tend to be healthy, some genetic disorders do occasionally occur. These are some of the more common genetic disorders in Labrador Retrievers:

- **Hip dysplasia:** This is the most common orthopedic problem in Labs (and in many larger dogs). Although not congenital (it isn't present at birth), hip dysplasia is probably due to a combination of genetic and environmental factors. If your dog develops hip dysplasia (the condition can be seen on an x-ray), she may suffer no symptoms at all. Or she may eventually experience severe pain and even lameness. Some Labs require no treatment, but if your Lab develops hip dysplasia and does require treatment, many excellent management strategies, treatments, and surgical options exist.

- **Progressive retinal atrophy (PRA):** This degenerative eye disorder eventually results in your dog becoming blind. A board-certified canine ophthalmologist can examine your dog's eyes if you suspect she is having any vision problems. PRA is a genetic problem involving a recessive gene. If a puppy receives the gene from both parents, she will develop PRA. If she receives the gene from only one parent, she will be a carrier and should not be bred to another Lab that is also a carrier. The location of the gene that involves PRA has been determined in Labs, and a blood test has been developed to determine whether a Lab is affected, a carrier, or clear. If you buy your Lab from a breeder who is diligent about eye testing, you probably won't encounter PRA.

- **Epilepsy:** If your Lab has epilepsy, that means she will have seizures. Epilepsy can be due to environmental or genetic factors and will probably show up relatively early if inherited. Seizures can be frightening for your Lab and for you. The most important thing to do for your Lab during a seizure is to keep her from hurting herself. Talk to your vet about the best strategies for managing seizures if your Lab has epilepsy. Depending on the frequency and severity of the seizures, your vet may recommend medication.

For more information on your Lab's health, see Chapter 6.

It's a Dog-Eat-Food World

One of the most common questions new dog owners ask veterinarians is, "What should I feed my dog?" Perusing the aisles at your local pet store or grocery store may only confuse you further. The choices are seemingly endless, and the range in price is dramatic. Is a basic, inexpensive food good enough? Are so-called premium foods worth the price? Can't you just throw your dog a bone?

Pet nutrition is a big industry right now, and it pays to know what's hype and what's important information. Although the science is constantly changing and the press releases from the various big-name dog food companies are relentless, in this section, we give you our down-to-earth take on the matter.

Reading labels

The dog food name, company reputation, and the nicely decorated package often influence which brands people tend to buy. Only one thing should influence you, however: the label. No matter the price, no matter how clever or cute the television commercial, and no matter what your friends or neighbors say, the label is the only thing that will tell you how good a dog food is.

What should you look for? First, look for approval by AAFCO, the Association of American Feed Control Officials. All dog foods must be approved by AAFCO if they advertise as being an acceptable diet. Only supplemental foods such as treats don't require an AAFCO statement, so most dog foods have it. But if the one you're looking at doesn't have it, put it back on the shelf. It isn't nutritionally adequate.

Homemade dog food?

Should you feed your dog a homemade diet? Homemade diets are particularly good for those few dogs who don't do well on commercial dog foods, either due to allergies or sensitivity to certain ingredients. However, homemade diets must be scrupulously prepared, and you have to know what you are doing. They take a lot more time to prepare than it takes to scoop out commercial dog food, and a diet lacking in any important vitamins, minerals, or other nutrients can seriously compromise your dog's health. For example, your dog may become very sick on an all-meat diet. If you like the idea of making your own dog food, read up on the subject, and don't skimp on ingredients. A few excellent books show you how to prepare a homemade diet that's nutritionally complete (see the Appendix).

But you don't want a food that's merely adequate, do you? You want a food that's good, a food that will help your dog be as healthy as possible. Many companies also have their own feeding trials so they can best refine their foods to help dogs thrive. Look for evidence of feeding trials on the label.

Take a look at your dog's teeth. Are they a little different than your own teeth? You bet they are! Dogs are carnivores. Sure, they can eat grains and vegetables (in the wild, they eat whole animals, including the animal's stomach contents, which often consist of grains and vegetables). But dogs need a higher level of protein than humans. Although grains and vegetables contain protein, it isn't in a form as digestible as meat. Therefore, we recommend looking for a food that lists at least two sources of meat in the first five ingredients.

Most dog foods list a few grain sources in the first five ingredients as well. That's fine. Grain is a protein source, too, although a few dogs have allergies to certain grains (try out a lamb and rice or other anti-allergenic dog food if your dog has trouble digesting her food). Just be sure grains aren't the only protein source. Grains are high in carbohydrates, and dogs don't digest carbohydrates as well as humans do. Too much of some grains may also hinder the absorption of other important nutrients. For example, iron absorption is hindered by diets high in soy protein.

AAFCO-approved dog foods also contain an array of vitamins and minerals. If the food is approved by AAFCO and especially if it has successfully passed feeding trials, the vitamin/mineral ratios should be adequate.

Look for how the food is preserved. Most foods these days are naturally preserved with vitamin E and sometimes vitamin C. Chemical preservatives such as *ethoxyquin* (a known carcinogen) can harm your dog's health and are best avoided.

After you find foods that meet these basic requirements, the rest is up to you. You can find all kinds of fancy foods out there. Some are loaded with delicious-sounding ingredients, lots of natural and organic vegetables, herbs, fancy oils, and high-protein grains. Others are strictly no-frills. As long as the food you choose meets the standards we set out, it should be fine for your dog.

The last, and perhaps most important, consideration: Your dog should think the food you feed her is yummy! If your dog eats the food you've chosen eagerly (and most Labs eat just about anything eagerly!), you have your dog food.

If your dog refuses to eat her food, she may be sick, or the food may be spoiled. If it smells of rancid fat, throw it out. Always check the food for expiration dates and bugs, and don't feed your dog expired or infested food. To avoid spoilage, keep dog food sealed in an airtight container and don't buy more than a month's supply at one time.

Although some people advocate giving dogs raw meat bones, we don't recommend it for Labrador Retrievers. Labs are chewers extraordinaire and even large raw bones can splinter in their powerful jaws. Bone splinters can cause internal injuries, so forego the raw bones for your Lab and stick to sturdy chew toys for chewing.

Feeding a puppy

Puppies eat puppy food, don't they? You may be surprised to discover that we don't recommend puppy food for your Labrador Retriever puppy. Although great for small dogs, the high protein and fat content of puppy food may encourage your Lab puppy to grow too fast. Several studies in the early 1990s demonstrated that larger breeds, including Labrador Retrievers, that grow too rapidly as puppies are at a higher risk for orthopedic problems, such as hip dysplasia, later in life.

A high-quality adult maintenance diet, however, is perfect for a Labrador Retriever puppy. You can also find puppy foods specifically for larger breeds. Just be sure you feed your Lab enough, but not too much. Your puppy should grow at a steady rate, stay slim and well-muscled, and have plenty of energy (your dog's condition is a better indicator of how much to feed than are the guidelines on the bag).

How often should you feed your ravenous little puppy? We don't recommend making food available all day long (called *free feeding*). Labs love to eat, and even on an adult-maintenance diet, a puppy could become overweight. Instead, feed your puppy three times per day for the first three or four months. Then, you can usually switch to a twice-a-day diet.

Avoid feeding your Lab, even when she's an adult, just once per day. Labs love to eat, so let them enjoy it twice each day. Just be sure to adjust portions accordingly so that your Lab doesn't get too fat! A number of recent studies have suggested that deep-chested dogs such as Labrador Retrievers may be more prone to bloating or stomach torsion, an extremely painful and life-threatening condition, if they're only fed once per day. Once-a-day feeding encourages faster, more frantic eating, which may contribute to bloating.

How much should your puppy eat? That depends on how active she is, how often she's outside in cold weather, and how old she is. The portions on the dog food bags may not be right for your dog. For puppies, we recommend starting with 1 cup of dry food three times per day. Take the food away after fifteen minutes. If your puppy doesn't finish her food, adjust the daily portion down by ¼ cup or so. If your puppy acts frantically hungry, adjust the daily portion up by ¼ cup or so.

Take time to experiment. Don't overfeed your puppy, but don't starve her, either. In general, if your Lab is energetic, looks healthy, has bright eyes and a shiny coat, and eats with relish but not so desperately that she acts as if she is starving, you have the right portion. Also, do a rib test once every month or so. If you can see your dog's ribs, she may be too thin. If you can't feel her ribs when you run your hands gently along your dog's ribcage, she may be too fat. If you can feel them under a light layer of flesh but they don't have a pronounced appearance, your dog is probably just right.

When your dog becomes more or less active, when she reaches adult height, or when the weather changes, you may need to adjust the food portion once again. The trick is to stay tuned in to your dog.

Feeding an adult Lab

If you've been feeding your puppy a high quality adult-maintenance dog food, you don't need to switch foods when she reaches adulthood. Labs continue to grow for two years or so, but nothing matches the growth rate of that first year. When your puppy reaches her first birthday, you can probably decrease portions slightly. But again, the best way to know how much to feed your dog is to pay attention to the way she looks and acts and to gauge her individual energy needs. The more energy she uses, the more quality protein and calories she requires.

Feeding an older Lab

Just because your dog is getting older doesn't mean she's getting sicker, slower, or any less hungry. The old school of canine nutrition once believed that older dogs (over the age of 8) should automatically be switched to a lower protein diet. Now nutrition scientists are discovering that unless a dog already has a kidney problem (and keep in mind that the kidneys process protein), senior dogs need just as much, if not more, protein than younger adult dogs.

Older dogs tend to lose lean body mass (muscle), so they need plenty of protein to stay strong. Protein doesn't cause kidney problems (some evidence points to too much phosphorous as the cause), although protein can aggravate an existing kidney problem.

If your older dog has become less active, she may require fewer calories than before. Decreasing portions slightly may be all you need to do. On the other hand, if your dog becomes inactive due to a health problem such as hip dysplasia, you may need to switch to a nutritionally dense food that offers more nutrition in each bite. Older dogs may not be as hungry, either, so nutritionally dense food may become important. If your dog's appetite changes or you feel she needs a dietary adjustment, see your vet for advice.

Supplementing a Lab's diet

Should you give your dog vitamin or mineral supplements? Most canine nutritionists say no, as long as you're feeding your dog a dog food that's nutritionally complete. Over-supplementation can compromise your dog's (and especially your puppy's) health by skewing the balance of nutrients. Unless your vet recommends supplements to address a particular health problem, stick to your regular dog food.

On the other hand, if you keep your Lab healthy and active, she may not show a single sign of slowing down even into her second decade of life. If your dog remains active and retains her appetite, there isn't any reason to change her diet.

Consider adding about ¼ cup of plain yogurt with active cultures mixed into your dog's food a few times a week. Yogurt helps to replenish your dog's intestinal flora and improve her digestion. Just don't use the sweetened kind. You may not like plain yogurt, but your dog will probably find it an interesting addition to her regular kibble.

Accommodating an active dog

Some dogs are extra rambunctious. Other dogs are true working dogs, whether avid hunters, trackers, or high-level obedience competitors. These very active dogs need extra protein and calories to give them enough energy and to maintain their muscle mass. If your dog is very active, you can feed her more than you would feed a normally active or sedentary dog.

The food you choose can be a high-protein food, as long as the protein is from a good source (in other words, meat). You may also want to supplement your active dog's diet with a little extra fat, especially during the winter months if your dog is often outside in very cold temperatures. One tablespoon of canola or safflower oil mixed with your dog's food and a scrambled or boiled egg once or twice a week will give your active dog a dietary energy boost. Remember to keep monitoring your dog. If she is getting too thin (if you can see her ribs), gradually increase her portions.

Checking whether your dog can pinch an inch

Labs certainly tend to be active, but because they love to eat, they also tend to get overweight. Some Labs prefer a relatively sedentary life which, coupled with the typical Lab appetite, can translate into extra pounds that may eventually compromise your dog's health. Overweight Labs are more prone to hip dysplasia and other bone and joint problems. They are more likely to suffer from heart disease (just like overweight humans). In addition, many other bodily organs and systems wear down faster in an overweight dog. As we mentioned before, it is particularly dangerous to overfeed a puppy because a too-fast rate of growth can seriously compromise bone and joint strength later in life.

One of the main reasons Labs (and other dogs) get to be overweight is from too many treats and/or table scraps. It's tempting to give your Lab the rest of that cheeseburger and French fries or the last of the vanilla pudding or meatloaf or lasagna. But after you begin feeding your dog just one bite of your dinner, extra feeding can easily get out of hand. Instead, make it a rule never to feed your dog any of the food the family is having for dinner, especially not right from your plate (it's unhealthy, and it encourages bad manners!). If you absolutely must feed her some people food, mix a cooked egg or some cooked vegetables into her regular food, in her regular food bowl. Remember, obesity is one of the most common health problems in dogs. Too much extra food, even healthy food, is bound to end up around your dog's middle.

To keep your dog from becoming overweight from too many training treats, use pieces of regular dog food taken out of your dog's daily allowance of food for training sessions. Reserve extra dog treats for special occasions.

How can you tell if your dog is too fat? First, look at your dog from above. Her waist should be narrower than her ribcage. If she looks like a barrel, she's probably overweight. Next, feel your dog's ribs. If they feel as if they are padded with a mattress (in other words, if you have difficulty finding them), your dog is probably overweight. Check with your vet if you suspect your dog has been packing on the extra pounds, and then work together to manage your dog's weight problem through a combination of dietary adjustments and exercise.

Helping ailing dogs recover

Certain health problems, such as kidney disease, diabetes, and heart disease, require dietary alterations. Your vet can best advise you on how to change your dog's diet to best manage a particular disease. If your dog is diagnosed with any disease or condition and your vet doesn't mention your dog's diet, be sure to ask if you should be making any changes in your dog's diet. And be forthcoming. If you've been feeding your dog pepperoni pizza four times a week, tell your vet. It may help him or her diagnose a problem.

Don't share that chocolate bar with your dog! Some dogs are allergic to chocolate and even a little can kill them. Don't risk trying to find out whether your dog can handle chocolate. Even if your dog isn't allergic, chocolate has no nutritional value and is bad for your dog's health.

Labs Are Movers and Shakers

Dogs need exercise, just like humans. Obese dogs need it, slim dogs need it, puppies need it, adult dogs need it and senior dogs need it. Exercise keeps your dog's muscles strong and her heart fit and provides a release for all that Lab energy! Labs who don't get enough exercise may wind up engaging in destructive chewing, or they may become jittery, nervous, and/or hyperactive. One or two nice long daily walks, at least twenty to thirty minutes, is all it takes, and you'll benefit, too! If you have a large fenced yard, don't think that's a substitute for a daily walk. Walking your dog is a great way for the two of you to engage in an activity together. This will improve your relationship. Extra time romping in the backyard is great for Labs, too.

Puppies need exercise

Lab puppies can be quite active. They need to have lots of outlets for that energy. If you expect them to lie at your feet all day, you'll probably end up getting the shoes chewed right off your feet! The fact that excess weight is particularly bad for puppies is another reason to make sure your pup gets lots of exercise.

Couch potato owners have couch potato dogs

If you're the sedentary type but have your heart set on a Lab, consider an older Lab who doesn't have the energy level of a puppy. Some older Labs love to sit around all day, although they should have at least one daily walk to keep in shape. If you never get any exercise, however, and can't even make yourself take that daily walk, either consider getting another type of dog (many small dogs can get enough exercise just running around the house) or hiring someone to walk your Lab for you. Otherwise, you'll end up with a couch potato dog who may suffer from serious health problems as she ages.

Dog daycare afternoon

Do you love dogs, but have to work all day and can't come home for lunch? Hire a dog walker, pet sitter, or doggy daycare center to fill in when you can't be there. More and more such services are popping up all over the country as people become increasingly aware of the importance of meeting their pets' needs. Check your phone book.

Or hire a trusted friend or family member to do the job. Your Lab will welcome the company, and you'll feel better, too.

Get your puppy used to walking on a leash right away. Put a collar and leash on your puppy as soon as you bring her home and keep it slack while following the puppy around in a safe area. Then follow the directions in Chapter 11 to teach your puppy to walk on a slack lead. Soon you'll be walking together like pros and getting the exercise your puppy needs.

Adults and seniors need exercise, too!

When your Lab is no longer a puppy, she may settle down a bit and require less exercise. On the other hand, she may not. Some Labs are highly energetic and enjoy lots of activity all the way through old age. Don't slack off on the walks just because your dog is no longer a puppy. Keeping your dog fit requires exercise every day, no matter your dog's age. Many old Labrador Retrievers are still happy to go on long, brisk walks, catch a Frisbee, or retrieve game on an all-day hunting trip.

To keep your Lab in good physical condition, allow him to get at least 30 minutes of exercise every day. To combat boredom (your Lab's or yours), alternate long walks; romps in the park; field trips to dog-friendly recreational areas, beaches, or hiking trails; and, of course, lots of retrieving activities.

However, if your dog begins to suffer from bone or joint trouble in old age, you may need to slow things down a bit. Swimming is an excellent exercise for dogs who have hip dysplasia and other bone disorders. Take the cue from your dog and be sensitive. Labs love to please, so they may push themselves too hard if they think you really want to run that extra mile. Be in tune to signs your older dog needs to slow down: panting, limping, slowing the pace, or signs of extreme exhaustion after exercise, such as sleeping for an unusually long time. Also, don't forget to check your dog all over during your daily grooming sessions. If touching certain areas elicits a yelp or a whimper, your dog is probably in pain. See your vet and take it easy on your dog, at least for awhile.

Puppies and older dogs alike can experience joint injuries and foot pad injuries from running on concrete. If possible, allow your dog to walk on grass, dirt, or any surface softer than a hard street or sidewalk. If you must walk your dog on concrete, slow the pace.

Some Beauty Is Skin Deep

The last important aspect of preventive care for your Lab is the daily grooming session. Labs are easy to groom and don't take much effort; there's no long coat to untangle or wiry coat to strip, for example. Daily grooming is important nonetheless. It is an important way for you and your Lab to bond, thus improving your relationship. It is also your chance to monitor your dog for any physical or behavioral changes. Consider it a chance to touch base with your best friend. Your dog will come to depend on it, and so will you.

Good grooming involves more than a clean coat. It also involves foot and nail care, eye and ear care, and a health check. A well-groomed dog is clean and beautiful. An ungroomed dog looks (and is) neglected. Keep your dog healthy and looking her best through vigilant grooming.

Saving your Lab's skin (and coat)

Every day, begin your grooming session by giving your Lab a good going-over with your bare hands. Massage her head, face, neck, back, chest, legs, and tail with your fingers, feeling for any lumps, bumps, dry patches, hair loss, or anything else abnormal. The more you do this, the more you'll get used to the feel of your Lab and the better you're able to notice when something changes. Massaging also loosen dead hair and skin so that it can be brushed away. In addition, your Lab will become accustomed to such a once-over and will be much easier for a vet to handle, when necessary.

Brush your Lab with a natural bristle or nylon brush. Although Lab coats don't require a daily brushing (they can get by with a weekly brushing), daily brushing feels great to your Lab and keeps her coat immaculately clean, free from shed hairs, and shiny. Be sure to also go over her coat with a flea comb, removing any dead fleas and checking for signs of infestation.

Labs don't need to be bathed frequently, and too-frequent bathing can dry out their skin, stripping it of natural oils. (Thank goodness, because bathing a Lab can be a challenging experience — see Figure 5-2.) Instead, make sure your Lab has plenty of time outdoors each day (outdoor air is good for keeping the skin moist) and stick to a good brushing for cleanliness. Bathe your Lab only when she gets really dirty; sometimes plain water will do the trick.

Figure 5-2:
Washing
your Lab
can also
mean a bath
for you!

© Nance Photography/AKC Stock Images

The eyes and ears have it

It's time to play vet. Check your Lab's eyes and ears so she becomes used to having them looked at. Your vet's job will be much easier if your Lab is used to this kind of prodding.

When you look at your Lab's eyes, check for discharge or irritation. If they look like they need it, you can clean gently around your Lab's eyes with a cotton ball soaked in boiled and cooled saltwater (use about a ¼ teaspoon of salt per cup of water). If you have a yellow Lab and the area around her eyes becomes stained due to the normal production of the tear ducts, rest assured that this is natural and not really a problem. It doesn't hurt your dog. If you want to remove the stains, ask your vet to do it or very carefully remove them with a cotton ball soaked in hydrogen peroxide. Always put a drop of mineral oil in each of your Lab's eyes first, however (see Figure 5-3). If you get hydrogen peroxide in her eyes, it will hurt.

If your dog's eyes look irritated, she could have a blocked tear duct, an over-active tear duct, conjunctivitis, or something in her eye. Call your vet for advice. If your Lab is showing signs of vision loss or if her eyes look cloudy, she could be developing cataracts. As long as you've been taking your dog for annual appointments, your vet can probably catch cataracts early, but don't hesitate to take your dog to the vet if you suspect that anything is wrong with her eyes.

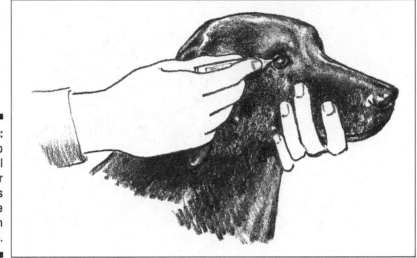

Figure 5-3:
Put a drop of mineral oil in your Lab's eyes before wiping with peroxide.

Never put your fingers or any other implement into your dog's eye.

Your Lab's ears should be clean and free of ticks and fleas (of course). If your Lab's ears look dirty or waxy, you can clean the outside with a cotton ball or cotton swab. Never put anything into your dog's ear canal! If your dog is scratching or shaking her ears quite a bit but you don't see any pests, or if you notice redness or a bad smell, take your dog to the vet. She could have mites, a yeast infection, or a bacterial infection, which your vet will have you treat with an ear cleaner or medication.

Getting off on the right foot

Foot care for Labs is as easy as coat care. Pick up each foot, moving each toe and pressing lightly on each foot pad to accustom your dog to having her feet examined. The most important thing to do in your daily grooming session is to make sure your Lab's nails aren't getting too long. Long nails force the footpads apart on hard surfaces, making it difficult for your dog to walk correctly. Bone and joint problems may result if your dog's nails remain untrimmed for long periods of time.

To trim your Lab's nails, use a trimmer made for large dogs, never a human nail trimmer (see Figure 5-4). Trim your Lab's nails frequently so you never have to trim off too much. This trimming will train the *quick,* the vein that runs through the nail, to recede. In nails that are never trimmed, the quick extends farther into the nail, and if clipped, they will bleed. (Keep a styptic pencil nearby to stem any bleeding just in case this happens.) You can see the quick in Labs with light-colored nails, but in black and chocolate Labs, you have to guess. Just don't clip too far up.

Figure 5-4:
Use caution
when
trimming
your Lab's
nails.

Clip off the nail tips, just where the underside of the nail starts to curve. Trimming your dog's nails every three to four weeks should be sufficient to keep them in good condition.

Some Labs develop cysts between their toes. A topical antibiotic ointment may help, or your veterinarian may choose to lance the cysts. Labs prone to cysts tend to develop them periodically, and a cyst takes about a week or a little longer to resolve. If your Lab is prone to cysts, make sure the cysts remain clean and uninfected. See your vet if you think that a cyst between your Lab's toes has become infected or if you aren't sure what to do about it.

Those pearly whites

The last important part of your daily grooming session should be a good teeth-brushing. Yes, dogs should have their teeth brushed, too! Dental plaque can get into your dog's bloodstream and into her heart, causing heart disease and dramatically shortening her life! If your dog has a serious problem with plaque or *tartar buildup* (that brownish yellow gook that sticks to her teeth), you can pay a vet to remove it. Sometimes this procedure requires an anesthetic. To avoid this problem, begin brushing your puppy's teeth on the first day you bring her home, and do it at least weekly (or even better, every day) to keep teeth their cleanest. (If you brush every day, shouldn't your dogs?) To maintain good bite inhibition, get your Lab used to having human hands in her mouth.

At your local pet store you can purchase a special long-handled dog toothbrush and toothpaste made for dogs (never use human toothpaste on dogs). Dog toothpaste tastes yummy to dogs, so at first, just let your dog lick the toothpaste off the brush. After a day or two of this, you can start carefully introducing the brush to her teeth (see Figure 5-5). Don't expect to be able to do a full, thorough brushing at first. As your dog gets used to the toothbrush, she'll eventually let you scrub away, revealing those pearly whites in their full glory.

Figure 5-5:
Brush your
Lab's teeth
daily.

Canned dog food is more likely to cause dental problems than dry dog food. The greater moisture content makes canned dog food stick to your Lab's teeth. Your dog will love dry dog food if she's hungry. Dry dog food is not only equally nutritious, but it cleans teeth and is more cost-effective. We suggest avoiding canned dog food.

Is your Lab healthy? A checklist

Just so you don't forget anything, we've provided you with a healthy Lab checklist. You can copy it and post it by your grooming area so you can go through it each day. Whenever you notice anything that may indicate your Lab is less than healthy, call your vet.

Today, my Lab had:

- A shiny, clean coat
- Smooth skin without dry patches
- Clean, bright eyes
- Clean, pest-free ears
- Short nails
- Healthy foot pads with no cracks
- Clean, white teeth
- No fleas or ticks
- A normal energy level
- A good appetite

Chapter 6

An Ounce of Prevention

*N*othing beats the effectiveness of preventive medicine. Incorporating a few basic routines into your life for the sake of your dog's health can go a long way toward minimizing health problems in the future. Even minor neglect and forgetting to pay attention to subtle cues from your dog can result in a lot of pain and suffering — not to mention financial cost — down the road. Establish a preventive routine when you first get your puppy and consider the small amount of extra time a worthwhile investment in your dog's future health (and in your future financial security).

You may have heard of pet health insurance. Before you sign up and send off that hefty check, make sure you know exactly what the plan covers and what it doesn't cover. Health insurance can be a great help with the cost of a major medical event such as surgery, chemotherapy, or a transplant. However, many plans have large deductibles, don't cover basic care, and don't cover past a certain age. Some plans may be perfect for you and your dog, but read the fine print — and buyer beware.

Finding the Right Care

It's a good idea to take your new puppy to a vet within the first two or three days after you bring her home, preferably right away. That isn't much time to spend choosing the practically perfect veterinarian, so it pays to do a little research even before you've chosen a puppy. If that first vet visit is with a vet who was a random pick from the Yellow Pages, don't feel you have to stick with him or her if you aren't comfortable.

Ideally, however, the same vet will see your puppy on her very first vet visit with you, and you will continue with that vet through her life. Although vet practices are beginning to resemble those large, human medical practices with multiple doctors (where you never know which doctor you'll get to see), there are plenty of smaller practices out there. We like these smaller practices, where the vet can get to know your dog and can help you to follow, keep track of, and maintain her good health.

That's not to say there aren't wonderful veterinarians in larger practices. Choosing the right vet and the right practice are important first steps in assuring a lifetime of good health for your dog. Don't be flippant about a decision like this. Take it as seriously as you would take the task of choosing a doctor for yourself or your children. After all, your Lab is a member of the family.

You probably aren't a vet. How are you supposed to know which among the many vets out there is the right vet for your Lab? The following sections show you how you can evaluate a vet who will tell you whether the match is right.

Asking around

Talk to the breeder about vets he or she likes. Talk to friends with dogs about their veterinary experiences. (You can learn a lot through the grapevine, although not everything you hear is necessarily true. Use your good judgment.) In most cities and many smaller towns, vets abound. Chances are, you'll have a wide variety from which to choose, so asking fellow dog owners whom they like and don't like helps you to narrow the field.

Considering some practical factors

After you've culled a list, pare your list down further by considering some practical factors:

- ✔ Which vets are closest to your home? In an emergency, a ten-minute drive to the vet is better than a 60-minute drive.

- ✔ Do you prefer a large practice or a small practice? A good small practice may have just the personal touch you like, but it may be easier to get an appointment in a larger practice because more vets are on hand (then again, it may not be; some large practices like to overbook).

- ✔ If your dog has a particular health problem, such as hip dysplasia or epilepsy, you'll want a vet with experience in that area.

Vets are people, too! When meeting vets on your introductory visit, be polite and ask questions in a friendly manner. Don't grill the vet or act as though you assume the worst. If you put the vet on the defensive, you won't get an accurate picture of his or her personality, and the vet won't think much of you, either!

Making a few appointments to meet the vets

Call the office and explain that you have a new puppy and are interested in meeting the vet to see whether he or she would be right for you. Don't apologize for a visit like this! Don't say something like, "I know this might be silly or a waste of your time, but I wanted to meet the vet before I decided which vet to choose." The vet works for you, and you have every right to meet him or her and evaluate the practice before handing over your hard-earned cash and your well-loved pet. On the flip side, however, if you take up the vet's time with an interview, expect to pay for an office visit.

Say something to the effect of, "Hello. I have a new Labrador Retriever and am in the process of choosing a veterinarian. I would like to make an appointment for my dog and me to meet Dr. So-and-So and find out a little about your practice." What kind of reception do you get?

- ✔ "He doesn't have time for that kind of thing unless you'll be wanting a full checkup and tests for your dog." Bad sign. This practice is probably more concerned with making lots of money than with getting to know its clients and providing a good service.

- ✔ "We can mail you a brochure, and then you can call us back to schedule a checkup." Another bad sign. This practice may not have time for you and doesn't want to provide the personal touch.

- ✔ "No problem, we have an opening five weeks from next Thursday." Red flag! Either this practice has more clients than it can handle, or it makes introductory visits a very low priority.

- ✔ "Can you come in right now?" Hmm. Could be a good sign — maybe they just had a cancellation. But it could also mean this practice is desperate for clients, and you have to wonder why. We don't mean to be suspicious, but your dog deserves the best.

- ✔ "Sure! Dr. So-and-So would love to meet your dog and tell you about his/her services. How about Wednesday at 3:00?" Now we're talking! This veterinary practice has passed the first test.

You may have to pay the price of an office visit for your introductory meeting with the vet. This is reasonable — you're paying for some of the vet's time, and he or she, in return, should spend some quality time with you, answering questions and telling you about the practice. You shouldn't pay for tests or time for examining your dog, however. This is just a meeting.

Don't be afraid to shop around a bit. The first practice you see isn't necessarily the best, and there isn't any reason to settle for so-so care from Dr. So-and-So just because that's what you happened upon first. And always take your dog with you when you visit a new vet. Labs are good judges of character!

Noting first impressions

Arrive for your introductory appointment ten or fifteen minutes early so you get a chance to fill out any necessary paperwork and survey the reception area. Is it clean? Does it smell good? Is the staff friendly and not too hurried? (All office staffs are hurried on some days, but if it looks like frantic chaos is the normal state of this practice, make a note.) Is the reception area a pleasant place to wait?

Make a note of how long you have to wait to see the vet. No one should have to wait an hour, or even a half-hour, in our opinion. If you've waited for over 20 minutes, you're justified in asking the staff if something is going on to delay your appointment and if the wait is always this long. How do they react? Ask politely and you should receive a polite answer. If they snap at you, take note. (And if you're writing everything down in a little notebook, they'll probably take note, too!) A wait of between five and 20 minutes is reasonable.

Also, pay attention to your Lab. Is she very resistant to entering the room? Does she cower, whine, or act afraid after she's in the room? Or does she act curious and interested? A bad reaction from your dog could be due to a bad experience at a vet before you brought the dog home. Or perhaps your dog is still shy and needs more socialization. But maybe she is reacting to something you can't perceive and is signaling you that this isn't the right place to be. Don't make a quick assumption if your Lab doesn't like where she is. But do notice.

Visit at least three different vets in your quest to find the right vet for you. If your dog acts negatively at each place, the problem is probably with your dog. If she acts friendly and happy in some places but fearful or hesitant in others, add your dog's opinion to the list of your own impressions. After all, it's her doctor you're choosing!

Examining your vet's bedside manner

Now it's your turn to see the vet. Continue to pay attention to your first impressions. Is the vet hurried? Does he or she seem annoyed or irritated by your questions, or is the vet friendly and open to your questions? Is the vet enthusiastic and willing to share information? Is he or she excited about the quality of the practice, or does the vet seem burned out or bored?

Most importantly, how does the vet react to your Lab, and how does the Lab react to your vet? Does the vet ignore your Lab? Does your Lab seem uninterested in or shy of the vet? Does the vet get down to Lab-level and immediately call your Lab over? Is the vet patient and gentle (see Figure 6-1)? Do you get the sense the vet is a true dog-lover and could develop a relationship with your Lab? If you like what you see, take note.

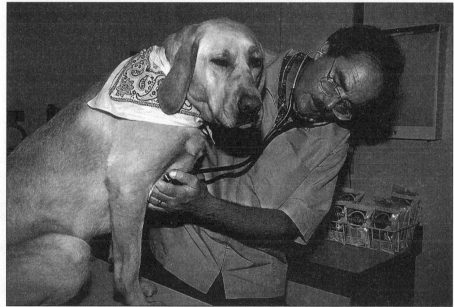

Figure 6-1:
A Lab and her vet should develop a good relationship.

© Kent and Donna Dannen/AKC Stock Images

When talking to the vet, you want to ask a few specific questions. These questions aren't unreasonable or nosy. They are perfectly legitimate requests for information, and your vet shouldn't be reluctant to answer them or annoyed by your asking them.

- How long have you been practicing veterinary medicine?
- Where did you receive your training?
- What animal is your specialty?
- How many Labrador Retrievers have you cared for over the years?
- Do you have dogs at home?
- What major health problems in dogs have you seen and treated?
- What health problems seem to be more prevalent in Labrador Retrievers? (Ask even if you know. Your vet should know at least as much as you do on the subject.)
- What kind of preventive care do you recommend?
- What is your philosophy of pet care?

When you visit a vet for an introductory visit, take notes. Write down the date; the name, address and phone number of the practice; and the name of the vet. Note your first impressions of the place, how the staff treated you, and how your vet responded to the questions you asked. Your notes will help you determine the vet who's best for you.

Doing your homework

After your visit, go over your notes to solidify the experience in your memory. Then do a little research. Look into the school where your vet did his or her training. Is it a good one? Look up any information your vet gave you about pet care in general or Labrador Retrievers in particular that you haven't heard before or that doesn't sound quite right. Spend some time considering your vet's answer to your last question about his or her philosophy of pet care. Do you agree with your vet's philosophy? Or did the vet's answer to this question confuse you? If your vet's answer to the question was, "Huh?," that's a red flag, too. A good vet should have a good answer to this question.

One final thing to think about during your entire introductory visit and afterward is how you feel about the experience. Just as you trust your dog's reaction to the practice and the vet, trust your own reaction. Did the vet or office staff make you uncomfortable in any way, even if you can't quite explain why? Or did you feel very comfortable and at ease during the experience? Your instinct about the place may be right on. If a place gives you a bad feeling or any kind of negative impression, keep looking.

The good vet checklist

To help you remember everything to look for and consider, we've assembled a good vet checklist. Copy it or photocopy it and bring it with you, or fill it out when you get home from your introductory visit, using your notes as a guide.

✔ Were you easily able to make an appointment for an introductory visit?

✔ Does the reception area look and smell clean?

✔ Is the staff friendly and polite?

✔ Is your dog curious and unafraid in the reception area?

✔ Do you have to wait longer than 20 minutes to see the vet?

✔ Is the vet friendly?

✔ Do you feel unrushed, as though you have as much time as you need with the vet?

✔ Is the vet willing to answer your questions about qualifications, experience, and philosophy of pet care?

✔ Does the vet seem genuinely to like and be interested in your Lab?

✔ Does your Lab seem genuinely to like and be interested in the vet?

✔ Do you get a good feeling about the practice and the vet?

Looking into holistic health practitioners

In case you haven't noticed, there is a movement in both human and animal health care. It's big, it's a moneymaker, and there just may be something to it. It's holistic health care, and it is increasingly recognized as a real alternative or ideally, a complement to, conventional (or allopathic) medicine.

Holistic health care treats the body as a whole, considering all possible factors that may contribute to a physical or emotional problem. Holistic health care takes the view that any illness, including emotional or behavioral upsets, is due to imbalances in your pet's whole self or life-force energy. A holistic health care practitioner asks you many questions about your pet that may seem unrelated to the problem at hand, such as what your pet eats, what her habits are, where she lives and sleeps, and her relationships with other pets and with people. Holistic healing seeks to balance the system as a whole, rather than treating individual symptoms, so that the body can best heal itself.

Allopathic medicine seeks to relieve symptoms and focuses treatment on the problem itself. Allopathic or conventional medicine typically treats a health problem without considering many other aspects of the system. (Most advocates of complementary medicine agree that holistic health care can be effective for many chronic or long-term problems, but allopathic care is best

Law & Order for pets

More and more lawyers are specializing in animal law. Lawsuits holding veterinarians and other animal caretakers liable for malpractice or negligience are on the rise, and lawyers are training to serve you if you and your pet become a victim. Law schools are even offering classes in animal law!

Critics argue that the legal system is already bogged down and doesn't need additional cases about dogs and cats. Proponents argue that such legal action will hold accountable those who provide pets with medical care and will raise the standard of care.

for acute or emergency situations.) For example, if your Lab has hip dysplasia or arthritis, allopathic medicine will seek to relieve the pain (a symptom) and perhaps perform surgery on a degenerated joint (treating the problem in isolation). A conventional vet may or may not ask you what you've been feeding your pet and probably won't ask you about your relationship with your pet or other factors not directly related to the problem.

In contrast, a holistic health care practitioner may view arthritis or hip joint pain as an indicator of an underlying energy imbalance. The arthritis or hip dysplasia itself is considered a symptom of this imbalance, not the underlying problem. Holistic care may treat this imbalance by altering your pet's diet, using herbal therapy to balance bodily energy, and providing pain relief through physical therapies such as massage, acupressure, acupuncture, or chiropractic manipulation.

The pet world is, in many cases, ahead of the human world when it comes to holistic health care, and this is both good and bad. It's good because certain new therapies may be available for your pet that can help her. It's bad because pet care isn't as regulated as human health care and, consequently, lots of therapies and products out there are at best a waste of money and at worst dangerous for your pet.

Should you choose a holistic health practitioner for your Lab, either as her primary vet or to consult in conjunction with your primary vet? That depends on a lot of factors. In many ways, your Lab is like your child. Her health care is in your hands, and it's up to you to make the best decision on her behalf.

Consider whether you're comfortable with the idea of holistic health care. If you are, if you use it for yourself and your own family, and if you've enjoyed positive results or find what you've heard about it intriguing, there is nothing wrong with pursuing this avenue of care for your Lab. However, do so with caution and with both eyes open.

Holistic health care and many of the therapies it calls for, such as herbal medicine and homeopathic remedies, are for the most part unregulated. For example, anyone can call himself or herself a homeopath (although not everyone can call himself or herself a homeopathic veterinarian; any kind of a vet needs a DVM or a VMD degree). Although homeopathic remedies are considered very safe, many herbal remedies can be quite potent and dangerous for a dog. Remedies that may be fine for you may be lethal for your pet. Just because herbs are natural doesn't mean they are always safe. For more information, take a look at *Herbal Remedies for Dummies* by Christopher Hobbs (IDG Books Worldwide, Inc.), a book about herbs for humans but with information about herbs for pets, too.

In addition, talk to lots of people. Get references and referrals. Question where your holistic health care practitioner was trained, what certification he or she has, if any, and how much experience he or she has. Just because a scientific study hasn't proved something works doesn't mean it won't work. Testimonial evidence abounds in favor of many holistic methods (some more than others, and some more trustworthy and believable than others). On the other hand, scientific studies may not have proven that certain methods are safe, either. Proceed with caution.

If you do choose to use a holistic health care practitioner for your Lab in conjunction with your regular vet, make sure your vet knows about it. Even if your vet doesn't necessarily approve or think the therapy you have chosen will work (although it is nice if your vet supports your efforts for complementary care), he or she must know about all aspects of your Lab's care. For example, some herbal medicine may react adversely with prescription medicines that your vet has prescribed.

Settling for nothing less than practically perfect

No matter what kind of care you choose for your Lab, conventional or alternative, allopathic or holistic, ask questions, do your research, and trust your

Use your noodle!

Use common sense about any kind of health care. Looking at your Lab's lifestyle, habits, diet, exercise level, and home situation certainly make sense when evaluating her health. Other approaches (holistic or conventional) may or may not sound right or seem sensible to you. If something sounds weird, suspicious, unnecessary, or otherwise wrong to you, follow your instinct and avoid that type of treatment.

Bodywork for pets

Another growing health field is bodywork for pets. Bodywork is any kind of physically manipulative therapy, such as chiropractic care, acupuncture, acupressure, massage, or energy work. Regular pet massage can desensitize extremely sensitive dogs to touch, making them easier to handle and easier for your vet to examine.

Experienced pet massage therapists are increasingly available in major cities, but you can give your Lab a massage yourself. Pet massage is a great way to bond with your Lab. She'll love the way it feels (doesn't everybody like a good, relaxing massage?), and you'll love being able to reward her for being such a loyal companion. Try this simple massage routine:

1. **Call your Lab to you and have her sit.**

2. **Begin by gently petting her in the way you usually do, so she doesn't immediately think you are doing something strange and shy away.**

3. **Pet your dog all over, head to toe, with a firm but light touch, using long strokes. This stroking prepares your pet's muscles for deeper work. Continue for about two minutes.**

4. **Move your hands to your dog's head. Gently hold her muzzle from beneath and stroke the top of her head with your other hand.**

5. **Stroke out over each ear.**

   Your Lab's ears are filled with nerve endings and stroking them will feel very relaxing to her. Continue for about one minute for each ear.

6. **Gently stroke your dog's cheeks, forehead and muzzle for about thirty seconds.**

7. **Work your way down to the back of your dog's neck. This skin is looser, and you can really feel the muscles. With your fingers, massage the muscles on the back of your Lab's neck, all along the back and sides (don't press on her windpipe).**

   Dogs hold a lot of tension in their necks, and your Lab may find this neck rub very relaxing.

8. **Move to your dog's back. With gentle pressure, stroke down both sides of your dog's spine (not directly on her spine) with both hands several times, and then stroke your palms along her sides for a minute or two. Then, gently walk your fingers up and down either side of your dog's spine. Follow with more long, firm petting strokes.**

9. **Have your dog lie down on her side. Gently stroke down each of her top legs five times, and then squeeze and hold each upper leg for about ten seconds. Gently rub your fingers between your dog's leg tendons.**

10. **Pick up each foot and massage on and around your dog's paw pads and nails.**

    Move each digit in small circles, and then flex and gently straighten each leg joint a few times. If your dog has hip dysplasia or other bone or joint problems, avoid painful areas. If your dog yelps or moves suddenly, you'll know you've hit a sensitive spot. Calm your dog (we would probably also apologize) and move to a different area.

11. **Have your dog turn onto her other side and repeat with the remaining two legs.**

12. **Finish your Lab's massage with some long, gentle, smooth head-to-toe strokes.**

    If your dog is asleep, great! You've done your job. If she isn't asleep, she is probably feeling very relaxed. Remain at your dog's side for a minute or two and let her get up when she is ready rather than calling her to get up. Let her bask in the relaxed feeling. If your dog jumps right up, that's fine, too. She's feeling energized!

instincts. In most places, you'll have more than your fair share of pet health care professionals to choose from, so don't settle for less than practically perfect.

That's not to say that you should reject every vet if a single aspect of his or her existence doesn't please you. An extra 15 minutes of driving, a bad choice of wallpaper in the reception area, or a haircut that went out of style in the 80s aren't worth rejecting a caring, friendly vet who has a great rapport with your Lab.

Unfortunately, just because someone is a vet doesn't mean that he or she is necessarily competent, honest, or always able to fix your pet. Wouldn't it be nice if that veterinary degree automatically conveyed perfection? Modern medicine has its limits, and humans have their faults. Don't be afraid to seek out a second opinion, switch vets, or completely change your approach if your pet's treatment plan isn't working or is making you uncomfortable. If you trust your vet, at some point, you just have to trust your vet. Let her do her job without questioning every move. On the other hand, everyone makes mistakes. If the holistic or the allopathic route you've chosen seems all wrong for your Lab and for you, be an advocate for your Lab's health and seek an alternative mode of care.

We talk a lot in this chapter about relying on your intuition, which may or may not make you comfortable. We think getting in touch with your own instincts about your pet can provide you with a great resource, but the key is to remain informed about your pet's health care needs and treatments and to form a bond of trust with your Lab's health care team. Whether that team consists of a homeopathic vet, an herbalist, and a pet massage therapist or a conventional vet and his or her office staff, all team members should be ready and willing to answer your questions, educate you, and work together with a common goal: the good health of your beloved Labrador Retriever.

To Breed or Not to Breed?

Another big issue in canine health is whether to breed your dog. People used to erroneously believe that a female dog would be healthier if she gave birth to one litter of puppies before being spayed. That's not true. Another common misconception is that a female dog must experience one heat before being spayed. But experiencing one heat means risking a pregnancy.

We don't mean to discourage potential breeders who are interested in learning everything they can about the hobby and engaging in dog breeding in a responsible, informed, and devoted manner. But if you're trying to decide whether it may be fun to breed your dog, we have a simple and heartfelt request: Don't!

When in doubt, don't!

Breeding is a time-consuming, expensive, and sometimes heartbreaking endeavor (puppies don't always make it). For truly devoted, die-hard dog lovers willing to do everything possible to ensure healthy, well-trained, well-socialized pups and who are willing to make the effort to place those pups in good homes by screening and educating potential buyers, breeding can be a labor of love. But it isn't going to make anybody rich, and your female Lab certainly doesn't need to give birth to a litter or even go through a single heat to be healthy.

We are in the midst of an epidemic of unwanted pets. Each day in the United States, 10,000 new humans and over 70,000 puppies and kittens are born. Shelters euthanize from five to eight million dogs and cats every year in the United States. Unless you have a really, really good reason for bringing more puppies into the world, please consider finding another way to experience the miracle of birth.

If you think your children should witness the birth of puppies as an educational experience, consider this: A routine birth can quickly turn into a scary emergency situation. Puppies are sometimes born dead, and the birth experience sometimes proves fatal to the mother. Instead, rent or purchase a video that shows the birth of kittens, puppies, foals, and other animals.

Breeding cons and pros

Although breeding has many cons, it also has some pros for the right kind of person. If you still think you have the right stuff to be a great breeder, survey our list of breeding cons and pros. (Yes, we put the cons first — we want you to know what you are getting into!)

Breeding cons:

- ✔ **Breeding is expensive.** You have to feed and house one or both parents and all the pups and get regular veterinary care for all including shots and worming, heartworm prevention, and pest prevention. You have to pay to advertise the puppies, which can be quite an expense. No matter how great your dogs are, you won't get rich breeding dogs. You may make enough to pay for your breeding expenses.

- ✔ **Breeding is time-consuming.** You have to care for, socialize, and begin training for all those puppies. Puppies need round-the-clock care, and you'll lose a lot of sleep when you have a new litter in the house.

✔ **You have to learn something about genetics and how to breed to best prevent genetic disease.** You need to understand the process of pregnancy and birth in dogs, how to assist with the whelping, how to prevent health problems in pregnant dogs and in puppies, how to keep conditions sanitary, what kind of equipment you'll need — the list goes on and on. Prepare to do a lot of reading and a lot of networking with other breeders.

✔ **Your time may often seem like it's no longer your own.** You have to be prepared to answer the phone at all hours of the day and night when you have an ad in the paper for your pups (and people will call at all hours). You need to be ready to answer the many questions people have, and you answer many of the same questions again and again.

You want to spend the time to screen potential owners of your pups on the phone. Then you have to invite the small minority of the folks you think may make good homes for your pups to your house. You should take at least a couple of hours of your time with each potential client or client family to show them the parents or parent of the pups, show them the pups, and give them all the information they will need to make a good decision.

Some people just like to drive around and look at puppies. After all your time, you may find out they have no real intention of buying. If and when you finally find good homes for all your puppies, you have to be prepared to be a continual source of information for the new puppy owner.

✔ **Breeding is more than just putting a male and female together and coming up with puppies.** Timing is very important. Finding the right stud (the male dog used for breeding) for your girl is very important. Stud fees can be expensive. Supervising the breeding to prevent injury to your dog is also necessary. Breeding isn't just a matter of letting "nature take its course."

✔ **Breeding can be heartbreaking.** Sometimes, the mother Lab dies. Sometimes puppies die. Sometimes they are born with serious genetic faults and have to be euthanized. If you can't even bear to watch a dog experience misfortune in the movies, you probably shouldn't take on the task of breeding.

✔ **Breeding is a big responsibility.** You're bringing life into the world. It is up to you to see that those puppies have proper care and socialization and go into homes that will provide them with a secure and happy existence.

Are you ready for all that?

Breeding pros:

If you love Labs and are ready to devote all your extra time to developing healthier, more beautiful, and better strains of Labs that make wonderful pets and can wow 'em in the show ring, go for it!

You'll find there is a lot to learn. Hook up with experienced breeders, read every book you can find on the subject (see the Appendix for some suggestions) and find out everything you can.

The Importance of Spaying or Neutering Your Lab

"Altering your dog," as sterilization is sometimes called, has lots of benefits and very few negative aspects. Here are some of the pros of sterilization:

- You won't risk bringing an unwanted litter of puppies into the world, contributing to the epidemic of pet overpopulation.
- You reduce your female dog's risk of breast, ovarian, uterine, and cervical cancer and your male dog's risk of testicular cancer or prostate infection.
- Your dog may become a little calmer and less agitated and less likely to escape in desperation to breed.
- Your male dog may become less aggressive toward other dogs.
- You never have to worry about the mess of menstruation in your female dog.
- Your female will be less likely to have mood swings.

The cons? There aren't many. You have to pay for sterilization surgery, but the cost is far less than the cost of taking on a litter of puppies or paying to have your dog treated for cancer. Many humane societies offer vouchers for significant discounts on sterilization that most vets will accept. In some areas, if cost is a problem, humane societies may even pay for the operation (although if you can afford to take on a dog, you should be able to afford to have it sterilized).

Deciding on the right time

The latest controversy in the spay/neuter arena is how early to sterilize your dog. Although it was once believed that dogs shouldn't be neutered until they were finished growing so they could fully develop their bones and muscles, more and more vets and humane societies are advocating juvenile or prepubescent sterilization (as young as eight weeks of age). Some vets still prefer to wait until six months, when a dog's bones are pretty much done growing, and research is still uncertain as to whether sterilization before six months affects growth in any way. Dogs can impregnate and get pregnant before six months of age in some cases. Talk to your vet about when he or she believes is the optimal time for sterilization.

If your female Lab is showing any aggressive tendencies such as growling, biting, or aggressive barking, see a canine behavior consultant or dog trainer experienced in aggression to determine whether you should work on the aggression problem before spaying. Some believe that spaying a female with aggressive tendencies may make her more aggressive.

Dogs recover from the surgery in a few days to a week or two and then will be back to their normal selves (Younger dogs tend to recover faster than older ones.) Sometimes a spayed or neutered dog seems a little more at ease and less agitated than before the surgery. Male dogs may be less aggressive towards other dogs and less likely to mark their territory with urine.

Contrary to popular belief, sterilization won't change your dog's personality, make him fat or lazy, or take away his guarding instinct. Nonsense! All sterilization does is take away that sometimes uncomfortable and overwhelming need to breed. Give your dog a break! If you aren't going to breed him responsibly, don't subject him to the urge to breed.

Vaccinations

Perhaps the most important thing you can do to prevent health tragedies is to have your puppy vaccinated. On that very first vet visit, your vet can provide you with a vaccination schedule for your puppy's first year. The purpose of vaccinations in the first year and slightly beyond is to gradually build up a puppy's immune system when he is no longer nursing and gaining immunities from his mother.

If you decide to administer your Lab's vaccinations yourself by buying the vaccines at a feed store, be aware that some vaccination mixes and different brands can differ in quality and in contents. Also, if you don't keep your receipts and careful records, you may not be able to convince a vet, a boarding kennel, or anyone else who needs to know that your dog has indeed been vaccinated. Taking your Lab to the vet for his vaccinations leaves a more reliable paper trail, and you can be assured of getting a quality vaccine. You may also be able to purchase vaccines from your vet.

A vaccine introduces a very small bit of a disease into your dog's system so he can build up an immune response to it. Later, if the dog is ever exposed to the disease, his body will be prepared to fight it off. The typical vaccination mix protects your puppy from several dangerous diseases and should be administered about once per month from about six weeks to about 17 weeks (certain vaccines may have different schedules; check with your vet). Most vaccine mixes protect your Lab from the following diseases:

- ✔ **Canine distemper virus (CDV):** This upper respiratory viral infection causes severe vomiting, diarrhea, and fever and used to be a leading cause of death in dogs.

- ✔ **Adenovirus-2:** This virus causes abdominal pain, jaundice, and clouded corneas.

- ✔ **Canine infectious hepatitis:** This liver virus causes fever, vomiting, and loss of appetite.

- ✔ **Leptospirosis:** This bacterial infection can be transmitted to you. It affects the liver, kidney, and bladder, causing fever, vomiting, loss of appetite, abdominal pain, and eye inflammation, among other symptoms.

- ✔ **Canine parainfluenza:** This is the flu virus in dog form.

- ✔ **Canine parvovirus:** Often called *parvo,* this gastrointestinal virus can be deadly, especially for puppies. Some breeds (Dobermans and Rottweilers) are particularly susceptible, but any puppy can catch it. Parvovirus can enter your home in a number of ways, including shoes, which are best left at the door in homes with puppies. Parvovirus causes diarrhea, fever, severe stomach pain, vomiting, and, when it isn't caught in time, death.

- ✔ **Coronavirus:** This intestinal virus is similar to but less serious than parvovirus. It causes vomiting, diarrhea, and fever. (The coronavirus vaccine isn't in all combinations; the virus is more common in some areas of the country than in others.)

You can also elect to vaccinate your puppy against other diseases and conditions, depending on where you live and how often your dog is outside. These include bordatella (kennel cough), a respiratory virus, and Lyme disease. The bordatella vaccine is often required for any dogs being boarded in a kennel because bordatella is so easily spread through kennels. Lyme disease, spread by ticks, is a good vaccine to get if your dog is often outside in wooded areas, especially in the northeast area of the United States. Lyme disease causes lameness, fever, loss of appetite, and swollen joints.

Your puppy should also receive his first rabies shot at around six months of age, and many vets will charge less for this shot if you have your puppy spayed or neutered by this time. Unlike the other vaccinations, rabies shots are required by law (although some cities have local laws requiring distemper vaccines). Rabies is always fatal for dogs. Please don't neglect your dog's rabies vaccinations.

If you find a stray dog who's acting strange in any way, including demonstrating uncoordinated or seizure-like movements and/or foam around the mouth, don't touch the animal. Call your local animal control agency. This type of behavior is a symptom of rabies, and you can easily catch rabies from an infected dog if he bites you or gets his saliva in an open cut in your skin. Rabies is often fatal for humans, too.

Understanding the great vaccination debate

After that first crucial year, should you continue to have your dog vaccinated every year? Some say yes; some say no. If you take your dog to obedience classes or have him boarded in a kennel while you're on vacation, you may need to provide proof of current vaccinations. But if you don't, what will happen if you don't vaccinate your dog? And what will happen if you do?

Some people believe that vaccinations are overadministered and unnecessary — and may even cause chronic health problems in some dogs. Others disagree, citing the low incidence of negative effects from vaccines and arguing that annual vaccinations will help to eliminate dangerous canine diseases from the population.

Both sides have convincing arguments, but we tend to agree that doing your part to eliminate disease from the general population is important. Vaccinating your dog is like vaccinating your child. Yes, there is a very small but real risk of a serious reaction and a slightly larger risk of a mild reaction. But vaccinations have drastically or totally eliminated some serious childhood diseases and have dramatically improved the health of children in general.

We've seen a similar occurrence in the dog world. One of the leading causes of death in dogs used to be distemper, but thanks to the distemper vaccine, few dogs die from it anymore. If your dog has a reaction to a vaccine or is in poor health, you have a good argument for choosing not to vaccinate your dog. If your dog is healthy and has never reacted to a vaccine, however, we encourage you to continue to vaccinate your dog, although you may be able to vaccinate only every two to three years after the first vaccination. Ask your vet.

New studies on vaccines

Recent research has argued that annual vaccines may indeed be overkill. At a recent conference of the Ohio Veterinary Medical Association, it was reported that vaccines probably have a longer term of effectiveness than once believed and that a two- or three-year interval between booster shots may be more appropriate than a one-year interval. Studies demonstrating how long immune effects from vaccines last are only required for the rabies vaccine. The protocol of the annual booster shots for other vaccines isn't based on research. Talk to your vet if you're concerned about overvaccinating your Lab. The two of you may be able to develop an alternate schedule of vaccinations every two to three years instead of once a year.

If you do decide to vaccinate less often than annually, don't let that be an excuse to ignore your dog's annual checkup. This checkup is an important preventive measure; it allows your vet to monitor your Lab's health, make sure you are doing all you can to keep your Lab healthy, and catch any problems before they turn serious.

Knowing what's optional; what's the law

Although standard vaccinations are legally optional, law requires rabies vaccines. Rabies can be transmitted to humans and can be fatal. It is always fatal to dogs. Although some dogs do experience reactions to the rabies vaccine, refusing the vaccine is a greater risk than a reaction to the vaccine. Keep your dog up-to-date on his rabies shots and always keep a current tag on your dog's collar showing that your dog has been vaccinated for rabies. In the unlikely event that your dog escapes and bites someone, there will be little doubt your dog is rabies-free.

If your dog bites someone — whether he's current on his rabies shot or not — he may need to be held in quarantine for ten days. (No vaccine is 100 percent effective, so even vaccinated dogs must be watched closely.) If for any reason authorities have reason to believe he does have rabies, there is only one way to test. You don't want to know. Suffice it to say, your dog won't come back to you in one piece. Play it safe and keep current on rabies vaccines! Always keep a tag showing your dog is current on your dog's collar and always keep that collar on your dog.

Don't Bug My Dog!

No matter where you live and no matter how seldom your dog goes outside, chances are at some time or another she'll encounter a flea or two. And it only takes two fleas to generate hundreds and hundreds of fleas. Parasite control is an important consideration for dog owners. Many dogs are extremely allergic to flea bites and can develop flea-bite dermatitis, a painful skin condition that is difficult to resolve. Fleas can cause anemia and tapeworms in your dog, and in rare cases, they can even transmit bubonic plague to you! Not to mention their nasty habit of infesting your house and living and breeding in your carpets, furniture, and bed mattress. Yuck!

Frightening flea facts

Only one to five percent of the flea population in an environment such as your home consists of adult fleas living on your dog. The remaining 95 to 99 percent are eggs, larvae, and pupae living in your carpet, furniture, and yard. Ten adult fleas can become 250,000 in 30 days under good conditions.

Ticks are another parasite common to dogs, and they are more than just a nuisance. Ticks can carry Lyme disease and many other diseases in your dog (and in you if you're bitten by the tick). For some diseases, including Lyme disease, the tick must remain attached to your dog (or you) for 72 hours to transmit the disease. But if you aren't checking your dog regularly for ticks, 72 hours can pass before you know it! Although many tick-borne illnesses are treatable, avoiding ticks is a more sensible, less costly, and less painful approach.

Worms and mites are other parasites you need to watch out for. Your dog can pick up these critters by sniffing the feces of another dog, eating fleas, getting bitten by a mosquito, or even by walking, because some worms can be absorbed through her feet (and yours, too). Always keep your dog on heartworm preventive medicine, even if she doesn't often go outside. Heartworms can kill. Your vet can test your dog for worms at each annual checkup.

Dogs can get several kinds of worms. Tapeworms and roundworms are easy to see in your dog's feces. Tapeworms look like moving grains of rice and roundworms look like spaghetti. Dogs get tapeworms from eating fleas, which carry them. Roundworms are common parasites and are contracted when a dog sniffs the feces of an infected dog. Hookworms are passed via the feces of roundworms. They burrow through skin and then move into the intestinal tract. Heartworms are transmitted by mosquitoes and are most common in warm climates where mosquitoes live year-round. Prevention is important because treatment is dangerous; many dogs don't survive the treatment.

Mites can cause *mange,* a very itchy and uncomfortable condition that can eventually be fatal if untreated. See your vet if your dog is very itchy or losing patches of hair.

Giardia is a protozoa, or one-celled organism, that can cause severe diarrhea in your dog. Giardia is common in natural bodies of water contaminated with feces from wild animals. Giardia will make anyone miserable (humans can get it, too), but it can usually be treated with a drug called Flagyl.

Checking for parasites

During your daily grooming sessions, check your dog for parasites. Because Labs have short coats, fleas are relatively easy to spot, although they are of course more difficult to see on chocolate and black Labs. Keep a flea comb handy and run it through your dog's coat. If you come up with nothing, great! If you find little black specks on the flea comb that jump back off, your dog has fleas. If you come up with little black specks that don't jump off, put them on a wet piece of white paper. If they turn reddish, they're flea dirt and digested, dried blood. Yuck! Your dog has fleas. Another way to check for fleas on your Lab is to run your finger through her coat so you can see her skin. If you see little black specks on her skin, she probably has a flea problem.

Ticks are larger, so they're easier to spot, but if you don't catch them and they remain attached, they can transmit diseases. The longer a tick is attached, the bigger it gets, because it becomes swollen with blood. Ticks aren't pretty. Removing a huge, swollen tick can be pretty grotesque and dangerous, too, if the tick bursts when you squeeze it (an experience most people would happily live without). That tick bacteria can be absorbed through the skin, so always wear rubber gloves or use a paper towel when handling ticks.

If you do find a tick on your dog, remove it properly to avoid infecting your dog or yourself. Here is the best way to manage ticks:

- Avoid places that could be infested by ticks, such as wooded areas. If you periodically take your dog to a wooded area, keep yourself well covered (wear a hat, long sleeves, and long pants) and check your dog immediately after your walk for ticks. You may be able to catch ticks on your dog before they have attached themselves.

- Keep the grass mowed in your yard and clear away brush.

- Remove ticks as soon as possible after you discover them.

- To remove a tick, wear rubber gloves, and use a paper towel, tweezers, or another device made for removing ticks. If the tick bursts, the bacteria could infect you.

- Grasp the tick close to the skin and pull straight up. If part of the tick remains under the skin, the remains could become infected.

- Always wash your hands thoroughly after removing a tick, even if you use gloves or tweezers and disinfect with alcohol the area where the tick was attached.

- Never cover ticks with petroleum jelly, nail polish, or other home remedies. Never burn a tick.

- Flush the tick down the toilet or drown it in alcohol. If you want the tick analyzed for Lyme disease, seal the tick in a bottle with moist paper and call your vet to find out where you can have the tick tested.

Preventing infestations

The easiest way to get rid of a flea infestation is to prevent a flea infestation. Fleas are stubborn little critters, and they don't take kindly to being asked to leave. So don't invite them in!

We suggest a three-pronged approach to preventing a flea infestation:

✔ **Keep your pet on an *insect growth regulator* (IGR) all year long.** Available in pill form or in spot-on forms (you apply a spot of liquid between the dog's shoulder blades and sometimes also at the base of the tail), IGRs don't kill fleas, but they affect either flea eggs or the larvae, preventing them from hatching or developing into adult fleas. Eventually, the fleas will die out. With an IGR, if your dog does get a few fleas, they won't be able to breed, and you won't end up with an infestation.

✔ **During flea season (which may be in the summer or, in warmer climates, all year-round), also keep your dog on an *adulticide*.** We recommend the spot-on treatments rather than the flea sprays and dips, which tend to be more toxic. Spot-on treatments move out, through different methods and across the skin and coat, and kill any adult flea on contact. Used in conjunction with IGRs, adulticides don't give fleas a chance!

✔ **During flea season, designate one day of each week as flea control day.** Wash all bedding (human and canine), vacuum all carpets and furniture (paying special attention to areas your dog frequents), clear all brush and pet waste from your yard (these attract fleas), groom your dog with a flea comb and, if necessary, spray an IGR spray made for carpets and furniture in your house and one made for yards in your yard (a professional can do this, too). However, if you've been vigilant, you probably won't need to spray anything anywhere. Modern flea control products work very well.

Be very careful about mixing too many flea products. Check with your vet before you use more than one type at a time (such as a flea shampoo followed by application of a spot-on adulticide).

Tackling infestations

If you do wind up with an infestation, you'll know it. Your dog will be scratching constantly, perhaps even waking you up at night with that thump-thump-thumping. She may end up with *hot spots,* those painfully itchy, red areas of skin that have reacted harshly to a flea bite or to the subsequent scratching. You may see fleas on your furniture or your bed. (If you let your dog sleep with you — it's okay, lots of us do it! — they may jump onto your arm and jump off again before you can catch them, and if you do catch them, you'll find them virtually indestructible unless you flush them.

Don't despair. Although it isn't easy, you can get the upper hand, but you need to get serious by doing the following:

1. **Secure your dog outside and clean house.**

   Vacuum every possible surface and vacuum well, including under furniture and furniture cushions. Dust all surfaces well. Wash all bedding, including your dog's bedding, in hot water. Spray the areas of carpet and furniture that your dog frequents with a flea spray safe for use indoors and meant for furniture and carpets. The best kinds contain an adulticide and an IGR.

2. **Now, it's your dog's turn.**

   If you haven't been treating her with an IGR and an adulticide, now is the time to start. After a good bath, keep your Lab outside until she dries but keep her from rolling around in the grass, where she may pick up more fleas. Groom her with a flea comb, apply the proper spot-on and if you're giving her an oral IGR, give it to her right away. Then bring her into the clean house.

3. **Continue to apply the adulticide and IGR according to the package directions and be vigilant about your weekly housecleaning sessions (but don't apply indoor flea sprays more often than recommended on the label).**

   Don't bathe your pet again for three or four weeks, until the spot-on is ready to be reapplied. If you keep up the effort, your house and your dog will soon be free of fleas.

If your dog is experiencing a reaction to flea bites, such as flea bite dermatitis, or if she is acting sick and you think she may have developed another flea-related problem such as tapeworms or anemia, take her to the vet as soon as possible.

If you're interested in taking the natural route to flea control, the only products scientifically proven to work are limonene and borate powder products. You can also purchase homeopathic flea sprays, herbal flea dips, food supplements (such as Brewer's yeast and garlic) meant to make your pet taste undesirable to fleas, sulfur-based products, citronella-based products, B-vitamin supplements, pennyroyal oil (careful: it's highly toxic if ingested), Fleabane, and Wax Myrtle branches and leaves. Not much research supports the effectiveness of these products, but testimonials abound. Never try to make your own natural products; use products already formulated for pet use.

When Emergency Strikes

No one like to think about terrible things happening to a dog, and we're sure you don't either. But sometimes terrible things do happen, and you can minimize the tragedy if you're prepared. If, despite your best preventive measures, your dog gets ill or injured, you can take certain measures to give your dog the best possible chance for survival and recovery.

If emergency does strike, try to remain calm. If you're frantic, you won't be able to help your dog.

Keeping tags on them

Never underestimate the importance of identification tags. Even a well-trained dog may get separated from her humans, and puppies that haven't been fully trained may wander away and be unable to find the way home.

Identification tags can mean your dog is quickly returned to you. Their absence can land your pet in the animal shelter, where you may not find her in time.

Being a Boy Scout (prepared, that is)

When your Lab is involved in an emergency, you need to act quickly. Knowing ahead of time what to do in any given emergency may save precious moments — even your dog's life! Keep a first-aid kit handy, take it on camping trips and vacations when your dog accompanies you, and always be vigilant. Keep your dog on a leash at all times, especially when near traffic. Always have your vet's number and an emergency number handy (memorize them!) and do everything you can to keep your dog away from hazardous situations and poisonous substances. Memorize what to do under certain emergency conditions and practice what to do. Your Lab is worth it.

Assembling your canine first-aid kit

To prepare for potential emergencies, assemble a canine first-aid kit. Keep it next to the first-aid kit you may have assembled for the human members of your family (and if you don't have one of those, why not make them both up at the same time?). Make sure everyone in the family and any pet sitters know where the first-aid kit is kept. Keep it well-stocked at all times, and if you ever use up any of the supplies, replace them immediately. Your canine first-aid kit should contain the following items:

- ✔ Gauze pads and strips to use as bandages (tape doesn't stick to fur very well, so be sure you have strips long enough to tie a bandage around any part of your dog's body).

- ✔ Cloth strips strong and long enough to use as a muzzle. Practice wrapping the strips around your dog's muzzle a few times and then tying them behind his head, but don't leave the muzzle on, of course. You don't want your dog to fear it. (An injured dog, no matter how well-trained, may bite out of pain.) Or you can buy a muzzle that fits your dog and keep it in your kit.

- A cloth strip and a wooden stick for use as a tourniquet or a tourniquet kit. (Use this only in cases of extreme bleeding or snake bite.)

- A large sheet on which you could carry your dog, stretcher-style.

- A blanket big enough to keep your dog warm, in case of hypothermia.

- A tourniquet rod (only for emergency bleeding situations).

- Hydrogen peroxide, for cleaning a wound and to induce vomiting.

- Syrup of ipecac, to induce vomiting.

- Mineral oil, for use as a laxative. Give 1 teaspoon for puppies under 25 pounds, 1 tablespoon if your dog is 25 to 50 pounds and 2 tablespoons for dogs 50 pounds and over.

- An antibiotic ointment or cream (the human kind works for dogs, too).

- An antihistamine such as Benadryl that your vet approves for use on your dog, in case of an allergic reaction. (To give a pill to your Lab, hold her upper teeth and insert the pill deeply into her mouth. You may also want to hide the pill in some cheese or other soft food.)

- Ice packs (keep accessible in your freezer) and heat packs (the kind you knead to generate heat are good).

- A snakebite kit, if you have an outdoorsy dog.

- Tweezers and pliers for removal of ticks, splinters, items on which your dog is choking, and porcupine quills.

- A thermometer appropriate for use on your dog (ask your vet which kind to buy and how to use it).

- Water and a bowl your dog can drink from.

- A spare collar and leash, in case his is lost, broken, or you don't have it with you.

- A card with the number of your vet, an emergency center for pets, and a poison center hotline that can answer questions about pets (call and ask).

LAB TIP

A large plastic or metal tackle box or toolbox is an ideal container to hold first-aid items for your dog. It is easy to carry, can be stowed in the trunk of your car on trips, and keeps smaller items separate. Larger items, such as a blanket, jug of water, and water bowl, can be kept separate, but don't forget them!

Keeping emergency information at your fingertips

An information card to keep in your first-aid kit can be a lifesaver if it has every number on it that you may need in an emergency and if you keep several copies in strategic locations: in the first-aid kit, by each phone, and in your wallet. This card is also great information for pet sitters.

Make up your own card after making the effort to find out and fill out all relevant numbers and information (see the following list). Some of the information we have in the following list may seem obvious to you, but you may be surprised what you suddenly can't remember in an emergency. Also, if something happens to you, someone else may need some basic information, and pet sitters will want all the information handy, too.

Our Labrador Retriever's name is _____.

He is _____ years old and weighs _____ pounds.

He is allergic to _____.

His owners are _____.

We live at _____.

Our phone number is _____.

Our vet's name is _____.

The number is _____.

An alternate vet's name and number, in case ours is unreachable, is _____.

An emergency pet care facility number is _____.

Poison control hotline is _____.

A friend's name and number, to call in case we need help, is _____.

Special information about our dog:

_____

_____.

Treating shock

If your dog suffers a trauma such as a car accident, electrocution, or losing much blood, he may go into shock. Shock itself can kill your dog. It causes a sudden drop in blood pressure that results in a consequent drop in oxygen to the body. If your dog is in shock, his heart rate will quicken because his heart is trying to compensate for the drop in blood pressure. His breathing will quicken (for the same reason), his pupils may dilate, he may have an intense stare, and he may lose consciousness or be only partially conscious. If you suspect your dog is in shock, keep him as still as possible, cover him, and get him to the vet immediately.

Helping your Lab survive a car accident

Few experiences are more horrible than watching your dog get hit by a car. Whether you have your dog off-leash or he somehow gets free from you, if a car hits your dog and you're with him, you're in a good position to get him immediate help. Labs are sturdy creatures, and unlike smaller dogs, they often survive a run-in with a car.

Whether your dog just has the wind knocked out of him or has a bone fracture or dislocation, approach him carefully. If he is in severe pain, he may bite even you. If your dog is lying down, don't try to get him to stand up. Cover him with a blanket to keep him warm, in case he's in shock. If you can summon help, you'll find it easier to move him onto the sheet you keep in your first aid kit, or you can use a piece of plywood or a board, if you can find them. Get your dog into the car and get him to the vet immediately.

If your dog gets up but is limping or yelping and seems very nervous, use a calm, soothing voice, secure him on a leash (muzzle him if you think he may bite) and get him to the car. If you can lift him without hurting the injured part, carrying him to the car is better than having him walk. He may want to do it himself, however. Use your common sense.

If your dog has run off and you don't see him get hit by a car but he comes home and is obviously injured, get him to a vet immediately. If you don't see your dog get hit and he doesn't come back, you may never know what happened unless your dog is wearing his ID tags. Better to make sure he never runs off.

If someone hits your dog with his or her car, you may feel like suing, but be careful. If your dog wasn't on a leash and you live where there is a leash or control law, and the car was damaged in any way, the person who hurt your dog could sue you and win. Keep your dog on a leash at all times to prevent this tragedy.

Managing broken bones and dislocations

A car accident or other accident such as a fall can cause broken bones or dislocations in your Lab. Be careful moving a Lab with a fracture or dislocation. Get him to a vet immediately because fractures and dislocations may cause shock, and the bone needs to be set or the dislocation corrected as soon as possible to minimize trauma and recovery time. Don't touch the painful area or try to set a fracture yourself.

Helping your dog when choking

Dogs can choke just like humans can, and because Labs love to retrieve things, they often have things in their mouths. If the dog is retrieving or playing with an object that's small enough, the object may easily get lodged in his throat. Never give a dog a toy smaller than his face. If your dog is choking, he will start to gag, paw at his throat, and salivate heavily.

Don't panic! Calmly try to see the object and determine how far back it is in your dog's throat. If your dog is choking on something sharp, such as a stick or a pencil, don't try to dislodge the object if there is any chance you could push it in farther or injure your dog. If he's choking on something you can see and easily remove, go for it! Just be careful not to lodge the object in farther. Use a hooking motion with your finger, tweezers, or pliers. (It helps if someone else can hold the dog still and calm him.)

If you can't dislodge the object, immediately rush your dog to the vet. On the way, you can try a canine Heimlich maneuver, but don't waste any time getting to the vet. If possible, do this maneuver in the car while someone else drives:

1. **Stand or sit behind your dog and clasp your hands underneath his abdomen just below his rib cage.**

2. **Thrust upward quickly, five times.**

3. **If the object isn't dislodged, try it again.**

In addition to choking, swallowing foreign objects presents other hazards to your dog. String or any string-like object can cause serious internal injuries to your dog. If your dog or puppy likes to chew, be very careful to leave all unsafe items well out of reach.

Alleviating heatstroke

Dark-colored dogs are more prone to heatstroke than light-colored dogs, but any dog left in a poorly ventilated environment such as a parked car (even with the windows open) or left outside in extreme temperatures without water can suffer from heatstroke. Heatstroke can be deadly, so take a few precautions.

✔ **Always make sure your dog has a sufficient supply of clean, cool water.** If the weather is very hot during the day and your dog is outside, make sure someone can replenish his water halfway through the day. Keep his water bowl in the shade and don't use metal bowls in hot weather (they heat up quickly). Or teach your dog to use one of those water dispensers that hooks right up to an outdoor faucet and provides a continuous source of cool water.

✔ **Let your dog stay inside when it's very hot and never take him on car trips if he will have to wait in the car on a warm day.** Even if you plan to leave the car running and the air conditioner on, the car could die, and the air conditioner could turn off. Before you know it, your dog could be another casualty of a hot car. It has happened too many times.

Heatstroke can also occur if your dog exercises beyond his capacity on a hot day. Dogs don't sweat, so they can't manage heat as well as humans. All they can do is pant. If you and your Lab are on a hunting or camping trip in hot weather, be sure to bring along plenty of water and watch your Lab for signs of overexertion and heatstroke. Signs of heatstroke include:

✔ Rapid, shallow breathing and panting

✔ Rapid heart rate

✔ Skin that feels hot to the touch

✔ Strange behavior, as if your dog isn't fully conscious or is very weak

Immediately cool your dog, but not too drastically. Sudden, rapid cooling may send him into shock. Put him in a bath of cool (not ice) water; put ice packs around his neck and head; wrap him in cool, wet towels; and give him cool water to drink. Then take him to the vet. Or, ideally, cool him while on your way to the vet.

Dogs need plenty of fresh water available at all times. In summer, put out two bowls. Fill one with clean water and the other with ice cubes that will end up as clean water. In winter, you can buy devices that will keep your dog's water unfrozen. Just make sure your dog won't chew through the electrical cord!

Handling hypothermia

On the opposite end of the scale is hypothermia, a condition in which a dog's body temperature drops too low. A dog's average body temperature is about 101.5 degrees. If a dog's core temperature drops more than a few degrees below this (it can even drop as low as 94 or 95 degrees), your dog has hypothermia.

The first signs of hypothermia are shivering and an increased heart rate. If your dog is shivering, immerse him in warm water or wrap him in warm towels or a heating pad. If hypothermia is advanced, the body systems begin to shut off circulation to the appendages to keep the vital organs warm. A blue mouth and blue tongue are signs that circulation is shutting down. So are lethargy, depressed behavior, and unusual sleepiness. If you suspect that your dog has advanced hypothermia, immediately warm him by giving him warm fluids and wrapping him in warm towels. Immediately take him to the vet.

Even the most experienced outdoor Lab can get frostbite in extreme conditions. Signs of frostbite include swollen and discolored (pink, red, purple or even black) ears, tail, or other appendages. As the area becomes warmer and blood flow returns, swelling will become more pronounced and the discoloration more intense. Never rub frostbitten areas; you may damage the tissue. Instead, pack the area with warm compresses.

Treating burns

Burns can be caused by chemicals, electrical appliances, contact with hot surfaces, or exposure to fire and are often the result of a dog exploring where he shouldn't be exploring. Severe burns can cause shock, and all burns are painful. If your dog is burned, run water over the burn in a gentle stream. Apply antibacterial ointment to superficial burns and keep the area clean. For second- or third-degree burns (those that affect more than the first layer of skin and bleed, blister, ooze, or reveal muscle tissue), immediately take your dog to the vet.

Attending to wilderness mishaps

Labs love the great outdoors, and many Lab owners do, too. If you take your Lab into the woods on hunting or camping trips, you'll need to be prepared for emergencies that could threaten your dog while you're far from a vet:

- ✔ **Snakebites:** Venomous snakes exist in virtually all areas of the country. If a venomous snake (a rattlesnake or a water moccasin, for example) bites your dog, help your dog to relax and stay still to limit the spread of the venom. If the bite is on his leg, use a tourniquet on the leg to keep the venom from flowing through his body (loosen it every ten minutes so the limb doesn't die from complete lack of circulation). Get your dog to a vet as soon as possible (sorry, this camping trip will have to get cut short). If you don't know what kind of snake bit your dog, even a description of its size and coloration may help. If you kill the snake, bring it with you.

- ✔ **Porcupine quills:** If your Lab tangles with a porcupine and gets shot with a quill or two (or more), don't try to pull the quills back out. Porcupine quills have tiny barbs at the end that can tear your dog's skin and make the wound subject to infection. Take your dog to a vet immediately so the quills can be removed in a sterile environment with your dog under sedation. If you can't get to a vet because you're deep in the wilderness, cut the quills so that they're about an inch long, and then pull them straight out with a pair of pliers. Immediately clean the wounds and cover them with antibiotic ointment.

✔ **Allergic reactions:** If your dog has an allergic reaction to a bite or sting, such as a bee sting, he may experience swelling. Call your vet. You may need to give your dog an antihistamine such as Benadryl. If you're going on a camping or hunting trip, talk to your vet beforehand about the proper dosage if this happens. A baking soda/water paste can help with pain and itching. Add just enough water to baking soda to make a thick, spreadable paste and then dab it on the sting.

Dealing with foot injuries

If your dog tears a dewclaw, splits a nail, or cracks his footpads, he will be in pain. If your dog's foot is bleeding, immediately clean the wound and wrap in gauze. If his footpads are cracked, clean them, rub them with antibiotic ointment, and cover them. If a nail or footpad is severely cracked or a dewclaw is torn off, clean the area, wrap it, and take your dog to the vet.

Salt and de-icing chemicals used on city sidewalks and streets in the winter can cause your dog's footpads to swell and crack. Snow itself can melt and refreeze between your dog's toes and footpads, causing irritation. Protect your dog's feet with doggy boots or keep a box of moist towelettes by the door so you can clean ice crystals as well as salt and chemicals from your dog's feet after a winter walk.

Combating poisoning

Sometimes you know what your dog has swallowed. If it's something from the following list, immediately follow the directions we provide. If you don't know what your dog has swallowed but he's showing signs of poisoning, such as severe vomiting, diarrhea, muscle trembling, and increased salivation, immediately take him to your vet or emergency pet care center. Some of the most common poisons dogs ingest are the following:

✔ **Antifreeze:** It leaks onto driveways, smells and tastes good, and can quickly kill your dog. Induce vomiting and take your dog to the vet or emergency pet care center immediately.

✔ **Rat poison:** Induce vomiting and take your dog to the vet or emergency pet care center immediately.

✔ **Insecticides:** If your dog has insecticides on his skin, wash his skin with water and vinegar and take your dog to the vet or emergency pet care center immediately.

- **Chocolate:** Some dogs can take chocolate, but it is highly toxic to many dogs. Induce vomiting and call your vet.

- **Lead:** If your dog ingests lead by eating lead paint, for example, induce vomiting and give your dog a laxative if it has been over two hours since the lead was swallowed.

- **Household cleaners:** For soap, induce vomiting and call your vet. For bleach, induce vomiting and call your vet. For ammonia, give your dog a spoonful of vegetable oil to block absorption of the ammonia and take your dog to the vet immediately. For furniture polish, induce vomiting or use a laxative if the polish was swallowed more than two hours before and take your dog to the vet immediately. For any other cleaners, call a poison control center and do what they say.

- **Human medications:** Ibuprofen (Advil, Nuprin, or Midol) is particularly dangerous. Acetaminophen (Tylenol) is also dangerous for dogs. If your dog swallows ibuprofen, induce vomiting and take your dog to the vet or emergency pet care center immediately. If he swallows acetaminophen, induce vomiting and call your vet.

- **Poisons or inedible substances in the garbage:** If you don't know what your dog has eaten but he's acting as if he is poisoned, take him to the vet. If he has eaten spoiled food and is vomiting, call your vet.

Stopping bleeding

If your dog is bleeding, you need to stop the flow of blood. For minor injuries (cuts, scrapes, and scratches), clean the injury and dab hydrogen peroxide on it with a cotton swab morning and evening to keep it clean. If a wound won't stop bleeding, take your Lab to the vet immediately. En route, try to raise the wound above your dog's heart while applying pressure with a bandage or towel (or both).

For gushing wounds on limbs or the tail that don't respond to firm pressure, you may need to apply a tourniquet. Tie a strip of cloth close to the wound between the wound and the heart, insert a stick, and twist to cut off the blood flow. Don't do this unless absolutely necessary, however, and never leave a tourniquet tied for more than ten minutes without loosening it. The limb or tail could die from lack of circulation and could then require amputation. A tourniquet is an emergency measure to be used on the way to the veterinarian.

Giving artificial respiration and CPR

If your Lab's breathing and heart are stopped, all may not be lost. You can administer artificial respiration and/or CPR to your Lab:

1. **Try to remain calm as you check for a heartbeat and obstructions in your dog's mouth.**

2. **Swipe your finger or a cloth in your dog's mouth to remove any blood, pull out his tongue, make sure his airway is clear, and then shut his mouth.**

3. **Pull your dog's lips over his mouth and hold them with your hand around his muzzle.**

4. **Wrap your other hand around your dog's nose, creating a tube. Blow into your dog's nose.**

   Make sure no air escapes between your dog's nose, hand, and your mouth.

5. **Inhale and exhale normally into your dog's nose, one breath about every five seconds.**

6. **After each breath, put both hands over your dog's heart and pump, a little faster than one pump per second.**

   If you have two people on the scene, one can do the breathing, and one can do the pumping.

7. **Keep it up until help arrives or perform these actions in the car as someone drives you and your dog to the vet.**

Chapter 7

Helping Your Lab Deal with Changes

*L*abs are creatures of habit. Your Lab loves his routine, his home, his yard, his doggy den, and his family. When any of these aspects of his regular life become upset, your Lab feels the stress of the change.

Major life changes are pretty stressful on humans, too, but we have the benefit of being able to understand, at least some of the time, why the change is taking place. Your poor Lab is at the mercy of whatever changes you inflict upon him. However, you can also manage your Lab in ways that will make major life changes easier to handle. If you help your Lab through life transitions, he'll turn right around and help you through them, too.

When You Move

Moving is a highly stressful event for humans. But don't let the stress of moving be an excuse to ignore your Lab. Imagine how your Lab must feel being suddenly uprooted from the home he knows and loves and transported to a whole new territory! He needs you right now, and even though you have boxes to pack and arrangements to make, you also have a responsibility to help your Lab maintain a regular routine and to spend your normal amount of time together. Don't leave him wandering around in the chaos without any attention from you, wondering what's happening.

Even if your Lab seems healthy, take him to your vet for a checkup a week or two before you move, and make sure he is up-to-date on all his vaccinations, tests, and heartworm pills. (You may even need a health certificate when moving from one state to another — check with your vet.) While you're there, ask your vet about anything that should concern you about moving with a dog. He or she may have some additional suggestions that will apply to your individual Lab and situation. He or she may even be able to recommend a good vet in the area to which you're moving.

Preparing your Lab (and yourself)

One of the best ways to prepare your dog to move is to keep everything as normal as possible. Take a break from moving preparations to engage in your normal grooming, training, and play sessions. Busy as you are, continue to feed your Lab at the normal times, keep his water bowl full, and take him on his walk. Keep bedtime about the same if you can.

Practice stress management yourself! If you're getting too stressed out, your Lab will think something's wrong. He'll worry. Really! Labs are perceptive, and if you're suffering, your Lab will suffer right along with you. Enjoy stress-reducing walks in the fresh air with your Lab. Take time out to just sit on the couch for ten minutes and pet your Lab. Remember, the more organized you are and the more you plan ahead, the less everyone in your family — your Lab included — will feel the strain.

Continue to take your Lab to different places. Socializing and traveling with your Lab (both locally and on longer trips) will make the move much easier on him. If you haven't been taking him to various locations and introducing him periodically to new people, it's time to start (see Chapter 13).

Ideally, you will begin training him in various locations and getting him used to riding in the car at least several months before the move. Make it as important a part of your moving plans as changing your phone service or booking the moving van. A Lab who's a veteran traveler will take a move to a new location in stride, especially if his routine remains relatively intact and you remain relatively calm about the whole affair. If your Lab is feeling good about the move, he'll be a source of comfort to you when you get to your new destination, too. Exciting as moving can be, it sure is nice to have a familiar and well-loved friend along!

When you're giving away stuff you don't use so that you don't have to move it, make sure you don't toss any of your Lab's things into the giveaway pile. Your Lab's doggy den, dog dishes, chew toys, retrieval objects, and even bedding — no matter how old and ratty they're getting — will be sources of comfort and reassurance for your Lab in your new location.

No dogs allowed?

If you have children and have to move, you would never say, "Well, it looks like we'll have to give up the kids. It isn't easy to find places that allow them, and it's such an inconvenience to move across country with kids in the car!" Don't get a dog if you aren't willing to make the effort to include him in your life changes. Finding places to live that allow dogs is tougher if you're renting, but it certainly isn't impossible.

 Although some landlords only accept small dogs, don't necessarily assume that a landlord won't accept your well-trained Lab on his or her rental property. Take your Lab with you when you look at possible rentals and let the landlord see how well-behaved and well-managed he is (see Chapter 8 for more on Lab management). You may just be able to seal the deal! Of course, in some situations, dogs are absolutely not allowed. Find this out on the phone beforehand and don't even waste your time looking.

Don't give up! If finding a place is taking longer than you anticipated, see whether a trusted friend or family member can temporarily house your Lab while you're looking for a more permanent situation. All of your positive training will pay off when you find the perfect place to live, where your Lab is welcome because of his good manners and friendly ways.

And Baby Makes . . . Four?

Your family is blessed with a baby, and you already have a well-trained Lab. This is a formula for success! Of course, bringing any new family member into the mix necessitates management. You can't just expect everyone to adjust without a little direction. Many couples have a dog before they have a baby, and until baby comes along, their dog is their baby. But guess what? After your new little human comes home to stay, your Lab is still just as much in need of your love and attention as he was before. As far as he is concerned, he was the first child, and the addition of a new pack member shouldn't downgrade his status any.

 An untrained Lab, no matter how well-meaning, can create a serious hazard to a new baby. Your Lab must be trained not to jump up and must be controlled around a new baby. Also practice the long down, coming when called, and the sit request (what we call "commands" — see Chapter 11). Train him every day, and by the time baby comes, your Lab will be a helpful "sibling" and ready-made best friend.

First-time parents may have difficulty making time for their old friend. Even die-hard dog lovers may feel, in those first hectic, sleepless, stressful weeks with a newborn, that their Lab has somehow transformed into "just a dog." The feeling that your Lab will have to do without your attention because you're spread so thin and feeling so stressed is natural, but is unfair to your dog. New moms, especially, are experiencing major hormonal fluctuations and may feel a little blue and extra emotional after baby comes home. It's easy to block out everything but the new baby and even to feel irritated and annoyed with your Lab, even though he doesn't deserve it.

All your Lab wants is to welcome you home. He is so glad to see you after your absence and so curious about the new little one! This is where Dad can help if Mom isn't quite feeling up to consistent management. New fathers are under a lot of pressure now, too, but managing your Lab can be an important part of the job. Give your Lab lots of love and attention, keep his routine consistent, and continue to train him. Plus, introduce him to the new baby in steps.

Introductions

The very first introduction between your Lab and your new baby should be scent-only. Your Lab knows something's up. Mom hasn't been home for a few days, and everyone is acting differently! He may not be worried, exactly, but he is probably extra alert for any clues about what's going on. You can help him by keeping his routine regular, but also by introducing him to the baby before the baby ever comes home.

How? Take a receiving blanket you can spare or a clean T-shirt or other soft cloth item to the hospital or birthing center and wrap the baby in it for a few hours. If the baby spits up on it, great, but that's not necessary. His scent will soon be all over the blanket. Then, Dad or another family member can bring the blanket home and offer it to your Lab. Let him sniff it, play with it, even sleep with it. Let it be his blanket. When he meets the baby for the first time, he'll already be familiar.

New parents are pretty exhausted for awhile. In spite of your fatigue, though, continue to train your Lab and spend time with him. When you first bring the baby home, take the next step. While one parent holds the baby, the other parent holds onto the dog. You've seen the way dogs greet each other, right? Let your Lab sniff the new baby's well-diapered rear. Your Lab doesn't need to lick the new baby, and of course, you don't want him to lick the baby's face, although he may try (he's just being friendly — no need to get upset about it). But let him sniff and encourage him with lots of positive words and gentle strokes, especially when he acts calm. Tell him the baby's name and explain that this is a new family member for him to love. He'll understand what you're saying, in his way.

After introducing him to the baby, let him take a nap in his familiar doggy den while you attend to the baby and show the baby around his new home. Don't feel guilty about confining your Lab when only one parent is home and is caring for the new baby. When baby takes a nap, you can do a lot of positive training with your Lab so he knows he is still an important member of the family.

Child-proofing your Lab

A well-behaved and well-trained Lab doesn't need much child-proofing (see the chapters in Part III). Labs are great with children (see Figure 7-1) and aren't naturally the jealous types. Your Lab will understand that the baby is like a puppy and will take a friendly interest in this new member of the pack. You may find he takes to sleeping outside the nursery door or standing nearby as a sentinel wherever the baby is playing or napping.

Figure 7-1:
Labs and kids usually become instant buddies.

© Nance Photography/AKC Stock Images

Take a few child-proofing precautions, however. Train your Lab to be conscious of the baby. If baby plays on the floor on a blanket, teach your Lab that he can't step on the blanket. If baby swings in a baby swing, you can teach your Lab to make a wide berth around the swinging seat so that baby and Lab don't collide. You may need to remind him that some toys are for babies to chew and others are for Labs to chew, and that toys aren't mutually interchangeable. Use the off request to teach your Lab what not to touch, the kennel request to teach him where to go when you need him to be out of the way, and the long down or long sit to keep him in one position while you move around — see Chapter 11.

An important part of training your Lab when you have children around, and even when you don't, is to teach him not to guard his food. It is natural, and a survival mechanism, for dogs to be protective of their food. In earlier times, dogs had to make sure they got enough to eat; otherwise, they wouldn't be able to pass on their genes.

It is best to feed your Lab in his doggy den away from toddlers and children until you teach him that your child is very rewarding to have around during meals. While you're still at the point of managing meals without training, remember that if your Lab gets used to eating alone, he may very well warn you or your child if you approach.

If you follow Joel's advice of using food as a lure and reward, you'll be using so much of your Lab's daily allotment of food for training that your Lab will not be eating much food out of a dish. When he's used to getting most of his food from your hand, you can train him to love the fact that your hand is near his food dish.

Make sure your dog is well-versed in the take it and off requests (see Chapter 11). Then, put a piece of food in your Lab's food dish and say, "Take it." What a great reward, getting to eat food out of a dish that you put in there with your own hands! Your Lab will never have the chance to think it is bad to have you around his food dish!

When he is used to eating some of his food out of his dish, occasionally and regularly take a tasty morsel (some kind of special treat your dog loves) and, while he is eating, reach your hand into his dish, add the treat to his regular food and then say, "Take it." He will love your approaching his food dish!

Because all relationships are unique, you must carefully train other family members to do the same training. Small children will have to be closely supervised during this type of training. If your Lab shows any signs of guarding his food, consult a qualified canine behavior consultant immediately.

Lab-proofing your child

When your baby develops an interest in your Lab and begins to reach out for him, do lots of positive training with baby and Lab together, teaching your baby how to handle your Lab gently and not to touch his eyes, pinch him, or hit him. Some babies are naturally gentle and would never hit. Others are more boisterous and tend to experiment with their environment in a more raucous manner.

If your Lab is already well-trained, your baby will probably need more training than your Lab! Always supervise your Lab and baby when together, as much for what your child may do to your Lab as anything! Continue to train and manage both kids and dogs to ensure a lasting, successful relationship.

Following are a few more management tips:

- ✔ Teach your child to leave your Lab alone when he's eating (except when training), drinking, and relieving himself outside. Even a friendly Lab has to have privacy once in awhile.

- ✔ Doggy dens are for Labs only. Teach your children that your Lab is off limits when in his doggy den. Keep your Lab's special, private place sacred, so he can escape the family fray and the prodding and poking of small children if he needs to.

- ✔ Keep dry dog food out of reach of small children. Kibble is a choking hazard.

- ✔ Babies love to play and splash the water in dog bowls, yet your Lab needs plenty of fresh, clean water available at all times. Always know where your baby is, and keep him away from the water bowl.

- ✔ If your Lab ever shows any sign of aggression towards your child, immediately separate dog and child and contact a canine behavior consultant. Depending on the cause, aggression can almost always be managed and doesn't mean you have to get rid of your dog. (By aggression, we mean a snarl, a snap in the air, a warning nip that doesn't break the skin, or a low growl.)

- ✔ Make sure your child (or anyone, for that matter) never comes into contact with dog feces. The accidental ingestion of roundworm eggs can pose a serious danger to humans. Have your Lab wormed regularly and talk to your vet about ways to minimize this risk.

- ✔ A child who can talk can learn positive dog training. Joel has seen children who learned their dogs' names and the sit request right after they learned to say Mommy and Daddy.

When teaching your children that dogs should be handled with gentleness and respect, also teach them never to approach a strange dog without first asking the owner's permission. Not all dogs are as well-mannered or well-socialized as your Lab, and many aren't used to children. Don't teach your child to assume every dog is friendly or let your child become a dog-bite statistic.

Pet Number Two (Or Three, or Four)

Many folks think it would be a good idea to get another dog, a friend for their Lab. The common thinking is, "We are gone all day. How nice if our Lab had company!" Well, maybe this is true, but maybe it isn't. If your Lab could talk

Rosie, Dominique, Buddy: Sit

If you have two dogs, you may wonder how they know which of them you are speaking to. Dogs understand that if you're looking at them, you're talking to them. If you have any doubt, go ahead and use your dog's name. Joel likes to have a way of requesting all the dogs to do something. Instead of saying, "Rosie, Dominque, Buddy: Sit," he will simply say, "Dogs, sit." It works!

and you asked him, he may say something to the effect of, "Another dog? Nah. You're all the company I need. When you can't pay attention to me, I'd just as soon take a nap." He may even say, "What? You don't spend enough time with me as it is, and now you want me to share you?"

If your Lab isn't yet very well-trained and you're still working out certain requests or the management of certain behaviors, getting another dog will only complicate the matter. It's harder, not easier, to manage two dogs than it is to manage one. The first dog won't train and manage the second dog for you. You have to do it all over again.

Remember all the work it took to get your puppy or dog house-trained and to get him to be a good member of the family? Remember those sleepless nights standing out in the middle of the front lawn in the wee hours of the morning while your puppy relieved himself? Remember all the work to manage your Lab's naturally exuberant behavior? Remember how nice it was when your Lab finally began to respond, behave, and understand what you wanted?

You'll have to do it all over again. You have to do the same great job with the new dog, put in all the same effort, and continue to manage your first Lab at the same time. Plus, you have twice the vet bills, twice the cost of pest control, twice the cost of heartworm pills, twice the cost of food, double the doggy dens, two collars, two leashes, two sets of tags, more grooming supplies and at least four chew toys. Is having two or more Labs impossible? No. Is it difficult? Time-consuming? Expensive? Chaotic? You betcha. Are you sure you're ready for that kind of commitment?

Another consideration when getting a second dog is the time you need to spend managing the relationship between your current dog and the new dog. You'll need to introduce the new puppy or dog properly, being careful to show more, not less, attention to your first dog whenever the new dog is present. Train your new pup when your first dog is sleeping securely in his doggy den so that he doesn't feel displaced and you can work with your new puppy or dog one-on-one. They both need their individual time with you, as well as time learning to get along together (if you have two or more kids, you know exactly what we mean).

Managed well, the relationship will probably work out just fine, but may present continual challenges to work through: squabbles over chew toys, battles for your attention, and the room-destroying menace of two frisky Lab pups playing an exuberant game of Labrador tag.

If your dogs are getting too boisterous, give them a dogs down request. If they do what you ask, they get to continue to hang out together. If they don't, do a time out with the one who isn't responding. You train two dogs by training them one at a time first, and then by training them both to follow requests when they're with you.

You also need to consider what gender to choose for your second Lab. Although the gender of your first Lab isn't as important as finding a Lab with the right personality, gender becomes more important when a second Lab enters the picture. The highest probability of success is having one male and one female. With proper introductions and training, this pair is likely to get along.

Two males can result in problems when the youngest reaches social and sexual maturity at about 18 months, although neutering one or both of your males may minimize this problem because the more different the two dogs are, the fewer problems they'll have. Two females are more likely to get along than two males, but if they do dislike each other, the fighting can be much more intense. If you do have problems between your two dogs, the sooner you seek the services of a qualified canine behavior consultant, the better! (To find a good canine behavior consultant, call the Association of Pet Dog Trainers, 1-800-GOODDOG.) Chapter 11 has more information.

If after a lot of soul-searching and planning, you decide that you are ready to manage a multidog household, welcome to an interesting and challenging way of life! You will learn a lot about doggy/doggy behavior. Sometimes, you may think that you do little else with your time at home than train, feed, groom, pet, and talk to Labrador Retrievers. But then again, some people think that's an awfully nice way to live!

Can you walk two dogs at once? Yes! Simply teach each dog to walk on a loose lead. Then connect a Y (available at pet stores) to the end of your lead so you can hook both dogs up to one lead. You can then walk two dogs at once. You can even walk four dogs at once, like Joel does, by having two leads with Ys.

Illness, Divorce, and Death

These subjects aren't pleasant, but they're all too often a part of life. If you help your Lab to cope when illness, divorce, or death strike your family, he'll help you to cope, too. You need each other!

When someone gets sick

When a new baby enters the family, it is a stressful yet joyful event consuming everyone's time. When someone becomes seriously ill, you have all the stress and none of the joy. Your Lab can offer you and your family love, companionship, and a positive focus for any family member who is ill.

Of course, when someone becomes ill, you probably have to make adjustments in your Lab's routine, especially if the person who is ill is the Lab's primary caretaker. But Labs are resilient, and although they love their routine, they love you even more. With good, positive training and quality attention, your Lab will be fine and will do his best to help you in whatever way he can.

Many Labs are used as service dogs for people with disabilities. (Chapter 20 covers this area in detail.) If someone in your home becomes ill or injured, consider training your Lab to help out. Labs can help pull wheelchairs, retrieve necessary items (such as telephone receivers and dropped utensils), and can even learn to open certain types of doors, turn light switches on and off, and fetch help. On top of all that, they're a great comfort and make superb confidantes.

The big D

One of the big reasons dogs are left in animal shelters or with rescue groups is divorce. Divorce happens a lot. But if you and your partner split up, please try to decide which of you can provide the best home for your Lab. Many folks work out joint custody arrangements. Getting rid of your Lab because you can't agree on who should have him is the worst possible outcome. Don't punish your Lab for your personal problems. Do what's best for him.

If your family is going through a divorce, your Lab probably knows something is wrong. Labs are very sensitive to their owners, and when people in the family are upset, angry, or distraught, the dog feels the same way. It may sound silly, but try to protect your dog from outbursts and arguments the same way you would protect your children. Labs are easily upset by family dissension because they're so sensitive to what their owners need and want. For the sake of your dog, as well as your children, keep it as friendly as possible.

Plan ahead for your Lab's future

If you're your Lab's only caretaker and you die, what will happen to your Lab? Please amend your will to specify who will take your Lab (make sure that person agrees). If you can't find anyone willing and qualified, consider leaving a donation to the local Labrador Retriever rescue organization along with instructions for your Lab to be placed there. They will find him a good home.

Part III

Training Your Lab with the MRE System

The 5th Wave   By Rich Tennant

Canine SAT exam

HIGH FREQUENCY WORD LIST

STAY!
SIT!
BAD!
DOWN!
FETCH!
OBSEQUIOUS!
SHUTUP!

In this part . . .

After over a decade of training dogs and their owners, Joel has developed a three-point system that summarizes the most important considerations for becoming the excellent owner of an excellent dog. Joel calls the system the *MRE system*, which stands for Management, Relationship, and Education. This system demonstrates the three most important aspects of handling dog behavior: proper management (M), a good dog-owner relationship (R), and continual training or education (E).

Dogs are dogs. They aren't people. Therefore, they come programmed with certain doggy behaviors that humans don't always find particularly appealing. They can't help it — as we say, they're dogs! But that doesn't mean these behaviors can't be managed.

In this part, we help you successfully manage your Labrador Retriever, the first step to guiding your new pet toward a happy and rewarding life with you. We also talk about the relationship between you and your Lab and how to maximize it at ever turn. Finally, we fill a good deal of space educating you about how to educate your Lab. You discover everything from how to teach your brand new puppy to sit using the lure-and-reward method to how to teach your older dog to understand and respond to more advanced requests, including the all-important "Come" request.

Chapter 8

M Is for Management

· ·

· ·

*J*ust about everyone has come into some kind of contact with a misbehaving dog. Maybe a neighbor dog liked to dig up your flower beds and chase your cat. Maybe you had a puppy as a child, and your parents ended up sending her to a farm or giving her away one day because she caused too much trouble. Maybe the dog sitting at your feet as you read this is doing her best to eat the soles off your slippers (and you're still wearing them).

But you never dreamed that uncontrolled rocket of black, chocolate, or yellow fur tearing through your home, stopping only to deposit a, um, mishap on your carpet, would belong to you. Dogs like that are other people's dogs, aren't they?

No dog comes pre-programmed with knowledge of how humans want her to act. Your puppy doesn't have a clue why you would care where she relieves herself or how fast she bolts through the house or what she chooses as a chew toy. No matter how nice or respectable or giving or affectionate a human you are, unless you manage your new dog, that adorable ball of fur with the melt-your-heart eyes will probably turn out to be more trouble than fun. Your new Lab means well, but she also means to be a dog (as well she should).

Management is the key, after which comes the development of the right relationship with your dog (see Chapter 9, where we talk about what the right relationship is) and training or educating your dog (see Chapter 10). How you manage different behaviors varies, so in this chapter, we break it down for you. But here's the key (remind yourself of it frequently): To properly manage your dog, don't let her get into trouble in the first place.

Managing Puppy Behavior

Boy, is that new Labrador puppy cute! And boy, is having a new puppy difficult! New puppies are indeed a challenge. The first few weeks with a new puppy aren't unlike the first few weeks with a newborn human. You probably won't get much sleep, you'll spend an inordinate amount of time cleaning up, and you'll sometimes think the unthinkable: "What on earth have I gotten myself into?"

Never fear, the end of the new-puppy intensity is near if you manage your new little bundle in a way that allows her to easily behave in the way you expect. Puppies do lots of things you probably don't care for. They whine and cry when you'd rather be in dreamland. They use the world as their toilet. They treat your fingers like chew toys. And oh, the energy! Just watching a Lab puppy can give you an overwhelming desire to take a nap. Can you manage all that behavior? No problem. Start out with easy management steps before you move on to relationship (Chapter 9) and training aspects (Chapter 10) to further develop and refine the behaviors you desire.

Barking and whining management

How can such a tiny pup make so much noise? And why, oh why, must she make that noise at 3:00 a.m.? Even when you do everything right, you won't get much sleep the first few nights with a new puppy. For one thing, puppies don't have the bladder control of older dogs and need to be taken out at least once during the night. For another thing, your poor puppy is confused, lonely, and scared. After all, she has just been taken away from her mother and littermates and the only home she has ever known. Sure, she may have acted like you were the answer to her prayers at the breeder's, but she had no idea what was in store.

Take pity on your puppy and recognize that whining and crying through the night are only natural. Then — and this is the hard part — after you've taken your pup outside for her midnight bathroom break, put her back in her doggy den and (gulp) ignore her.

Easier said than done (and it wasn't even easy to say). We know you didn't get a puppy so you could ignore her, and that whining, crying, whimpering sound is almost unbearable to a confirmed dog lover. But you have to be strong. You have to stick to your guns. Why? Because your puppy has a very important early lesson to learn: How to be by herself.

If you respond to your puppy's cries during the middle of the night, your puppy will learn some lessons, all right:

- ✔ Whining works.
- ✔ She doesn't have to sleep through the night.

Those aren't the lessons you want to teach your puppy. You want to teach her that:

- ✔ You don't respond to whining unless it's for a good reason (the puppy needing to relieve herself is a necessity).
- ✔ Nighttime is for sleeping. Daytime is for playing.

Actually, letting your puppy whine it out is easy (if you have a good pair of earmuffs). It requires no action whatsoever on your part, and after a night or two, the puppy will realize that her strategy isn't working. Sooner or later, she will realize she is tired, and she will go to sleep. Before you know it, your dog will eagerly hustle into her den come bedtime or whenever she wants to escape the family and take a little personal time.

Of course, reinforce your nighttime management with daytime management. When your puppy has slept well and quietly with only one or two trips outdoors during the night, take your pup out, have a training session, and praise her.

New puppies can't be expected to make it through the night without a trip or two outside to relieve themselves. Puppies under four months old shouldn't be expected to go more than four or, at most, six hours without a potty break, and no dog should be left in her den for more than eight hours.

One last point about nighttime management: We strongly recommend the use of a *doggy den,* which is a nicer name for a *crate* or *kennel.* Doggy dens are wire or plastic enclosures used to give your puppy a safe, secure place to go. Dens also keep your puppy out of trouble at night and when you aren't home.

Lots of people think doggy dens are cruel and will tell you so if you mention that your dog has one. The opposite is true. Dogs are den animals and need a small enclosed space to feel safe. Without one, they may feel anxious and insecure. You can often find den-less dogs underneath tables, chairs, or desks, looking for a place to call their own. Make it easy on them. Give them a den just big enough to sit, stand, turn around, and lie down in comfortably, and your dog will likely love to sleep, rest, or just hang out in there.

Remember, the doggy den is a place for your puppy to sleep. If you start feeling that you're putting your pup in the doggy den too often, make sure that you're spending lots of time doing positive lure-and-reward training. Remember, pups sleep a lot, and it is more humane to do a time-out then to keep yelling at the puppy for being overactive and overtired.

House-training management

Puppy owners always want to know, "When will my puppy be house-trained?" It would be nice to be able to give an answer like "two weeks and three days," but here is the straight scoop: Your puppy will be house-trained just as soon as possible, if you do everything right.

Doggy dens are a great management tool for house-training puppies and even adult dogs that haven't yet been taught the skill. When you first bring home your new puppy, watch her carefully. When she looks ready to relieve herself, whisk her outside. When she urinates and/or defecates, praise her gently and sincerely. When you can't watch your puppy continuously, put her in her den (not for more than four to six hours when your puppy is younger than 12 weeks, including at night). As soon as you take her out of her den, take her outside. Puppies won't soil their dens unless they have no other option, so keeping your puppy in her den will teach her to exercise bladder control.

After you get to know your puppy a little better, you'll recognize the signs that she is ready to relieve herself. Some puppies start to sniff the carpet, some will wander away from you, some will just get that look. Catching the signs every time will make for a smooth house-training transition because your dog will soon learn that outside is the acceptable place.

Another way to manage house-training is to be familiar with the *gastrocolic reflex*. This reflex (which human babies also experience) causes defecation to occur approximately 30 minutes after a meal. If you feed your puppy at consistent times each day then take her out 20 to 30 minutes later, you may be successful in preventing an accident every time.

Of course, accidents do happen. You look away from your puppy for just a minute to read the mail and uh-oh! If your puppy does urinate or defecate in the house and you catch her in the act, immediately pick up the puppy and take her outside. If she continues to eliminate outside, praise her.

If you don't catch your puppy in the act, never punish her and never, ever rub her nose in the waste. Your puppy didn't make a mistake — you did. But don't feel you have to punish yourself, either. Just resolve to do better next time.

Immediately and thoroughly clean indoor accidents with an active enzyme cleaner (ask your local pet supply store manager for the best brand). Dogs tend to eliminate in places where they smell previous elimination, and enzyme cleaners remove the scent. If you don't want to spend time mixing concentrate when you're in a hurry to clean up a mess, buy the slightly more expensive ready-to-use variety.

Play-biting management

Puppies bite. Not to be nasty, mind you. For puppies, play-biting (sometimes called mouthing or puppy biting) is a way to explore the world. Just as a human baby grabs with her hands and explores with her mouth, puppies explore and grab through biting. They play with their siblings using their teeth, and their siblings hardly notice. Play-biting isn't a sign of aggression; it is a sign of play, and puppy play is good. Puppy play is how puppies learn.

But to humans, puppy bites hurt. Those tiny teeth are as sharp as needles. The puppy doesn't know that, of course. She doesn't have any idea that you aren't covered in tough canine skin. You need to do two jobs while the puppy is mouthing:

- Teach the puppy not to bite hard.
- Teach the puppy not to bite at all.

Your puppy must learn that human flesh is much more sensitive than the flesh of puppies and dogs. This is one of the most important things that you will teach your pup. An adult dog may bite if she has pain inflicted on her. Just imagine that your beloved, well-behaved dog is asleep on the family room floor. A 3-year-old child comes running over, falls on your dog, and sticks a finger in the dog's eye or ear or causes pain to your dog in some other fashion. If your dog bit the child at this point, that would be normal behavior. If you were sleeping on the sofa and someone woke you up by slapping you hard on the face, you would wake up in an aggressive fashion, and nobody would say you have a bad temperament! Teaching the puppy that human flesh is sensitive (bite inhibition) is like buying insurance. You will be glad you did it, and hopefully, it will never be tested.

One way to help your puppy learn is not to give her the opportunity to bite you. Don't hold out your fingers or feet for your puppy to bite! When your puppy does bite you (because she will find those fingers despite your efforts), say "Ouch!" sharply to startle the puppy into recognizing that you are reacting. Immediately withdraw your hand or whatever the puppy is biting. Then immediately train your puppy or do a time-out. Do this consistently, and your puppy will learn that she needs to be careful when playing with humans. You may have to endure a few uncomfortable nips during this process, but isn't it worth it? See Chapter 10 for more on how to train your puppy not to play-bite.

Chewing management

Puppies also chew to explore the world, and they chew like a wood chipper when they're teething. In Chapter 11, we talk in more detail about how to teach your puppy what's appropriate to chew, but the best way to manage chewing is to limit your puppy's access to things she isn't allowed to chew.

Labrador Retrievers seem to have a particular penchant for chewing. Even adult Labs will chew destructively if not given a proper outlet for their energy and if left unsupervised for long periods of time. An adult Lab can easily destroy large items of value, such as bicycles, swing sets, and even parts of your car. Better to teach your Lab early on about chewing etiquette.

Just as you child-proof a home against a toddler, puppy-proof your home against a chewer. Before you bring your new puppy home, walk through each room of your house trying to see with the eyes of a puppy. Then take the following precautions:

- Hide or tape up all electrical cords.
- Keep shoes in closed closets.
- Secure cords from window blinds so that your puppy can't reach them.
- Keep garbage out of reach.
- Police the floor on a daily basis for choking hazards such as paper clips, rubber bands, and pieces of string.
- Keep everything of value to you that could possibly be destroyed by chewing out of puppy's reach.
- If you have stairs in your home, make sure everyone in the family knows to keep the door at the top of the stairs closed. If you don't have a door, keep a baby gate in place so that your puppy won't fall down the stairs.

Because you'll be watching your puppy 100 percent of the time for house-training purposes when she's on the loose, also watch her for chewing tendencies. Whenever your puppy shows any indication that she's preparing to chew on something forbidden, remove the item and give your puppy a quality chew toy, preferably one that can be stuffed with treats (see Chapter 11).

Orbiting management

Orbiting refers to the behavior of dashing wildly around the house. Older puppies and sometimes adolescent dogs orbit with joyful abandon, and nothing is safe that lies in the path of destruction. The bigger your puppy is, the more damage orbiting can cause.

Your puppy isn't trying to destroy your coffee table or your antique tea set. She is simply burning off some of that incredible supply of puppy energy. The key to managing orbiting behavior is to provide your puppy with plenty of opportunities for both physical and mental stimulation. For very small puppies, exercise in the house and the yard should be sufficient, but the bigger your puppy gets, the more she will need a daily brisk walk out in the fresh air. Tired puppies are happy puppies, and they're less destructive, too.

To further manage orbiting, pay attention to the time of day when and/or the types of situations in which your puppy tends to experience an energy overflow, and then apply the following techniques when the orbiting time or the situation approaches:

✔ Put a leash on your puppy in the house.

✔ Engage in a vigorous lure-and-reward training session (see Chapter 9), take your puppy outside to relieve herself, and then put her in her den.

✔ Teach your puppy to come when you call (see Chapter 10). A puppy can't come to you and orbit at the same time.

Control orbiting by rechanneling energy, and you'll soon have a well-behaved dog who knows when to romp and when to wait patiently for the proper time to romp.

Managing Your New Adolescent or Adult Dog

One of the advantages to bringing an older dog into your family is that she may already be trained in certain desirable behaviors. On the other hand, many adolescent and adult dogs have developed undesirable behaviors because their owners didn't train them and then gave up on them. Therefore, the best way to manage a new older dog is to treat her just like a puppy. Don't assume that your dog will know better. She may not have any idea what you expect. If you manage her in the same gentle, positive manner you would apply to a puppy, she will soon learn the house rules and how to stay out of trouble.

Consider that you have been blessed with a dog who wasn't handled correctly in the past. A dog treated with love and supported in the managing and education process is similarly blessed and will return your caring management and education with years of love and devotion. We've seen it happen again and again. And if you find during the management and education process that your adult dog already has many skills and positive behaviors, you're doubly blessed.

Managing the transition

Adult dogs may come with some additional challenges not present in puppies. For one thing, dogs are creatures of habit. If they're used to being in one place for several years and are suddenly moved, or if they have been shifted around a lot, they may come to you full of insecurities and anxiety. Begin good management and positive training immediately, so that your dog has the chance to understand the rules and expectations as soon as possible. Show your dog that she can be happy and successful in her new home and that this home is a home for keeps.

Adult dogs commonly act relatively subdued during the first week in a new home. You must gain the dog's trust. When your dog begins to demonstrate more energy, even in negative behaviors, take heart in knowing that your new family member is feeling more secure and comfortable. Now all you have to do is educate your dog so she will become a good companion (see Chapter 10).

Managing the separation

You may have heard a lot about separation anxiety. Separation anxiety is actually a clinical diagnosis that isn't as common as people think. Most trainers refer to barking, digging, and other destructive or annoying behaviors a dog exhibits when the owner is away as learned behaviors that can be modified by good, positive training. Rather than experiencing anxiety, your dog may be bored out of her mind or having fun while you're away. In Chapter 10, we show you how to train your dog about what she is and isn't allowed to do when she's home alone.

Here are some good ways to begin to manage this type of behavior:

- ✔ If you work all day long, come home for lunch to walk your dog (or hire someone to do this).
- ✔ Provide your dog with lots of stuffed hollow chew toys (see Chapter 11) to chew and play with in your absence.
- ✔ Spend a lot of quality time practicing lure-and-reward training with your dog when you're home.
- ✔ Don't leave your new dog too often or for too long a stretch until you have solidified your relationship (see Chapter 9).

With proper management and training, your dog will be well-behaved even when you aren't looking. True *separation anxiety* (in which a dog becomes extremely distraught when the owner leaves) is sometimes exhibited by adult dogs who have had insecure or abusive pasts. It may also be caused by a medical problem. The dog may become extremely destructive, even injuring herself, and may require medication and behavioral treatment. If you suspect that your dog suffers from true separation anxiety, see your vet.

Chapter 9

R Is for Relationship

*T*he second part of the MRE system is the relationship between you and your Lab. Good relationships between dogs and humans don't just happen. Sure, you can have great chemistry to start with. You can adore each other. But until you really know each other and develop a rapport based on mutual trust and communication, you won't have a true relationship.

Unfortunately, there are many ways to compromise your relationship with your Lab, and most of them happen completely unintentionally. You may not have any idea why your Lab puppy suddenly stops listening to you or doesn't greet you with affection when you return home. Relationships take work. You probably know that about human relationships, but human-dog relationships aren't that much different. What can you do to get the most out of the relationship between you and your new friend? This chapter tells you!

Your relationship with your dog will be stronger and more stable if you can keep in mind one cardinal principle: Bad behavior is never the dog's fault. Dogs don't misbehave on purpose. Revenge or ill humor doesn't motivate them. They want to be rewarded, and they depend on you to show them how.

Creating a Bond with Your Lab

After you get your new dog home, it's time to get acquainted. You surely have some first impressions of your Lab, and he probably has some first impressions of you, too. It is important for you to spend the majority of your day with your new dog during the first few weeks he comes to live with you. You'll both have adjustments to make, but you also need to bond in order to build the foundation of a relationship that you hope will last for a very long time.

Taking stock

Bonding with your new Lab is even easier when you're properly supplied. Make sure you have these items:

✔ Doggy den

✔ Water and food bowls that are heavy enough to stay put when your excited and hungry Lab devours his dinner

✔ Collar, identification tags, registration, and rabies tags

✔ Leash

✔ Several very sturdy chew toys

✔ Brush and nail clippers for grooming

✔ A good quality adult dog food (see Chapter 5)

The day you bring your Lab home, begin observing him. Notice how he acts when you behave in certain ways. Notice when he gets tired, when he gets hungry, and when he needs to go out. Notice what he seems to enjoy and what seems to scare him. As you play with him and cuddle him, notice when he enjoys it and when he seems ready to be left alone. In other words, tune in to your dog. This is the only way to really know him.

After your dog has been with you for a few days, answer the following questions to get a clearer picture in your mind of your dog's personality. (Writing often helps to clarify what you already know.) This information can also be transferred into your pet records for future reference (or just keep this book with your pet's vaccination and other health records).

✔ My Lab is _____ months/years old.

✔ My Lab eats _____ times per day. I feed him _____. His appetite is _____.

✔ At night my Lab sleeps for about _____ hours before he needs to go out. I would characterize his sleep patterns as _____.

✔ My Lab's overall health seems _____.

✔ Something the vet said about my Lab:

_____

_____

✔ My Lab's favorite toys are _____.

✔ My Lab is most active in the _____.

✔ I think his favorite thing to do is

_____

✔ He seems to have a tendency to _____.

✔ He is very good about _____.

✔ Something I think we'll need to work on is

_____.

✔ When teaching my Lab what's expected of him, my confidence level is

_____.

✔ I'm a little worried about handling _____.

✔ I don't think I'll need to worry at all about

_____.

✔ We are spending _____ minutes _____ per day on training exercises.

✔ My Lab reacts to training sessions by

_____.

✔ My Lab's favorite reward for doing a good job seems to be

_____.

✔ When it comes to training, I'm very comfortable about

_____.

✔ When it comes to training, I need to work on my tendency to

_____.

✔ He's a typical Lab when it comes to

_____.

✔ He doesn't seem so Lab-like when he

_____.

✔ I'm good at managing him when I don't give him the opportunity to

_____.

✔ I've slipped up a few times by letting him

_____, but I plan to avoid that in the future.

✔ One thing I can't resist letting my Lab do is

_____.

✔ I'd also like to remember the following story or stories about my Lab's first few weeks with me:

_____

_____

_____.

Feeling bonded yet? We hope so! But as you know by now, bonding is only the first step toward relationship success. You also have a few more responsibilities, and they are your responsibilities, not your dog's. Dogs are pack animals by nature and are hardwired to get along with other living beings they consider their pack or family. The dog is doing his part. The rest is up to you.

Building a good relationship

If you've just brought a dog home or are getting ready to bring one home, you're smack in the middle of a great opportunity. You have the chance to forge a wonderful and rewarding relationship with a loving pet who can bring you years of happiness and devotion.

But how do you make it happen? Think about the good relationships with others in your life. Do you tend to have better relationships with the people who praised and rewarded you when you did something right? Did these same folks keep you out of trouble while you were learning what was expected of you? When you misbehaved, did these people show you how to behave correctly?

Now, think about the people with whom your relationship isn't so great. Did these people punish you harshly when you made a mistake? Did they punish you even when you weren't sure what you did wrong? Do they tend to ignore you, put you at the bottom of their priority lists or act irritated by you?

In many ways, dogs are like people. They tend to prefer the people who are kind, affectionate, and keep them out of trouble. They like to know the rules, and the people who make the rules clear without harsh or cruel punishment are the people to be trusted. Dogs won't behave as well if they're treated meanly, punished excessively, or punished when they don't know what the punishment is for. They don't like to be ignored or treated like an irritation. They want to be loved. Doesn't everyone?

Your dog can move his jaws five times faster than you can move your hand. If you make your puppy or dog fearful by harsh behavior (yelling, hitting, and so on), he may bite you. This obviously isn't good for your relationship, and if a dog learns that biting is the only way to defend himself, he could eventually end up in dire circumstances.

Use this little trick to help to reinforce good behavior in your dog. When he's behaving the way you want him to behave, look at him. When he is doing something you don't like, don't look! (You probably don't want to see that trash spread all over the kitchen, anyway!) Dogs notice where your attention is directed and just looking at your dog can be a form of reinforcement.

A relationship is a relationship, whether with child, spouse, friend, or dog. Respect your new dog and pay attention to him so that you can guide him in the best way.

The ten commandments of dog-human relationships

Keep these ten commandments in mind:

I. **Thou shalt have fun with your dog.** Dogs, and especially puppies, relish fun. Play with your dog, walk him, romp with him, and make training sessions fun, too. The couple that has fun together, stays together!

II. **Thou shalt allow your dog to be good at something.** Give your dog something to do. Whether it's training sessions, obedience classes, fun tricks, hunting, or running in the park with you each morning, dogs like to have a purpose and a task at which they can succeed. Let your dog excel at something, and he'll love you for it.

III. **Thou shalt give your dog companions.** Dogs are social animals, and although some dogs do well alone all day, most dogs like to have someone to see every few hours. Come home for lunch if no one will be home all day. Have friends, relatives, or a professional pet sitter visit and walk your dog when you won't be around much. If you can handle the added expense, commitment, and training time, you could also consider bringing home another dog.

Never get a second dog just to keep your first dog company. Every dog deserves love, attention, and proper care. If you can't afford two dogs, find another way to give your dog something to do. On the other hand, if you can afford it and are willing to spend the time training both dogs, a second dog can be fun for the family and a great pal to your first dog (see Chapter 7).

IV. **Thou shalt keep your dog out of trouble.** Your dog can't misbehave by chewing your new shoe or forgetting his housetraining, for example, if you don't give him the opportunity.

V. **Thou shalt teach your dog what you expect.** How can your dog know those new shoes aren't chew toys if you don't show him, in ways he can understand, that some things are off limits for chewing, but other things are okay for chewing? Similarly, how will he know where it is acceptable to relieve himself unless you show him?

VI. **Thou shalt not reward your dog for doing something you don't like.** Even if you don't realize it, your reactions to your puppy's behaviors could be reinforcing the behaviors you dislike the most. For example, if you don't pay attention to your dog very often, he may discover that an accident on the carpet is the only way to get your attention, even if the attention involves getting yelled at.

VII. **Thou shalt praise and reward your dog when he does something right or well.** Praise and treats are big payoffs for good behavior as far as your dog is concerned. When he pleases you, let him know it.

VIII. **Thou shalt know what you want your puppy to do.** You can't show your puppy what you expect unless you have your expectations clearly in mind.

IX. **Thou shalt confine your dog in his doggy den or some other safe area when you can't pay attention to him.** This is not cruelty, but kindness. You're keeping your dog out of trouble and letting his energy and hunger renew so that the next training session will be productive. (And sometimes your dog needs a rest from you.)

X. **Thou shalt not ever yell at, jerk, hit, grab, pinch, shock, squirt, or kick your dog.** Not ever. There is always a better way. Labs were not bred to take abuse; no dog is bred to take abuse.

Keeping that relationship

Forming a solid bond with your dog and teaching him the ropes and the rules is an important beginning, but if you want to maintain that relationship, remember that dogs are a lifelong commitment. You can cement that commitment if you:

✔ Remain consistent in the way you relate to your dog.

✔ Remain consistent about what your dog can and can't do.

✔ Provide a home full of rewards, benefits, and good things for your dog. (We don't mean you should spoil him. We mean you should create an environment in which he is happy.)

✔ Continue to educate your dog so he can enjoy a lifetime of learning and has continual chances to be rewarded by your praise and attention and by play, toys, and treats.

✔ Keep loving him!

That's all it takes. Not so complicated, is it?

Dogs take a cue from your body language. When you want your dog to relax and calm down, act relaxed and calm yourself. Don't run around frantically, waving your arms and screaming, "Down! Stop it! Calm down!"

Disciplining Like a Parent

Even if you aren't a parent, you had parents or parental figures in your life. Parents are important for children in their roles as lawmakers, guidance counselors, moral supporters, disciplinarians, and sources of unconditional love. And these are exactly the same roles you'll play with your new puppy! You make the rules and teach your puppy how to follow those rules, all the while offering your unconditional love.

But what about discipline? Discipline can mean many things to many people. Look at it from an educational perspective: You want your puppy to learn to behave in a certain way and also to learn how not to behave. There is a well-established scientific *learning theory* involving two types of discipline: reinforcement and punishment. This theory can help you understand how to help your pup be a good citizen.

Reinforcement makes behaviors more likely to occur:

✔ Positive reinforcement is doing something pleasant or nice for your pup right after he does something good for you. For example, if you say, "Sit," and your pup sits, you give him a treat.

✔ Negative reinforcement is stopping something bad when the dog does something for you. For example, you stop constricting the choke chain on your dog's neck when you ask him to sit and he sits.

Most progressive trainers prefer to use positive reinforcement and little or no negative reinforcement. Why would you want to cause discomfort to your puppy if you don't have to?

Punishment is something that makes a behavior less likely to occur:

✔ Positive punishment means that you add something unpleasant when your dog does a behavior you want to decrease. For example, if your dog barks at another dog, you give him a leash jerk. If the positive punishment works, he may be less likely to bark at that dog the next time he sees it. Positive punishment may sound sensible, but it is always risky. What if your dog interprets your action to mean that in the presence of that other dog, you become nasty? You may help your dog learn to dislike other dogs. Joel has seen this happen time and time again.

✔ Negative punishment means taking away something good to decrease the likelihood of the behavior. For example, to help your dog stop barking at other dogs, you could immediately turn around and walk away from any dog that is the object of his barking. If your dog likes to meet other dogs, taking away his chance to meet them will be negative punishment and will make him less likely to bark at dogs in the future.

Positive reinforcement and negative punishment are the preferred methods because they don't involve doing anything nasty to your dog. Even if you think withholding reinforcement is a little nasty, it only makes sense. If you don't work or obey the law, good things are taken away from you. Your dog can learn that basic principle, too.

On the other hand, negative reinforcement and positive punishment are best avoided. Why do something aversive to your dog if you don't have to? Remember, if you do choose to use negative reinforcement and positive punishment and you don't see positive results at once, you're not using the learning theory correctly. Even if you don't intend it, you're being abusive.

Aversive action toward your dog can have many unpleasant and even tragic side effects. It can ruin your relationship. It can make the dog fearful or aggressive. You certainly will not be as happy a person if you're causing discomfort to a beloved family member.

Focusing your parenting efforts on the positive rather than the negative is the sure way to teach your dog right from wrong and good from bad. It also cements your relationship for good. Your dog will know that good things come from you, and who wouldn't want a relationship with someone like that?

Chapter 10

E Is for Education

In This Chapter

▶ Introducing your dog to lots of people

▶ Using lure-and-reward training

▶ Understanding reward training

▶ Teaching your dog not to bark, play-bite, or have accidents in the house

Can you imagine what you would be like if your parents had sat around on the couch looking at you until you were 18 years old just to see what you would pick up on your own? Instead, your parents spent a lot of time training (educating) you, so you would know the house rules and the rules of life, too. Your parents also sent you to school so that experts (teachers) could further educate you.

Imagine, too, the absurdity of the argument, "This kid doesn't know how to do anything! Must be bad breeding." Of course, you wouldn't know anything if your parents didn't teach you anything. While you may have figured out some basic survival tactics, you certainly wouldn't be very good at anything, and you wouldn't have any manners.

But that little puppy or dog you have just brought home has a smaller brain than you do. How can you expect her to figure out everything on her own? Dogs need your guidance so that they know what to do and how to act. Puppies are more self-sufficient than human infants when it comes to survival, but they certainly aren't preprogrammed to be housetrained, let alone to heel on a leash or sit at your feet at your request.

And that brings up part three of the MRE system: education. It's your responsibility to educate your dog if you want her to be a good companion. Education isn't as hard as it may seem. You need to know what you're doing, make a plan, and know when to ask for help.

Your Canine Eliza Doolittle: Socialization

Socialization is a fancy term that simply means this: Your pup has to meet every kind of person and situation that you want her to accept as an adult, starting when she is a little puppy and continuing until she is an adult. If you properly socialize your pup, there is a very good chance that she won't be fearful or aggressive to all of the nice folks she meets as an adult.

You not only have to socialize your pup with lots of folks, you also need to manage the interactions so that they're positive for your puppy. You have to be able to control what the people your pup meets are going to do. Bad experiences with strangers can teach your puppy that some folks aren't acceptable.

Young puppies are very susceptible to certain diseases, especially before they have received all their vaccinations, and humans can subject puppies to diseases. You don't need to keep your puppy isolated, however. When having people over to meet your new puppy, simply have them remove their shoes at the door and wash their hands before they hold the puppy.

If you don't have the kind of house where people are frequently coming and going, consider having a few puppy socialization parties. Invite friends over, have everyone remove their shoes and wash their hands, and then have people approach your puppy one at a time and introduce themselves. Let your puppy get to know each party guest. In return, you provide the snacks.

Danger: Kids ahead

If you're a couple without children and you get a Lab puppy, you want to look ahead to the time when you will have children. (Even if you aren't planning to have children, you never know what the future holds.) If you're trying to socialize your puppy to children but you don't control the interactions, your pup may very well learn that children are loud, obnoxious, and downright dangerous.

Socializing your pup to children doesn't mean leaving her alone in a room with seven toddlers. Young children aren't any more trained to handle a puppy than the puppy is trained to handle them. When socializing your puppy to young children, hold the puppy and control the interaction by carefully monitoring how and how much the children touch the puppy and how much noise they make while doing it. If your puppy seems fearful, don't restrain her and force her to accept being touched. This will make her more fearful, not less. Just as you would be very careful with a baby or a toddler around a strange dog, you must be careful with your puppy to make sure that the vast majority of her interactions with children, and with adults, too, are positive — see Figure 10-1.

Figure 10-1:
By training
your Lab
and your
child to
accept each
other, you
can
encourage
a great
friendship.

© Close Encounters of the Furry Kind

Preventing problems is much easier than solving them. A dog that wasn't socialized well can still be trained, but it is a much longer road. In any situation where your pup is going to meet someone new, make sure you can control the situation. It is better to pass up the chance to socialize your puppy if there is any chance that it is going to be frightened by the new person, such as a screaming child, a person with a cane, or someone who may tend to grab the puppy unexpectedly. Just make a note to find the same kind of person to socialize your pup in the future.

The ABCs of socialization

When socializing your pup to someone new, try the following steps:

1. **Make sure the puppy is hungry and the new person is seated in a comfortable chair with treats that you know your puppy likes.**

2. **Wait for the puppy to approach the person, and then have the person silently offer the puppy a treat.**

3. **After the puppy readily take treats from the new person, the person can gently talk to the puppy while she takes the treat.**

4. **Have the person lure the pup into various positions (you may have to show the person how to do this) and then reward the pup.**

   If you want your pup to obey other people, have the person give the same requests you use.

Petting the puppy gently on the head or chest is a good reward after she obeys a request. Sometimes, however, petting will activate a Lab pup, and you may see some jumping up or play-biting.

Earliest Lessons

Training your new puppy doesn't start at six months of age. It starts the minute you bring your puppy home. If you show your pup right from wrong at the very beginning, it won't feel as if you are suddenly changing the rules just when she gets to know you!

Relief is in sight!

You want the pup to relieve herself outside? As soon as you get out of the car after that very first drive home, take your puppy to the designated bathroom location outside. Set her down and watch her, but don't interact with her. She'll probably sniff around for a minute or more. When she starts producing urine or feces, gently praise her. Congratulations! You just took that important first step in the house-training process.

How much is enough?

Knowing how often your puppy will need to relieve herself gives you a better idea of how often to take her outside to her spot.

- Between the ages of 6 and 14 weeks, puppies need to go out about eight to ten times in 24 hours.

- Between 14 to 20 weeks, when bladder control gets stronger, your puppy will require about six to eight trips outside.

- Between 20 and 30 weeks, four to six trips should do the trick.

- From 30 weeks to adulthood, your dog should do fine with three or four trips outside each day.

Despite what you may have heard, it isn't healthy for any dog, no matter how old, to have only one chance in twenty-four hours to eliminate.

Many young puppies will make two puddles or two piles when you take them outside, so don't rush your puppy in immediately after she has relieved herself. After a couple of minutes, when you're pretty sure your puppy is finished, take her back inside.

The puppy-proof room

After your puppy is finished relieving herself, take her into the house to the room where you're going to spend most of your time together (usually the living room, den, or kitchen). This should be a room where you feel comfortable, too, so that you will enjoy being in here with your puppy.

Remember to puppy-proof your house, doing the most careful job in the room where you and your puppy will spend the most time together. You want your new puppy to be able to explore the room without the chance of injuring herself by chewing on an electrical cord or swallowing a rubber band. Remove or put everything that she could possibly damage or destroy out of puppy's reach.

Let your puppy do some exploring on her own. During her explorations, she'll probably come back to you periodically. Gently pet and praise her. Reassure her that she's in a safe and wonderful place. If she starts to chew on something off-limits, give her a safe object to chew like a sturdy, hollow chew toy, and then gently praise her when she chews it. If she shows no interest in the chew toy, stuff it with a few safe goodies (puppy treats), and she'll quickly get interested.

Young puppies are easily excited, and when they get excited, they have to urinate. Always keep this fact in mind as you vigilantly watch your puppy play and explore. Whenever your puppy starts to get excited, take her outside to her special spot so you can praise her again when she urinates there.

Watch your pup for signs of fatigue. Like young children, young puppies will play like mad and then suddenly collapse. Don't let your pup overtire herself. After about ten or fifteen minutes of exploring (see Figure 10-2) and/or chewing, take her outside to her spot and then bring her back in. Toss a few pieces of her dry dog food in her den and gently place her inside.

Figure 10-2:
Like young children, young puppies like to play. Nap time will be necessary afterward.

© Close Encounters of the Furry Kind

The doggy den

Your pup's doggy den is the safe place where she can hang out when you can't watch her. Dogs are den animals, so forget the idea that you're being cruel by caging her. It would be more cruel to let her get in trouble or injure herself by chewing inappropriate objects.

You now have the physically easy yet emotionally challenging job of getting your puppy used to spending time in her doggy den. This is as physically easy as training gets: Put her in her den and do nothing. Oh, how badly you'll want to take her out when she begins to whine! But do nothing! If you respond to her vocalizations, she will train you to let her out, and she won't learn to accept and love her den.

Many of Joel's clients ask, "How do I know whether the pup is fussing because she has to go to the bathroom?" It's pretty simple. Always take her outside just before you put her in her den. If you just took her out to potty, she's not fussing because she has to go to the bathroom.

After she has been asleep in her den for awhile and wakes up, take her outside before she starts fussing. The key is to keep a watchful eye on your puppy at all times, even when she's in her den. If you anticipate her elimination needs, training her to love her doggy den and to be house-trained will both be much easier.

The daily schedule

When teaching your pup to love her den, your daily schedule should go something like this:

- ✔ In the morning, take your puppy out of her den and immediately take her outside to relieve herself. You may need to carry her at first to prevent her from making a mistake on the way to the door.

- ✔ During the day, keep her out of her den when you're ready to train her, play with her, and watch her 100 percent of the time. When one responsible person can watch the pup every second to make sure she isn't getting into trouble and to watch for signs that she needs to be taken outside to relieve herself, she can stay out of her den. When no one is available to play puppy watcher (which could be a full-time career), put the pup in her den.

- ✔ At night, your puppy should get used to going to sleep before or when you go to sleep. Put her in her den at night, set your alarm if necessary for the middle-of-the-night potty run (especially if your puppy sleeps in another room and her cries won't wake you) and let her cry it out. It isn't cruel. The sooner she learns that night is for sleeping and day is for playing, the better off you'll all be. Labs are social animals and will be most comfortable sleeping near you. That doesn't mean you have to let your Lab sleep in the bed with you, but if you can keep your Lab's doggy den in the room where you sleep, your Lab will probably rest easier.

How Dogs Learn

Knowing how your dog learns is an important part of knowing how to teach your dog. One key truth about dogs may help you in almost every aspect of training: Dogs do what benefits them right now. If your puppy comes to you and you talk sweetly to her, gently stroke her, and give her a piece of her food, she will be more likely to come to you in the future. If she comes to you and you ignore her, or worse, yell at her when she tries to get your attention by jumping on you, she may not be as likely to come to you next time. If she jumps up on you and you smile and laugh and say, "What a cute puppy!," she will be more likely to jump up on you next time. It's that simple. When it comes to dogs, you reap what you sow.

Dogs are motivated by rewards. They are social animals and have a very predictable list of things they find rewarding:

- Comfortable temperature
- Water to drink
- Attention
- Food
- Air to breathe
- Sex (when they mature, females for a few weeks each year and males any time)

Knowing what pleases your dog is the first step in training. The second step is using those rewards in a method. The two best and nicest methods for training any puppy or dog are

- Lure-and-reward training
- Reward training

These methods are covered in the two following sections.

Lure-and-reward training

If your puppy is both hungry and well-rested, you can hold a piece of food in front of her nose and use it to lure her into various positions (the basis of the Start Puppy Training Procedure described in Chapter 4). Here's how it works:

- **The sit:** When your pup is standing, slowly move the lure up and slightly to the rear, and she will sit. Say "Yes" and give her the food reward.
- **The stand:** When your pup is sitting, slowly move the lure straight away from her, parallel to the ground at her nose level, far enough so she has to stand up. When she stands, say "Yes" and give her the food reward.
- **The down:** When your pup is sitting, slowly lower the lure straight down from her nose to the floor. When she lies down, say "Yes" and give her the food reward.

When you're ready to bet $100 that you can lure your puppy into a position, you're ready to start giving the positions names and teaching the pup to perform them on request.

- Say "Sit," lure the dog into position, say "Yes," and then reward the dog.
- Say "Stand," lure the dog into position, say "Yes," and then reward the dog.

✔ Say "Down" (from sit), lure the dog into position, say "Yes," and then reward the dog.

✔ Say "Sit" (up from a down), lure the dog into position, say "Yes," and then reward the dog.

The beauty of the lure-and-reward method is that the breeder can teach it to pups as soon as they start eating solid food. You can start this type of training on the very first day you bring your puppy home. Why wait? It's fun for you and the puppy. You immediately start to request things of your puppy and reward her, rather than letting her decide what she wants to do (which will inevitably get her into trouble).

Here are a few tips for lure-and-reward training:

✔ Always practice lure-and-reward training when your puppy is hungry.

✔ When your pup is following the lure (the piece of food), don't say anything. If you talk, you'll distract your puppy from the task at hand.

✔ Make sure the pup is paying attention to the lure before you move it, and then move it very slowly.

✔ Hold the lure with two fingers and your thumb. You want the pup to see, smell, and be able to touch the lure, but not to be able to take it away.

✔ At first, use your puppy's regular dry dog food as a lure. If she loses interest, move on to something more exciting, such as tiny pieces of bland cheese or low-fat meat slices. If you use anything besides the pup's dry dog food, flavor the dry food with the cheese after the pup catches on and gradually switch back to the dry dog food.

Using pieces of your dog's regular food for training is the best way to avoid excess calories. Take the training allotment out of your dog's regular ration of food.

✔ If you try all of these tips and still can't get lure-and-reward training to work, find someone skilled in this type of training to help you.

Reward training

For most puppies and dogs, lure-and-reward training is the best way to teach your dog to follow requests that are easily lured. But some behaviors or requests aren't lurable. How do you use a moving piece of food to make your dog learn a trick, for example, or for house-training? You don't. For these types of behaviors, reward training is best.

How can you use reward training to get your dog to perform a behavior on request? Suppose your dog yawns when she gets up from her nap, and you think it would be great to get your dog to yawn every time you say, "Bored?" The first step is to let your dog know that, whenever she hears a specific word or sound, she will get rewarded. The reward could be a verbal "Yes" followed by a treat or a click from a clicker followed by a treat. A *clicker* is a simple device that makes a click when you press it. It is a plastic box with a thin metal tab in it that makes the clicking sound. You can buy them in some pet stores, and Joel says they used to come in Cracker Jack boxes. (Sort of dates Joel, doesn't it?) Practice this whenever you can. Say "Yes" or click the clicker throughout the day, and then offer your dog a treat afterwards.

As soon as your dog figures out that when you say "Yes" or click the clicker, she gets a treat, she'll start looking for her treat. Now you can begin to associate the praise/reward with a behavior.

To teach your dog to yawn on request, you will need to wait for her to wake up (knowing her typical schedule will make this a lot easier). Whenever your dog wakes up and yawns, say "Yes" or click the clicker, and then give her a treat. After you practice this for awhile, your dog will start yawning more often because she has figured out that yawning results in a reward. You may be amused by how much she yawns!

When you're willing to bet $100 that your dog is going to yawn (by watching your dog, you'll learn the signs), begin to say, "Bored?" just before she yawns. When she does yawn, say your "Yes" or click your clicker, and then give her a reward. Keep practicing! Before you know it, your dog will be yawning on request.

Lab Basic Training

Reward training is the best way to approach the elimination of undesirable behaviors, as well as the addition of desirable behaviors. But knowing some other techniques will help, too. The following sections describe some of the most common behaviors in puppies that humans tend to dislike and also tell you how you can teach your dog better ways to spend her time.

Whenever your pup is behaving unacceptably, the right thing to do is train her or do a time-out (put her in her doggy den). Punishment hurts the relationship and isn't very effective. Letting your pup continue the behavior will make the behavior worse and hurt the relationship, as well.

Barking

"Help, Joel! My puppy barks!" "Joel, what do I do? My dog barks!" Well, of course she does. Dogs bark. When you were a child and first began to figure out that you could communicate verbally, did your mother shriek, "Doctor! Help! My child talks!" Of course not! She probably bragged about you, proudly declaring, "My child can talk!"

Talking and barking aren't exactly the same, of course. But people talk and dogs bark for some of the same reasons. Sometimes your dog barks to communicate something to you. For example, your puppy may bark when you leave her alone in her doggy den. She is used to spending most of her time with her littermates, and it is perfectly normal for her to protest, "Hey! Where is everybody? I'm lonely!"

As much as you love your puppy, you must teach her how to be alone some of the time. The best way to do this is to ignore the barking. This is both good management (see Chapter 8) and good education. You took her out to relieve herself before you put her in the den, so you know she isn't barking for that reason. Let her bark. Behaviors that aren't rewarded decrease in frequency. Puppies and dogs are smart enough to know that if the barking doesn't work, it is better to conserve energy for more important things. It may take your dog a little while to figure this out, but she will figure it out eventually.

Tiny puppies can make big noises. Try to arrange it so that your barking puppy is in her kennel during a time when the noise won't disturb anyone and get you and your puppy evicted.

When your dog does stop barking, she'll take a nap. Be sure to be there when she wakes up so you can take her out of her den and outside before she starts barking. She will have to go out, and you want to make sure you take her out, but you don't want to combine this necessary action with an inadvertent reward for barking.

Some folks confine their pups only when they leave the house. This usually results in a puppy or dog who will bark if she ever does have to be confined when the owners are home. It makes house-training more difficult than it has to be, and it takes away a great management tool to prevent mouthing, jumping up, and other behaviors. Teach your pup that it is normal to be confined in her doggy den occasionally when the family is home. It doesn't mean she will be confined all the time. She can be out whenever she will be watched so that she doesn't get into trouble.

Play-biting

Play-biting is normal puppy behavior and the method by which puppies explore their worlds. Puppies play by grabbing each other with their teeth; such biting isn't a result of aggression or fear. If you watch your puppy when she is play-biting, you'll see that she is relaxed, not fearful or aggressive. She's having fun!

However, just because play-biting is normal doesn't mean you should let your puppy bite anything she wants. Most humans find play-biting obnoxious at best and painful at worst. Yet you must avoid punishing this behavior. You don't want to take a puppy that's playing and turn her into a fearful or aggressive dog.

A two-step approach to play-biting is usually the best approach. First, teach your puppy that human flesh is very sensitive by saying "Ouch!" sharply every time your pup's teeth make contact with your skin. Every puppy/human pair requires the right tone and volume that will be effective for getting the puppy's attention. You may need to experiment to find yours. Your goal is to startle and momentarily stop the play-biting. It is important to understand that you will be doing this for weeks and that you will probably not see immediate results as far as a decrease in the frequency and the force of the play-biting. Be patient. Over a period of weeks, you'll see a change.

You're teaching your puppy *bite inhibition,* a fancy term meaning you're teaching your dog not to bite too hard. All dogs will bite as adults if they are given the right (or sometimes the wrong) reason. Teaching them bite inhibition can avert disaster.

The second step is being able to tell your pup not to play-bite even before she does it. You accomplish this by teaching her the "Take it" and the "Off" requests:

1. **Hold a small quantity of her dry food in your hand.**

   Say "Take it" as you give her one piece.

2. **Close the rest of the dog food in your fist and hold your fist right in front of her nose, about an inch or two away.**

   Say "Off" in a sweet and gentle voice. She will mouth or paw at your hand to try to get the food.

3. **Wait until she stops mouthing or pawing for three to five seconds.**

   Say "Take it" again and give her another piece.

4. **Continue this process until her meal is done.**

   By doing this, you are teaching her that "Off" means not to touch. After you see her responding well for a few days at this, you can start to tell her "Off" when she looks like she is going to play-bite you.

In the wild, puppies and dogs have two peak activity periods: dawn and dusk. This corresponds with the times when you tend to be home: in the morning and in the evening after work. You will probably notice a lot more play-biting during your puppy's peak activity period. Be prepared to tell her "Off" and then either train her or do a short time-out (put her in her den).

House-training

If you follow the management advice for house-training in Chapter 8, your pup may already be house-trained. Lucky you! If not, however, have no fear. You can complete the process now.

The goal is to have your puppy at the preselected elimination spot when she has to relieve herself. These times tend to be:

- Whenever she wakes up
- After she drinks water (the younger the pup, the sooner after drinking)
- After she eats (the younger the pup, the sooner after eating)
- Whenever anything exciting happens (like five minutes of training)
- Whenever you play with her for five minutes (training is play; do it whenever you can)
- If she hasn't been out for awhile
- First thing in the morning
- Last thing at night

A good way to make puppy duty a family affair is to make a rule: Whoever gets up first in the morning has the job of taking the puppy out to relieve herself. Whoever is the last person to go to bed at night has the job of taking the puppy out to relieve herself.

Always take your puppy outside on a leash. It is very important that she learn to potty on a leash. You want to be able to take her with you on vacation and your other travels. Stopping at a rest area for both of you to potty can be very frustrating if she hasn't learned to potty on leash. And you certainly don't want her running loose near the interstate!

Just before you take her through the door to the outside, say "Let's go outside." Walk directly to the potty area. Stand there and don't interact with your pup. Watch her carefully. When she starts to give signs that she is going to urinate or defecate, say "Go potty," and then while the urine or feces is flowing, gently praise her: "Good potty!" (Not too loudly. You don't want to scare her into stopping!) Make sure you give her an extra minute or two in case she needs to go more.

If you always take her back in right after she goes, she may learn to "hold it" so that she can stay out and play longer. If you play for a few minutes *after* she goes, she'll learn to go quickly so that she gets to play sooner.

If your puppy doesn't relieve herself within five minutes of being outside, take her back in the house. Train her if you can, watching her like a hawk, or return her to her den (watch her in there, too). The next time you take her out, she'll probably relieve herself right away. If she doesn't, that only means she can hold it longer than you thought.

When your pup is back inside, don't forget: One responsible person must watch her 100 percent of the time, or she should be in her doggy den. When Joel tells this to her clients, they usually nod their heads, "Yes, yes, 100 percent of the time." Joel likes to stop them and explain that house-training a puppy requires full-time attention. We can't emphasize this enough! It isn't easy to be so vigilant, but it is by far the fastest and easiest way of getting your pup housetrained. If she never has a chance to have an accident in the house, she'll learn very quickly.

Also, remember to say "Let's go outside," just as you open the door to take the pup out. She will soon catch on to the meaning of these words. While you're watching your pup in the house, if she starts to sniff or circle or goes to the door, put on her leash immediately and take her outside at once. You and your puppy are doing a great job!

If your pup starts to squat in the house, say "Go outside" with a slight edge in your voice, and then whisk her outside at once. If she has done anything in the house at this time, or if you find a little puddle or pile that you didn't see her make, wait until after you put her in her den to clean it up. Remember, punishment would be pointless. She obviously hasn't learned where her potty location is yet, and it was your job to take her outside on time. Don't blame her, and don't punish yourself. Just do your best to avoid a future incident through better management. Don't forget to clean up the mishap with a good enzyme cleaner to eliminate the smell that may signal your dog to eliminate in the same spot again.

One of the best times to train your puppy is when she has just come in from going to the bathroom. Just remember that training is exciting for your puppy, so if she shows any signs of wandering off, she probably has to go potty again. Take her outside — better safe than sorry!

Chapter 11

Training Tips, Tricks, and Techniques

. . . .

In This Chapter

▶ Teaching your dog what to chew and what not to chew

▶ Training your dog how to greet people

▶ Mastering sit, stand, down, take it, off, and kennel

▶ Using training requests: come, long sit, and long down

▶ Walking on a loose leash and heeling

▶ Hiring a trainer or canine behavior consultant

▶ Attempting to reach Canine Good Citizen status

▶ Understanding the ins and outs of obedience competition

. . . .

*T*raining your dog and giving him new things to learn and do is a lifelong process. Positive training does more than help you with barking, play-biting, and housetraining. It can also help you teach your dog not to jump up on people, what he can and can't chew, how to listen to you, and a whole range of typical dog behaviors: sit, stand, down, take it, off, come, long sit, long down, walking on a loose lead, and heel. Are you ready? Take your pup out for a potty break, bring him back in, and get your treats ready. Here we go!

Mastering Good Behavior

If you've been consistent in your management of your new puppy and especially if you've also been trying some lure-and-reward training, your puppy is behaving better and better. He has more to learn, however, and positive training is the key.

Chewing

Chewing is perfectly normal puppy and dog behavior. Puppies and dogs chew for many reasons, such as the following:

- Teething
- Boredom
- Exploring a new object
- Stress
- Fun

It makes sense to teach your puppy or dog what to chew rather than to not chew at all. To do this, you need to use chew toys. The best kind to use is a sturdy, hollow, rubber one.

Joel's favorite chew toy to use is the Kong chew toy, a virtually indestructible object that's perfect for the boisterous chew sessions for which Labs are notorious.

Some puppies/dogs chew these toys the first time they get one. If your puppy or dog doesn't seem interested in chewing his toy, stuff it with tasty treats to pique his interest. When you stuff a hollow chew toy, the idea is to put in something desirable that your puppy or dog will have to work for to get out. Wedging in a hard treat such as a big dog biscuit works well. Then put in a few smaller pieces that your dog can get out with some work. Last, put in a small handful of his dry food that will fall out as soon as he touches the chew toy. You can also add a small amount of peanut butter, if necessary, for an even bigger incentive.

After you have a chew toy that definitely interests your dog, hold it in your hand and say, "Chew your toy," and then give him the toy. Praise him for chewing the toy. By teaching him to chew his toy every day, you will help him develop a strong preference for chewing his chew toy rather than the furniture, your shoes, your children's toys or whatever else you would prefer didn't make contact with doggy teeth. Always make sure you have a chew toy handy (it pays to keep several around the house). If your dog begins to chew anything else, say "Chew your toy!" Then make sure he does.

Keep the stuffed chew toys for when your puppy or dog is out of his den. When your dog is in his den, a regular, unstuffed chew toy will satisfy his urge to chew.

Jumping up

Most people don't like when a dog jumps up on them, although with a puppy, the behavior is easy to forgive. You may even feel flattered. "Oh look, he likes me! Good dog!" Silly human! You've reinforced a behavior that won't be so cute when your dog weighs 75 pounds and comes barreling across the kitchen to greet you.

Puppies and dogs jump up on you because they want to look into your face. Dogs can tell what mood you're are in and whether you're in the mood for fun by looking at your expressions. But the poor dogs are way down there on the floor! You can't blame them for jumping up to get a better look. After all, they can't ask you, "How are you feeling today? Are you going to play with me or would you rather I left you alone just now?"

Jumping up is another one of those normal doggy behaviors that you can manage through positive training. Look at it from a human point of view: Imagine coming up to a good friend and putting your arm around him or taking his hand and giving it a friendly squeeze. Now imagine that in return, he slaps you in the face. That would probably hurt your relationship. Would you do such a thing to your best canine friend? To your dog, jumping up on you is the equivalent of a friendly hug. Don't punish your dog for being friendly! That doesn't mean you can't teach your dog not to jump, however.

Puppies often jump up so that they can see what's going on. And most people pet a little puppy who puts his little paws on their legs, wags his tail, and looks up with love in his eyes. Six months later, someone will be advising you to knee your dog in his chest or try other silly, unpleasant, or even nasty things.

Instead, try this:

1. **Put a *buckle collar* (a standard collar with a buckle closure) and a leash on your pup.**

2. **Get him to sit.**

3. **Have the person he wants to get to know gently stroke his chest in a calm manner.**

If you practice this management and training method, you'll wind up with a dog that sits to greet people. If sitting gets him the reward of lots of attention and petting, he'll be glad to sit for you and anyone else who gives him affection.

Getting Your Lab to Listen

As a trainer, Joel hears a lot of people complain that their Labs won't listen. Do you have the impression that your puppy or dog doesn't listen to you? Before you throw your hands up in despair, ask yourself just what you want him to listen to. It would be wonderful and convenient if dogs understood English (or any human language). Then you could just explain to them what you wanted them to do. That's what you do when human children finally learn to speak, right?

Of course, puppies and dogs don't understand English, but they do read you in other ways. They interpret your facial expressions, your body language, the tone of your voice, and some of the words you say, after you've carefully taught them the meaning of those words through training. Dogs get to know you and how you tend to act in different situations. They watch you for cues. They want to be rewarded, so they're paying attention. You can take advantage of all this attention by learning how to communicate in a way your dog understands. And by continuing to give rewards.

When we say your dog can't understand English, we mean he'll never be able to understand English in the complex way humans understand it. You can teach him the meaning of certain words, however. These words, often called *commands,* are most effectively taught as requests. Why command when a request will do? A request is all you need, if you ask in just the right way. You remember the old saying: You catch more flies with honey than with vinegar!

Even though we like to call commands *requests,* they shouldn't be spoken as questions (as a true request would be spoken). Speak your requests with the inflection of a pleasant and friendly request but without raising your voice at the end.

After going through reward-based training, if your dog doesn't obey a request the first time it is asked, he probably doesn't understand your request. If you repeat the request before the dog has a chance to do it, you may condition your dog to obey the second — or fifth! — request. Instead, train that request in a positive manner until he wants to do it the first time.

Sit

"Sit" is probably the first request that comes to mind when people envision training their dogs. To teach your dog to sit using lure-and-reward training, first make sure your dog is well-rested and hungry. Then do the following:

1. **Using your dog's dry dog food as a lure, grasp a piece of food with your first two fingers and your thumb.**

   If dry food isn't enough of a lure, use a more tempting treat such as low-fat cheese sandwich slices.

2. **When your pup is standing, hold the piece of food directly in front of his mouth, almost touching his lips.**

3. **Very slowly raise the piece of food so that it moves in an arch from in front of his lips to slightly above his head.**

   Most pups will follow the food with their noses and wind up with their rears on the ground.

4. **Say, "Yes" and give the pup the treat.**

   That is a sit! Well done!

5. **After you do this a few times, add the verbal request, saying "Sit" in a sweet tone of voice before you move the piece of food up.**

6. **When your dog goes into the sit position, say, "Yes" in a sweet tone of voice.**

7. **Give your dog the piece of food.**

Some people dislike the idea of training with food, claiming that praise is adequate reward for any dog. Sure, praise is nice. You like it when your boss praises you for a job well done. But a raise is a lot bigger motivation, isn't it? Your dog loves praise, but when you back it up with a little gastronomic "raise," you'll be speaking your dog's language!

Stand

Lots of dogs pick up the sit request fairly easily, but many dog owners don't think to teach the stand request. The stand request is handy when you want to groom your dog, when you want him to get ready to go out or when you want to try a new training exercise.

Here's how you can get your dog to stand:

1. **When your pup is sitting, hold the lure (food) so that it's almost touching his lips.**

2. **Draw the lure forward, parallel with the ground and far enough so the pup has to stand up to get it.**

   Make sure you don't lower or raise the treat.

   When the pup stands up to get the treat, he is doing a stand.

3. **When he's got it, add the verbal request, saying "Stand" in a sweet tone of voice.**

4. **When your dog goes into the stand position, say, "Yes" in a sweet tone of voice.**

5. **Give your dog the piece of food.**

Down

"Down" is a great request when you want your dog to lie at your feet and behave himself. Everyone will be impressed with how well your dog is controlled, but you and your dog both know you have a mutual understanding about when to play and when to lie down and relax.

Follow these instructions:

1. **When your pup is sitting, hold the lure (food) directly under his nose.**

2. **Slowly lower the lure straight down to the ground under his nose.**

   Don't move the lure forward. Most pups will follow the lure down and get into the down position.

   If your pup doesn't lie down after a few tries, make sure you're moving the lure as slowly as possible. If he still doesn't lie down, you may have to move the lure slightly toward him or slightly away from him. Experiment and see if you can find a place that works.

   If you still can't lure your dog into a down, move on to other requests and then go back to the down on another day after he has a better idea about what it means to follow the lure (in other words, it means "reward"). If it still doesn't work, seek out a good, positive dog trainer or canine behavior consultant to help you.

   When the pup goes down to get the treat, he is doing a down.

3. **After your dog has the idea, add the verbal request, saying "Down" in a sweet tone of voice.**

4. **When your dog goes into the down position, say, "Yes" in a sweet tone of voice.**

5. **Give your dog the piece of food.**

Take it/off

"Take it" and "Off" are two wonderful requests you can use to teach your dog to take something from your hand and not to touch something.

To teach your dog to take anything from your hand, use the take it request. You can also use the take it request to ask your dog to pick up anything off the floor. Drop your keys? Ask your dog to "Take it!" Labs love to carry anything around in their mouths. That's what they were bred to do. Use your imagination, and you'll have a companion to help carry things for you. Remember that a dog with something in his mouth can't pick up a forbidden object.

You can manage many normal doggy behaviors with the off request. Playbiting, mouthing, jumping up, picking up forbidden objects (such as people food), nose prodding, licking, and other behaviors all respond well to a properly timed off request.

You can teach your pup the take it and off requests together.

1. **Take a small handful of the pup's dry food.**

2. **Say, "Take it," and give your pup one piece of dry food.**

3. **Close the rest of the food in your fist and say, "Off," in a nice tone of voice.**

   The pup will probably lick, gnaw, or paw at your hand. Such temptation so close at hand! But stick with the technique.

4. **Hold your hand steady and wait for him to stop touching your hand for three to five seconds.**

5. **Say, "Take it," and give him one piece of food.**

   This process works almost like magic. The pup learns that if he stops touching you when you say, "Off," he will get the take it request and then a food reward. And he learns this amazing feat without a single harsh word from you.

Kennel

The kennel request is a handy way to teach your pup to go into, through, or to some place or area. We use "kennel in your den" as an example of teaching the kennel request. You might also choose to call this a "den" request.

1. **Place yourself and the pup in front of his doggy den, with the doggy den door propped open.**

2. **Hold a piece of dry food in your right hand with the puppy sitting next to you on the left side, your left hand gently holding his collar.**

3. **Say, "kennel in your den," toss the treat into the kennel, and release your pup when he pulls forward to go into the kennel.**

4. **Close the doggy door and say, "Good kennel."**

5. **If the puppy doesn't pull forward to go into the den, gently place him in the den, close the door, and give him a treat.**

Come

The come request is among the most important that you can teach your dog. If you can get your dog to come on request, you may someday be able to avert danger or even save his life. A dog who comes to you is also much easier to manage, and that improves your relationship.

Teaching your pup to come to you using the lure-and-reward method is fun and easy. Make sure your pup is hungry and rested and that you're holding a desirable treat. (Your pup's regular dry food should be your first choice.) Train your dog to come in a safe location where there's nothing more rewarding than you and the treat (no tempting squirrels to chase, kids to play with, or other dogs to visit with).

1. **Hold the lure (food) with two fingers and your thumb with the back of your hand resting against your thigh, near the center line of your body with the food towards the pup.**

2. **Smile at the pup and say, "(Your dog's name), come," in a sweet tone of voice with just a hint of excitement.**

   Don't overdo it, but don't sound bored, either.

3. **If your pup doesn't come running over to you, look down at the food treat and wait for one minute.**

   Almost all hungry puppies or dogs will come running over to you at once — see Figure 11-1. If not, you might show him the treat. If he still isn't interested, try a more rewarding treat.

   If he still refuses to come, squat down (or sit in a chair you have placed right behind you). Your pup will be much more likely to come to you when you get down to his level. Wait another minute. If he still hasn't come, walk away from him. When he follows you, lure him into a sit and reward him while touching his collar and saying, "Yes," just as if he had come right away.

4. **When the pup does come to you, slowly lure him into a sit, give him the treat with your right hand, and slowly caress his neck with your left hand, very near his collar. Say "Yes" as you do this.**

   If your puppy or dog gets away from you in an unsafe area, calling him to you will become very important. You don't want him to shy away when you reach for his collar because you will need to do this to get him on his lead and under control. So always gently put your hand on your dog's collar when he comes to you. See Figure 11-2.

Figure 11-1:
Most Labs
will come
quickly for a
reward.

© Ken and Donna Dannen/AKC Stock Images

Figure 11-2:
Stroke your
Lab's neck
near his
collar when
he comes
to you.

© Nance Photography/AKC Stock Images

Getting him to come is the important job at this point, even if it takes a minute or two. Every time you get him to come and he gets rewarded, he will be more likely to come the next time.

Long sit

A *long sit* is a sit that your dog holds for an extended period of time. In Joel's experience, people tend to use the stay request with a puppy, punishing him as soon as he moves. But this is hardly fair! Your pup doesn't know what "Stay" means.

Instead, use this nice and very positive way to get your pup to stay in the sit position. After you have taught your dog to sit, you can start teaching him that "Sit" means he should remain in a sit position until you give him another request or a release. Before you try the long sit, make sure your dog knows how to do the sit request well.

Here's how to train your dog to do a long sit:

1. **Begin with a small handful of treats in your left hand behind your back.**

   Always have one treat in your right hand when you're ready to give your pup a reward. You have taught your pup to follow a treat with his nose and body (this is what the lure-and-reward method is based upon). If you have more than one treat in your right hand and you give him one and then move your hand away while still holding a treat, he will follow your hand. It's what you've taught him to do!

2. **Give your dog the sit request, and then after a few seconds, say, "Good sit," and give your pup one treat.**

3. **Have your pup sit several more times, gradually increasing the amount of time between when your dog sits and when you say, "Good sit."**

   Give him the reward immediately after saying "Good sit."

You will probably want to work up to a two- or three-minute long sit. Use the long sit while waiting to cross a road or while talking to a neighbor on your daily walks. If you want your puppy or dog to remain in one place for a long time, use the long down request (covered in the following section), which is more comfortable for your dog.

While being trained in the long sit, your pup may get out of position. If he gets back into position within thirty seconds, wait five seconds, say, "Good sit," and reward him. Make sure you wait five seconds before you say, "Good sit" and reward him, or he may learn that getting up and then getting back down is what you want. If your pup doesn't get back into position within thirty seconds, say, "Sit," and lure him back into position.

Long down

The *long down* is like the long sit (see the previous section). It means that your dog will lie down and wait for a long period until you release him or give him another request. The long down is taught the same way the long sit is taught. You say "Down," wait a few seconds, and then say "Good down" and offer the reward. Gradually increase the time between saying "Down" and saying "Good down." This method is so much better than requests taught with reprimands (or worse, punishments) when the pup gets out of position.

You can work up to 30 minutes or more on the long down. Joel uses this request with his pups when he's working at the computer. They will happily remain lying next to him for as long as he likes. They often gaze up at Joel fondly, and he can see them thinking, "Joel is going to give me another treat, sometime."

You can use any release word you want for the long sit and the long down. Joel likes to say, "Go play," and toss a treat. Remember the release word is just that. It means your dog can go do whatever he likes. If your puppy or dog wants to keep lying next to you, that's his choice. You should feel flattered!

Walking on a loose lead

One of the biggest problems dog owners have is walking their dogs on a loose leash. You can see puppies and dogs pulling their owners down any street. Why do dogs do this? Because it works. When they are young, they pull on their leads, and their owners go where they want to go. What a great system! Why would a pup stop?

Joel devised a simple method for training dogs to walk on a loose leash years ago. He calls it the *Zen method of walking on lead.* Follow these steps:

1. **Stand outside with a buckle collar and a six-foot lead attached to your dog, whom you've put into a sit.**

2. **Pick a path that's a straight line leading to some landmark (a tree, for example), and start walking toward it.**

3. **If the lead is slack, continue to walk. If the lead becomes tight, stop and become a tree.**

   Becoming a tree means you stand with your knees slightly bent and the end of the lead (the loop) in both hands at your waist.

4. **Stand there until the puppy sits, lies down, or gives you slack in the lead.**

5. **Start walking again.**

The logic behind this method is that the dog is getting continuous positive reinforcement by keeping slack in the lead (he gets to walk with you). If he tightens the lead, he gets continuous negative reinforcement (it's no fun to be tied to a tree-like owner; it's boring).

If your dog lags behind, just keep walking. He will almost always decide to go with you. If you find yourself dragging him across the ground, change the area or direction you're walking. If he still won't go with you, try using a tasty lure.

If you can't seem to make this method work, either because you can't get yourself to be a tree for a longer time than your dog can wait or because you can't help dragging your dog in frustration, stop and consult with a positive dog trainer or canine behavior consultant who can demonstrate the right way to teach your dog to walk on a loose lead.

Heel

After you teach your dog the sit, down, and stand requests using the lure-and-reward method, you're ready to teach him to heel off-lead; that is, walk at your left side with his collar even with the seam in the side of your pant leg without a lead or leash. (Yes, off-lead! You don't need a lead when the puppy wants to work with you. And he wants to work with you because you're very rewarding!) By heeling, your Lab learns to keep pace with you and stay in that position. Just think of how many leash jerks a dog gets before he learns this concept — none with this lure-and-reward method!

1. **Hold one treat in your left hand in front of your dog's nose after you have him sitting on your left side.**

2. **Say "(Your dog's name), heel."**

3. **Step off on your left foot, take four and a half steps.**

   If you hold the treat in the correct location, your pup will be in the heel position. If you have trouble getting the pup to go with you, make sure he is hungry and use a more attractive treat. Keep trying. Eventually he'll figure out what you want and be happy to oblige (and to follow that treat).

4. **Lure the puppy into a sit.**

5. **Say, "Yes," and give the pup a treat.**

Practice heeling off-lead in a safe location — no busy streets or distractions! Keep the conditions safe for your dog.

Finding a Good Trainer

Sometimes, your dog just won't behave the way you expect, no matter how closely you follow the training instructions. Whether your dog has had a difficult past or is just very independent, you may need to consider hiring a good dog trainer or canine behavior consultant who uses positive methods. An expert can demonstrate techniques and help you to establish an effective line of communication with your dog.

Finding a good trainer or behavior consultant may be more difficult than finding a good veterinarian. Veterinarians are licensed and have a well-defined education. Dog trainers and canine behavior consultants aren't licensed (although some are certified), and you can't be sure what kind of education they have.

When looking for a trainer or canine behavior consultant, find someone who has the following characteristics:

- ✔ Understands how dogs learn. This well-defined science is not in the realm of speculation.

- ✔ Trains you to train your puppy or dog in a positive and non-confrontational manner.

- ✔ Is familiar with and uses lure-and-reward training and/or clicker training.

- ✔ Understands that eight-week-old puppies are fully capable of learning all of the requests that will make them good companions.

- ✔ Understands that you need help managing your pup and keeping him out of trouble while you train him in a positive manner.

- ✔ Is familiar with the work of pioneers in the field of positive reinforcement training, such as Dr. Ian Dunbar and Karen Pryor.

- ✔ Is a member of a professional organization such as the Association of Pet Dog Trainers.

- ✔ Offers private lessons and/or classes.

- ✔ Can give references. Make sure you check these references. Your vet may be able to refer you to a trainer or behavior consultant.

Joel is often amazed when someone says he has taken his dog to an obedience class but doesn't know the name of the trainer. You know the names of your children's teachers, don't you? Develop a relationship with your dog's trainer to better develop the relationship between you and your dog. Obedience classes and private lessons are both good options for training your dog, as long as the teacher uses and teaches positive training methods.

Does your Lab need a canine behavior consultant?

If you aren't sure whether your dog and your situation warrant professional guidance, ask yourself the following questions. If you answer yes to even one, you could benefit from a professional behavior consultant or animal behaviorist:

✔ Have you had your puppy or dog for more than a few months and he's still urinating and/or defecating in the house?

✔ Is your dog having behavior problems that are getting worse?

✔ Are you seeing any signs of fearful behavior? For example, has your dog become afraid of someone, such as the mailman, delivery men, or family members whom he wasn't afraid of in the past? Or maybe he just looks afraid. You're the expert when it comes to your dog's behavior.

✔ Are you seeing any submissive urination or urination due to excitement?

✔ Is your dog behaving aggressively? Is he barking aggressively at people, growling at you, or biting?

✔ Are you having serious problems managing your dog's behavior?

✔ Are you finding yourself wanting to punish your puppy or dog?

✔ Is your relationship with your dog getting worse?

✔ Is your dog risking his life (and/or your possessions) by indiscriminate chewing?

Calling a professional doesn't mean you have failed at anything. Good professional behavior consultants and animal behaviorists have years of experience in handling problems that you may never have encountered before. They can make your job much easier and your relationship with your dog much better.

Obedience classes are less costly than a private trainer, but there are benefits to both methods. Many behaviors are best dealt with by a qualified canine behavior consultant who can come to your home and help you with housetraining, jumping up, chewing, play-biting, and other issues. If your dog has exhibited any aggressive or fearful behavior, you certainly want to find a well-qualified canine behavior consultant (covered in "Does your Lab need a canine behavior consultant?" sidebar) who has a good record dealing with these problems.

Ignore trainers and books that suggest you wait until your puppy is six months old before you can expect much. What a waste of precious learning and bonding time! These sources often advocate the use of choke collars and other punishments, and this age requirement is only given because such harsh punishments may be dangerous for young puppies.

When looking for a trainer, always inquire into the methods used before you sign up. Sadly, abusive training methods do work with some dogs, so some trainers continue to use outdated, punishment-based methods.

Continuing Training throughout Your Lab's Life

Behavior is always changing, either improving or getting worse, depending on what's happening in the dog's life. If you use rewards to improve your dog's behavior, chances are, the behavior will improve. If some behaviors are getting worse, you need to work specifically on those behaviors. Be vigilant and committed. Dogs, like humans, need to learn throughout their entire lives. Keep it fun and keep it up!

As your Lab puppy becomes less demanding, you may be tempted to spend less time with him. Now you can finally catch up on all that living you've been missing! Well, that's partly true. Puppies do demand a lot of time, but after they become fully house-trained and well-behaved, you can just return to your pre-Lab life. But why would you want to? Life with a Lab is a joy, especially when you take full advantage of all the ways your Lab can fit into your life at home, at work, and during your free time (see Chapter 12). All of these times offer opportunities for training, bonding, and just being together.

Training at home and away

A wonderful thing happens when you train your Lab both at home and away from home. Your Lab becomes better behaved and will be welcomed in more places than you may imagine.

Another wonderful thing happens when you train your Lab wherever you are. Your Lab obeys you wherever you are. "My Lab knows his requests. He'll obey them wherever we are!" you may protest. Trust us, dogs that are trained at home only tend to obey only at home. Follow our advice on training wherever you are and you won't be one of those frantic and apologetic dog owners who has to keep insisting, "He really does do it right at home! No, really!"

Don't assume that when you and your Lab are both home, you're spending time together. Bring him into your routine and he'll become a part of it. Pretty soon, you won't know how you ever brushed your teeth, watched television, or worked at your computer without him!

The thirty-minute (plus) Labs-only daily break

Daily mini training sessions aside, reserve one training session for when you aren't doing anything else at the same time. During this special, you-and-your-Lab-only time, you devote all your attention to your beloved companion and the training activities you're working on together.

Young pups may not last for thirty minutes, but after your Lab is approaching his first birthday, you'll probably be able to work for half an hour. Just be sure to watch your Lab for signs of boredom. Training sessions should be fun for both of you. If your Lab tires of training before the end of his thirty minutes, make your training more fun!

The training walk

Because the health benefits of walking have become widely known, many people make a daily walk part of their regular routine. You can include your Lab in this health-bestowing daily activity by turning your walk into a training walk. Training your Lab during a walk is a great way to teach your Lab to obey your requests wherever you are, not just in the house. A daily training walk reinforces this behavior until it becomes second nature.

As you walk, stop occasionally and have your Lab do a few position changes: sit, stand, sit, down, and so on. Then continue the walk. Do this about every 25 yards or so or whatever makes sense in your neighborhood. You can designate certain landmarks as training spots, such as street signs, trees, or corners. The continuation of the walk will serve as a reward, and your dog will learn to follow requests at lots of different locations. What a fun way to teach good behavior.

Training Your Good Citizen

If you and your Lab would like to pursue some obedience work and have already mastered the basic classes, a fun and useful endeavor is to let your Lab try for a Canine Good Citizen award, a sort of feather in your Lab's cap. Any dog can take the Canine Good Citizen (CGC) certification test, but only dogs well-trained in basic obedience will pass. This is one award that even a mixed-breed dog can win, so if you have a Lab mix, go for it! (Note that a CGC certificate can also help convince a reluctant landlord that you and your Lab will make good tenants.)

Unlike obedience competition, the CGC award doesn't involve any competition. Your Lab is on her own, and she either passes or fails, regardless of how any other dogs perform. In obedience competition, however (covered in the following section), you and your Lab compete against other dogs for placement and ribbons.

Many dog organizations, including AKC clubs and other organizations such as 4-H, offer the CGC test, so call your local All-Breed Obedience club, Labrador Retriever Club, or the AKC office to find the nearest opportunity for testing (see the Appendix). The test is a non-competitive, one-time, pass-or-fail set of ten tests designed to recognize those dogs (and owners) that have such excellent control of their behavior that they make excellent citizens. The ten tests are as follows (so start practicing):

- ✔ **Accepting a friendly stranger:** In this test, your Lab must remain quiet and well-behaved when a friendly person your Lab doesn't know approaches you and speaks to you. You will shake hands with the stranger and talk pleasantly. Your Lab must not show any sign of guarding you, of shyness, or of moving towards the stranger. She must stay in position next to you.

- ✔ **Sitting politely for petting:** In this test, your dog sits at your side, and a friendly stranger approaches and pets your Lab on the head and body and walks behind and around you and your Lab. Your Lab must not show shyness or any resentment.

- ✔ **Appearance and grooming:** The purpose of this test is to show that your dog can be safely and easily examined and handled by a stranger, such as a vet, groomer, or friend. The evaluator will comb or brush your Lab and lightly examine her ears and each front foot. Your Lab, of course, must allow it and not act shy or aggressive.

- ✔ **Out for a walk on a loose leash:** In this test, you demonstrate that you're in control of your Lab. Your Lab must walk on either side of you on a loose leash. Together, you must make a left turn, a right turn, and an about turn, stopping once during the middle of the test and again at the end. Your Lab must stay in a good heel and can either sit or stand during the stops.

- ✔ **Walking through a crowd:** In this test, your Lab must show that she can remain under control in a public place. You and your Lab must walk around and by at least three people. Your Lab may show interest in the people, but she shouldn't get excited, shy, or resentful. You may talk to your dog, encouraging her, praising her, and giving her direction during this test, but your Lab must not strain at her leash and should remain next to you and under control.

Testing administration

Individual dog lovers can administer the Canine Good Citizen test to others. If your Lab passes with flying colors and you think you would like to help other dogs become good citizens, too, write to the American Kennel Club for a free information kit or to purchase a Canine Good Citizen test kit: The American Kennel Club, Attn: CGC, 5580 Centerview Drive, Suite 200, Raleigh, NC 27606 (919)233-9767 or e-mail at info@akc.org.

✔ **Sit and down on request, staying in place:** In this test, your Lab demonstrates her knowledge of basic requests. You request a sit and a down. You're allowed to make the request more than once and to use more than one word to make the request (such as, "Come on, Shivers. Would you please sit?"). Then, when instructed, you ask your dog to stay and walk down a 20-foot line away from your Lab. She must stay in place, although she can change position.

✔ **Coming when called:** In this test, your Lab shows that she understands the come request. First, you must walk ten feet away from your dog. You can ask her to stay, or you can simply walk away if the evaluator is petting her or distracting her. Then you turn, face her, and call her to you. She must, of course, come.

✔ **Reaction to another dog:** In this test, your Lab shows how well-behaved she can be around other dogs. You and your Lab must approach another handler and dog from about ten yards away. You and the other handler will stop, shake hands, talk pleasantly, and then continue on for another five yards. Both dogs should show casual interest in each other, but they shouldn't break position or act shy or aggressive.

✔ **Reaction to distractions:** In this test, your Lab proves that she is confident and well-behaved in distracting situations. The evaluator will set up some common distractions, such as a loud noise (like a large book being dropped to the floor) or a person running by in front of the dog. Your Lab must show some natural interest and curiosity and may appear a little startled, but she shouldn't act panicky, fearful, or aggressive. Your Lab must also not try to run away or bark.

✔ **Supervised separation:** In this final test, your Lab shows that she can behave herself when left alone and will continue to demonstrate good manners and training. The evaluator will say something to the effect of, "Would you like me to watch your dog?" and you will agree. Hand the leash to the evaluator and walk out of sight. The dog will be held for three minutes, and although she doesn't have to maintain a position (such as a sit), she should not spend the whole three minutes barking, whining, howling, pacing, or acting very nervous. She can, however, act slightly agitated. After all, you're such a wonderful companion and have trained her so well that she misses you!

If you pass, congratulations! If you don't, you can try again another time. Keep working with your Lab. When she does earn her CGC certification, you can both be very proud.

Obedience Competition Is Fun!

What could be nicer than a happy, well-trained, well-behaved dog? If that describes your pal, and if you're running out of things to do in your training sessions because your Lab has mastered all the basic requests, why not consider a little friendly competition?

Obedience competition can be great fun for you and your Lab and can also get quite competitive, depending on the types of trials you choose. The best way to start is through obedience classes (although be absolutely sure they only employ positive training methods before signing up with your Lab). Obedience classes range from puppy classes and Canine Good Citizen classes to advanced obedience classes that train you to train your dog for the Companion Dog (CD), Companion Dog Excellent (CDX), and Utility Dog (UT) titles.

If you're looking for titles for your Lab, you need to attend trials and tests sanctioned by the American Kennel Club (AKC), in which your Lab can earn points towards obedience titles. If you're just looking for some fun, attend fun matches and matches sanctioned by the AKC and UKC (United Kennel Club, Inc., the second oldest and second largest all-breed dog registry in the United States), that don't count for points towards titles.

The purpose of obedience trials is more than just to prove that your Lab obeys. Obedience is meant to show how useful purebred dogs are as companions to humans. In obedience trials, dogs are expected to show they can behave themselves in all venues, including in the presence of other people and other dogs. Advanced obedience work includes tracking, which demonstrates your Lab's natural ability to follow a scent. Tracking is a rigorous sport requiring lots of energy on the part of both your Lab and you, so if you'd like to try it, be sure you're both in good shape!

Obedience is a sport, and both you and your dog must exhibit good sportsmanship while participating. Obedience can get mighty competitive, so make sure you're as good a citizen as your Lab. Your Lab must also be willing and happy to participate. If you get so competitive that you forget to make sure your Lab is having fun, you've lost the meaning of the game.

The rules

To earn obedience titles, your Lab must qualify by earning over 50 percent of the points in each exercise and attaining a final score of at least 170 out of 200 possible points. Your Lab must then earn qualifying scores under three different judges at licensed or member obedience trials meeting all requirements. (If your Lab performs perfectly and wins every prize but the trial isn't official, the points won't count.)

Your Lab's appearance doesn't have any bearing on points in obedience work. Obedience trials are far more lenient about who can participate than are regular dog shows in which dogs are judged for *conformation* (physical appearance). Spayed and castrated dogs and dogs that are surgically altered to correct a congenital defect may all participate.

Not every dog may qualify for an AKC-sanctioned obedience trial, however, including

- Puppies under 6 months of age
- Female dogs in heat
- Lame, hearing-impaired, or sight-impaired dogs
- Dogs who are bandaged or have any medical device attached to them
- Dogs who are powdered or dyed (people do strange things in the name of beauty)
- Any dog that attacks another dog
- Dogs from breed that aren't recognized by the AKC
- Mixed-breed, non-pedigreed, or unregistered dogs (although these dogs can earn obedience titles in trials put on by organizations other than the AKC)

The full scope of obedience rules is complicated and beyond the scope of this book, but the best way to learn is to start attending obedience trials. Read the literature, hobnob with dog people, and ask questions. Look for books devoted solely to obedience and start practicing. If you and your Lab are having fun, keep it up. You may end up with an obedience trial champion!

Titles

In obedience, your Lab may earn certain titles, each of which requires the performance of certain exercises. Titles are earned in different classes, including Novice, Utility, and Open. Exercises for titles become progressively more difficult, of course.

After your Lab has earned a title, you can list her title after her name, like a degree. For example, Holland Cliffs Sweet Cocoa CD, Golden Boy Maxwell CDX or Walton's Kiri Dearie UD. Talk about prestige!

Companion Dog (CD)

A CD is the first, most basic obedience title in the Novice class. For this title, your Lab must perform the following exercises:

- **Heel on leash and a figure eight:** Your dog must know the following requests: forward, halt, right turn, left turn, about turn (always to the right), slow, normal, and fast. Fast means you and your Lab run! Halt and turn requests are only given when moving at a speed of normal. Orders are to be given in sequence and repeated when necessary.

  You can hold the leash in either hand or in both hands, but you mustn't tighten or jerk the leash or give the dog any other kind of assistance beyond the verbal request. When you enter the ring, the judge will ask if you are ready.

- **Stand for examination:** In this exercise, the judge examines your Lab.

- **Heel free:** In this exercise, your Lab must heel and do a figure eight but without the leash.

- **Recall:** For a recall exercise, your Lab stays while you walk away from her and then comes when you call.

- **Long sit:** For a CD, the long sit must be held for one minute while the handler stands across the ring.

- **Long down:** For a CD, the long down must be held for three minutes while the owner stands across the ring.

Companion Dog Excellent (CDX)

The CDX is the next level of title, after the CD part of the Novice class, for dogs who have already earned their CD. Your Lab's next challenges are as follows:

- **Heel free and figure eight:** This exercise is identical to the first exercise for the CD (see the previous section), except that your Lab won't be on a leash.

- **Drop on recall:** For this exercise, after walking away from your Lab, she must come running when you call her. Then, on request, she must drop into a full down.

- **Retrieve on flat:** For this exercise, you throw a small dumbbell at least 20 feet, and your dog must, upon request, run straight to the dumbbell, pick it up, and bring it straight back to you.

- ✔ **Retrieve over high jump:** For this exercise, your Lab must jump over an obstacle to retrieve the dumbbell. For the high jump, the minimum jump height for a Labrador Retriever is set at the nearest multiple of 2 inches to the height of your Lab at the *withers* (the highest points of the shoulder blades — see Chapter 5), with no dog jumping less than 8 inches or more than 36 inches.

- ✔ **Broad jump:** For this exercise, your dog must jump over four hurdles on request. The height and length of the hurdles depend on the size and breed of dog.

- ✔ **Long sit:** For the CDX, your Lab must hold a long sit for three minutes while the handler is out of sight.

- ✔ **Long down:** For the CDX, your Lab must hold a long down for five minutes while the handler is out of sight.

Utility Dog (UD)

The next level is to earn the title of Utility Dog, and it's available for dogs who have already earned their CDX. This title is in the Utility class. To earn the UD, a dog must earn the sufficient points in the following exercises:

- ✔ **Signal exercise:** For this exercise, you and your dog must work as a team to demonstrate your dog's knowledge about how to respond to the signals stand, stay, drop, sit, and come given by hand (without benefit of speech). The orders given by the judge to dog and handler are the same as for the heel on leash and figure eight exercise (see the "Companion Dog (CD)" section). Your Lab must heel during this exercise without a leash, and throughout the exercise, you may only use hand signals to make your requests.

- ✔ **Scent discrimination:** This exercise demonstrates that your Lab can distinguish something of yours from a group of other objects and can then deliver that object back to you. The judge will ask if you're ready and then takes an article from you. Your dog must then find your object by scent alone. You will have handled it so your scent will be on it — a scent far too subtle for you to distinguish but obvious to your dog.

- ✔ **Directed retrieve:** For this exercise, you must provide three white cotton work gloves that the judge has approved. Your dog stays until you direct her to retrieve a designated glove. After she's directed, she quickly moves to the object and then retrieves it. The orders are "One," "Two," or "Three," "Take it," and "Finish." Each number refers to one of the gloves.

- ✔ **Moving stand and examination:** For this one, your dog must heel, stand while the judge examines her, and stay on request while you move around.

✔ **Directed jumping:** This exercise requires that your dog move away from you in the direction you indicate, stop, and then jump as directed over both a bar jump and a high jump, one at a time. The judge decides which jump goes first. Your Lab must not anticipate your request, but waiting, instead, for you to give the request before making a move.

Advanced titles

After your dog has achieved CD, CDX, and UD titles, she can go on to bigger and better titles. The Utility Dog Excellent (UDX) title is for dogs who have already earned their UD titles. This title is in the Utility class. To earn this title, dogs must qualify in ten separate events in both Utility and Open classes and have earned these qualifying scores at ten licensed or member obedience trials.

To qualify for an Obedience Trial Champion (OTCh.) title, a dog must have earned her UD. This title is in the Open class. Your Lab must win 100 points and one first place in Utility and Open classes, plus a third first place win in either class, totaling three first place wins. These wins must also be under three different judges.

Tracking

Tracking exercises test your Lab's ability to track a scent. They are strenuous, athletic events for both dog and handler. The AKC offers three different tracking tests, and your Lab only has to pass one time to earn a tracking title.

✔ The Tracking Dog (TD) is the entry-level test.

✔ The Tracking Dog Excellent (TDX) test is for dogs who have earned their TD and is more difficult.

✔ The Variable Surface Tracking Test (VST) is the most difficult of the tracking tests.

✔ If your dog has earned her TD, TDX and VST, she automatically earns her Champion Tracker (CT) title.

Obedience competition serves many purposes, not the least of which is providing you and your Lab with a great opportunity to meet other dog enthusiasts and spend time together playing. If your Lab takes to obedience and seems to enjoy the sport, and if you can afford the time and the cost (you have to pay to attend trials), you'll have a fun, exciting mutual pursuit. Fun like that can only strengthen the relationship between you and your Lab.

Labrador Retriever puppies come in all shapes, several personalities, and three colors.

A yellow Lab puppy is, quite possibly, the cutest dog in the world.

Choose a puppy who is neither aggressive nor passive. Be sure her personality fits yours and your family's.

Lab puppies aren't ready to go home with you until they're about eight weeks of age.

Labs make good indoor dogs but will require plenty of outdoor exercise as they get older.

Lab puppies grow quickly during their first few weeks in your home.

Introduce your Lab puppy to a small pond as soon as she seems interested in water.

While your growing Lab needs plenty of rest, chances are, she'll be able to wear you out when playing outdoors.

Be sure your Lab puppy has access to plenty of water.

A "teenage" Lab is always ready for action.

Throw floatable toys into water, and your Lab's retrieval instincts will kick into high gear.

© Gail Painter.

Combine a game of fetch with water and you've mixed two of a Lab's favorite activities.

© Close Encounters of the Furry Kind

© Close Encounters of the Furry Kind

A Lab's coat dries quickly even after a thorough drenching.

A well-trained Lab can sit at attention next to her master while he hunts.

At her master's command, a trained Lab delicately retrieves a downed bird.

Running in a field is the stuff of dreams for a grown Lab.

Add water to the mix, and you'll have a devoted Lab in your family.

Now add a toy for your Lab to fetch, and you'll be a hero!

Nothing's out of reach for an athletic Lab.

Part IV
Your Lab: A Member of the Family!

The 5th Wave   By Rich Tennant

"That's ENOUGH, Misty! I'm not going to keep throwing that thing for you!"

In this part . . .

If you're like us, your Lab is a full-fledged member of your family. But how often can you include him in your activities? More often than you think! In this part, we give you lots of suggestions for involving your Lab in your daily routine at home, at play, while exercising, and sometimes even at work.

We also give you lots of hints and tips for traveling with your dog, whether around town running errands or including your Lab in your family vacation. People are doing it more and more often!

Chapter 12

Involving Your Lab in Your Life

*H*umans thrive on routine and so do dogs. If you can incorporate your Lab into your daily routine, he'll know just what to expect and how to behave. You'll also find that you have more opportunities to spend time with your Lab than you thought you did. What a happy surprise! This chapter shares ten — well, make that nine — ways to spend more time with your Lab.

The *long down* is one of the most useful skills you can help your Lab develop (see Chapter 11 for instructions on how to teach your Lab the long down). You'll find the skill invaluable as you go about your daily routine, especially if your Lab likes to follow you around the house. When dealing with a younger Lab, make sure you do a few sit, stand, sit, and down position changes before the long down so you burn up some of that Lab energy. That way, he'll welcome getting to lie at your feet.

While Surfing the Net

These days, most people spend at least a little time on the computer each day. If you're like us, you may spend quite a bit of time sitting there hammering those keys. But you don't have to work alone! Computer time is a great time to train your Lab to do a long down. When practicing the long down, you should be stretching the time between request and reward. When you become engrossin your work, you'll find this easy to do.

If your Lab pup wants to find something more rewarding to do than the long down when you're seated at your desk (and you know he can't yet be trusted to wander around the house on his own), put a 6-foot lead on his buckle collar. Secure the end of the lead under your foot or a sturdy piece of furniture and let him explore the immediate area.

When Making Phone Calls

If you tend to get involved in long phone calls, a long down with your Lab is a great way to get the most mileage out of that time. Remember, you don't have to praise your Lab verbally every time you give him a food reward or stroke his ears.

On Take Your Lab to Work Day

If you run your own business or work for yourself, you can take your Lab to work with you! If you don't run your own business, however, you may still be able to convince your boss that your Lab can be a well-behaved member of the team. After your boss meets your well-trained Lab, you may be surprised by his or her response.

Certainly, some workplaces aren't dog-friendly, but many are. Follow our recommendations for training while at the computer and on the phone and your Lab will be the practically perfect office companion. In work situations where you or others move around a lot, consider bringing along your Lab's doggy den to keep him out of trouble (especially if he is still a pup). After he has mastered the long down (see Chapter 11), he may not have to use the doggy den, except when you're away for a long time. Many office environments are potentially Lab-friendly — here are a few we have seen that work well:

- Many types of retail stores.
- Any pet-related profession, from veterinarian to dog groomer. Make sure your Lab is socialized well to other dogs.
- Informal offices (and even some formal ones).
- Landscaping, building, and other outdoors work. (Be sure to keep your Lab under close supervision so that he doesn't run loose and get into trouble at construction sites.)
- Drivers of all kinds — Labs love to ride along. (See Chapter 13 for safety tips.)
- Sales — if your clients are dog lovers, they'll take to you right away; if not, you can leave your Lab in the car (never on warm days!) or in his doggy den.

If you think your Lab would do well at work but you aren't sure how he'll respond at first, take him there for one or two weekend practice sessions before you try him out on a workday. Show him around while he is on his lead and then do some training so he gets used to obeying you in your work environment.

If you do bring your dog to work, you may also find that the time spent driving to and from work is more fun with your Lab along for the ride. Just be sure to follow the Chapter 13 safety tips for riding in a car with your Lab.

If your work environment is unsuitable or unsafe for dogs, or if your boss just doesn't go for the idea of you bringing your Lab to work with you, don't feel guilty. Dogs usually sleep when they don't have anything to do and are generally happy to keep an eye on the house for you.

However, your dog will certainly love to see you over the lunch hour. When your Lab is a young pup, you have to go home for lunch or have someone stop in to let your Lab out for a potty break. But even after your Lab can hold it all day, it's nice to come home so you can to spend a little time together. What a lovely break in the middle of a grueling workday.

While Eating

Labs are very motivated by food, so aren't you just asking for trouble if you ask your Lab to hold a long down while you sit there eating all that delectable people food? If you never give your Lab treats from the table, he won't expect them. You can reward him with pieces of his own food, but as long as you refrain from tossing him a T-bone because he's being "So good!," you won't have a problem on your hands (or under your feet).

On the other hand, if you want to enjoy your dinner Lab-free and you spend a lot of time with your Lab throughout the rest of the day, don't feel guilty about confining him to his doggy den or, if he can be trusted, letting him amuse himself in another room while you have your meals. You have every right to devote some time to the other humans in your life!

When You're in the Bathroom

Yes, we said in the bathroom. After all, you're just sitting there with nothing else to do, right? What a great time for your Lab to practice position changes, or if you want to read, a long down. Talk about using your time efficiently!

As You're Grooming

We mean you! When you're grooming yourself each morning (brushing your teeth, washing your face, combing your hair, and taking a shower), bring your Lab into the bathroom and let him wait for you by your side. This is also a good time to groom your Lab. Don't forget to brush his teeth! (But remember, use doggy toothpaste, not your toothpaste, for him.)

While Watching Television

When you're watching television and your Lab is with you, do a few requests at every commercial break. You don't want to waste your time watching those commercials anyway, and they're on so frequently that you'll get lots of opportunities for training breaks.

As You Run Errands

As you drive around, running errands, consider taking your Lab in the car with you. Commuting with the dog gets your Lab out of the house, gives him a change of scenery, provides companionship for you on the trip, and as a further benefit, discourages carjackers, who are more likely to pass up a car with a dog in it.

When Shopping

No, your dog can't go with you to the grocery store (there are health regulations), but many stores will be glad to let you and your Lab come in and browse. Just ask — you may be surprised how many retailers will welcome your Lab. Pet supply stores almost always welcome dogs.

The nice thing about bringing your Lab shopping is that people who want to sell you something have an extra motivation to be nice to you and your dog.

Chapter 13

Traveling with Your Lab

· ·

In This Chapter

▶ Keeping your Lab safe in your car, minivan, or motorhome

▶ Vacationing with your Lab

▶ Making arrangements when she can't join you

· ·

*W*hat could be more fun than driving all alone in a car? Having your Lab along when you drive around town or go on a family vacation can make the ride much more enjoyable and can even make your trip safer (evil-doers don't want to tangle with people who have big dogs in their cars). Plus, you can rest easy knowing your dog is with you rather than home alone. Everyone will be happier.

In this chapter, we give you some ideas about how to travel safely with your Lab and how to make the most of your car trips, whether they're around town or on the road. We also help you to find more ways to spend time with your Lab by taking her with you, even to places you may not have considered.

Taking Your Lab around Town

Take a few minutes to make a list of the trips you take on a regular basis in your local area. Where do you typically drive? The grocery store? The bank? The post office? To pick up your kids from school or from their extracurricular activities? Put a star by the trips you think would be made more fun with your Lab along. (Don't worry about the details, all the "But how will I's?" that may be popping into your head.) What? You have a star by every item on your list? So do we!

Your Lab may be able to accompany you to more places than you think. Joel trains families to train their puppies and dogs all around the Washington, D.C., metro area and the suburbs. He does lots of driving and spends an hour or two at each of his client's homes on a weekly basis. For over a decade, he has brought at least one Lab with him, and now he usually has two Labs and a Rottweiler (that's another book). He does this year-round, and it works great with lots of planning. If you become a client of Joel's in the summertime, he'll be asking you, "Where can I park my vehicle in the shade?" You, too, can take your Lab just about anywhere if you plan ahead.

Always be alert to the dangers of heatstroke. When the temperature is just 85 degrees, the temperature in a parked car, even with the windows partially open, can easily reach 102 degrees in ten minutes and 120 degrees in 30 minutes. A dog can withstand a body temperature of 107 to 108 degrees for only a short time before irreparable brain damage or death occurs.

In the winter, you probably don't have to worry about heatstroke unless you live in a warm climate; plenty of dogs in Florida, for example, can get heatstroke on a warm day in January. Although Labs are more cold-tolerant than heat-tolerant, you don't want to freeze your buddy on a particularly frigid winter day.

Choosing the Right Vehicle

Who would buy a vehicle just for their dog? Plenty of people! Although you can buzz your Lab around town in that little sports car, you won't want to leave her in there for very long.

Baby, you can drive my car (because it's too small for my Lab)

Most cars have a relatively small airspace, and when your Lab is with you and will have to wait in the car, even for a short time, you have to think about ventilation and temperature. If you leave the windows open enough to ventilate a car and keep it cool, they'll probably be open enough for your Lab to escape after that squirrel in the parking lot. If you keep your Lab in her doggy den, you can crank the windows wide open, but then someone could steal your car and/or your Lab. You certainly don't want that to happen!

Station wagons offer more air space than cars, but they aren't particularly well-ventilated. Your Lab may have more room to move, but she can still get heatstroke easily in the back of a station wagon when the only air is coming through those little vents in the back windows. Even better than a station wagon or any kind of car is a minivan, van, or motorhome (see the two following sections).

Never allow your Lab to ride in the back of a pick-up. Even a small accident or sudden stop could kill your friend. Also, don't let your Lab hang her head out the window as you drive. Flying debris may injure your dog, and she could also distract other drivers and cause an accident. You can't be too safe on the road.

Cocoa chooses a Caravan

Many years ago when Joel's Lab, Cocoa, started to have trouble jumping into his utility vehicle, Joel and Cocoa went vehicle shopping together. Guess what? Not one single car dealer said, "Get that dog out of here!" (That could have meant a missed sale!) When Cocoa stepped into the back of a Dodge Caravan, laid down on the seat, and looked at Joel as if to say, "Okay, buy this one," Joel did. Cocoa spent many happy years riding around in Cocoa's Caravan, and somewhere out there is a salesperson who probably remembers with great fondness that incredibly easy sale!

Vans and minivans

If you go to a dog show (a fun family activity, by the way), you'll see that the parking lot looks like a minivan dealership (you'll also see some full-sized vans and more than a few motorhomes). Minivans are great for every kind of dog because they offer lots of airspace; multiple windows that can be opened for ventilation; and plenty of room to haul the kids, the dog, and all the stuff that both need on any kind of trip.

Regular vans and sport utility vehicles offer lots of room and airspace for your Lab, too, but check to see how easy it is for your Lab to get in and out. If your Lab is aging and/or suffering from arthritis, hip dysplasia, or any other painful condition, a low-to-the-ground minivan may be just the ticket — it's easy to enter, easy to exit, and very comfy.

Motorhomes

Motorhomes aren't cheap, and you may find the price to be more than you can justify for your life right now, no matter how much you love your Lab. But boy, do Labs love motorhomes! Motorhomes are the ideal vehicle for transporting your Lab. You may have trouble explaining why you drive a motorhome around town, but you and your Lab will be happy!

Of course, motorhomes make more sense for longer trips. If you're at a stage in your life where you would like to travel comfortably around the country with your Lab, a motorhome may be the ideal purchase. You'll have fun traveling from town to town, seeing the sights, meeting new people, and relaxing in your home-on-wheels.

Joel goes to lots of seminars, so when it came time for him to get a new, safe vehicle for his dogs when traveling both locally and far from home, he

Looking for grass

Even veteran travelers can face new challenges. Back in 1993, Joel and his Lab, Cocoa, drove from Maryland to California for a meeting of the Association of Pet Dog Trainers conducted by Dr. Ian Dunbar. Cocoa was an old pro at traveling, having accompanied Joel to many seminars. When Joel made the first potty stop in the desert, however, Cocoa looked around, puzzled, and then looked at Joel as if to say,

"Well, where's the grass?" Joel laughed and said, "You're in trouble if you hold out for grass!" Cocoa decided to hold out for grass and convinced Joel, with her Labrador Retriever wiles, to stop at casinos along the way instead, where they had plenty of nice, lush grass. When Cocoa pottied, she gave Joel the look that meant, "Good job! Now clean it up, and let's get going."

decided he'd better do some research. On the Internet, he found what looked like the perfect vehicle: the Volkswagen EuroVan Camper by Winnebago. At first, it looked like this motorhome was only available in Europe, but after calling around, Joel found one in the Virginia suburbs of Washington, D.C., and bought it. The Volkswagen EuroVan Camper by Winnebago has lots of ventilation, including a vent in the roof and a couple of screened windows. For hot days, the top pops up and becomes a screened tent! The biggest drawback is the price. It isn't an inexpensive ride.

Your vehicular pick

Much of your decision will depend on your individual needs and the way you travel. But do consider your Lab when choosing your next vehicle. Here are some factors to consider when choosing a Lab-friendly vehicle:

- ✔ Does your Lab's doggy den fit inside?
- ✔ How well can it be ventilated?
- ✔ Does it stay cool in the shade (light-colored cars stay cooler)?
- ✔ Can your Lab easily get in and out?
- ✔ If everyone in your family is in the vehicle, is there still room for your Lab?
- ✔ Can your Lab be safely secured in the vehicle?
- ✔ Does it have room to pack all your Lab-related accessories, such as your canine first-aid kit, water, dog bowl, and items for retrieving?

If you have children, you may have noticed that sports cars don't look quite as appealing as they once did, and if you bought one back in your pre-parent days, you may now find it pretty inconvenient. Now that you're a dog owner, give your dog the same consideration, and your life will be easier when you take your Lab along. Spend some time looking around, trying out options, and choosing a vehicle that will allow you and your Lab to spend time together on the road.

Practicing Vehicle Safety

Every time you drive in your car, you risk the possibility of having an accident. You put your seatbelt and shoulderbelt on to prevent injury (at least, we hope you do!). But what will prevent your Lab from getting injured if you're involved in a car accident?

As a dog owner, it's your responsibility to see that your Lab remains as safe as possible. Also, consider that your Lab could seriously injure you and the rest of your family in an accident if she becomes an unguided missile inside your car. Take all precautions and secure your Lab inside your car whenever she travels with you.

If you can't safely confine your Lab in your car, either because you don't have a doggy seatbelt or because her doggy den won't fit, leave her home. Don't take chances with your Lab's safety or your own.

You have two options when deciding how to confine your Lab inside your car. If your Lab has reached the point in her training where she chews only her chew toys, your best option is the doggy seatbelt. Available in pet stores and pet supply catalogs, these harnesses have a loop on the back through which you thread the seatbelt/shoulderbelt of your car. Your Lab can sit, lie down or stand up on the back seat and still be safe in a fender-bender.

If your Lab still chews, follow the training advice in Chapter 11 to teach your Lab what to chew and what not to chew. Seatbelts, of course, are in that not-to-chew category. Meanwhile, your pup should be secured in her doggy den while riding in your vehicle. Make sure the crate is secured to the vehicle with the seatbelt or by some other means so that it doesn't become a missile in your car in the case of an accident. The doggy den should be just the right size for your pup: big enough for her to stand up, turn around, and lie down in, but not so big that she gets thrown around every time you turn a corner.

The crate is the only acceptable option for a Lab who still chews. Don't give your Lab the opportunity to get in trouble by chewing up your car. That's proper management! Allow your Lab to ride along outside the crate in a doggy seatbelt only when you're absolutely sure that she can behave and not destroy your car.

Taking Family Vacations with Your Lab

When you brought home your Lab, you did so with the intention of making her a part of your family. You include her in your daily routine, so why not bring her along on the family vacation? She is family, right? Although we understand that not every vacation is suitable for dogs, we hope that you'll try to make your family vacations Lab-friendly whenever possible so you can bring your dog along. She wants to be with you, and the whole family will have a great time if your Lab is well-trained and well-behaved (as yours certainly is or soon will be — see Part III).

Labs add a special quality to a family vacation. Many people who wouldn't normally talk to a stranger on the road will warm up and strike up a conversation with you when they see your Lab. You'll get the chance to meet fellow Lab lovers and dog lovers wherever you go, and you just may forge some lasting friendships.

If you're a single person with a Lab, the enjoyment of traveling can be enhanced by having a buddy with whom to share your vacation. People won't think twice if you discuss things with your Lab — at least not other dog lovers! ("Just look at that spectacular view, Skippy!") Your Lab can also keep you safe from people with less than good intentions, too. Nonetheless, use common sense and caution when traveling alone with your Lab.

Keeping your dog's routine as normal as possible while on vacation will help her to feel secure and happy. Groom, train, feed, and put her to bed at the same times as you normally do. In between, have lots of vacation fun that includes your Lab: hiking, camping, swimming, and retrieving.

If you know you won't have any time for your dog on your vacation or if the place you're going just isn't right for a dog, leave her home. Don't feel guilty. Just make sure she is well taken care of while you are away, and do something special for her when you get back. Next time, you can plan a more dog-friendly vacation.

Success is in the planning

Labs are creatures of routine, and your Lab will have the same needs and will prefer the same schedule on the road as she has at home. Of course, your vacation schedule can't exactly mirror your schedule at home; otherwise, why take a vacation? But you can still plan to feed your dog and take her outside for potty breaks at the same times each day. If your dog normally sleeps in her doggy den, bring it along so that she can feel secure at night. If she normally sleeps with you, don't suddenly banish her.

You'll need to be prepared for emergencies. What if your dog gets sick? Be prepared to find a veterinarian in a strange area. Don't forget to take along your canine first-aid kit.

Part of the fun of a vacation is the planning. With a Lab, you may have a little more planning, but that just adds a little more fun! Enjoy the process.

Water differs all over the country, and your dog's digestion may be sensitive to changes in the water (yours may be, too). Bring along a couple of gallons of the kind of water you give your dog at home and keep them in the trunk or the back of your van. To prevent a sudden bout of intestinal distress, give your dog "home water" only.

Vacation checklist

Whenever you travel with your dog, you absolutely must be prepared by taking the following precautions. The extra preparation time will be well worth it if emergency or misfortune should strike. Before you lock that front door and set out for destinations known or unknown, don't forget the following:

- A buckle collar complete with readable identification tags and a license and a tag showing your dog has a current rabies vaccine. Make sure your dog is wearing this at all times.

- An extra set of car keys. If you have to leave your dog in the car in very hot or very cold weather, you can leave the car running with the air conditioning or the heat on and still keep the car locked. Still, don't leave your dog unless you absolutely have to — the car could stall, which would mean that the air conditioning wouldn't work, and your Lab could die in just a few minutes.

- At least two gallons of water from home. Give only this water to your dog.

- A water bowl. The kinds that have a weighted bottom or that are heavy enough not to spill are good for in-the-car (or minivan or motorhome) thirst quenching. Or teach her how to drink out of a sports bottle or squirt gun.

- The doggy den and, if your dog is able to keep from chewing up your car, a seatbelt harness.

- Enough dog food for the trip, plus some extra in case of spills or other mishaps.

- A canine first-aid kit.

- A chew toy or two.

- Something to retrieve. Hey, it's your dog's vacation, too — she should be able to have some good fun!

- An extra collar and an extra leash, just in case.

- A retractable leash (also called a Flexi-lead) for safe romping.

- Any medicine and/or vitamins that your dog requires. Don't forget to keep your dog on her schedule of flea/tick control and heartworm pills (those little critters don't take vacations).

- Grooming supplies. Keep your grooming routine the same, even when on vacation. Bring along the brush, nail clippers, flea comb, toothbrush, and so on.

- Old towels, blankets, and other clean-up items in case your Lab romps right into a muddy river, for example, and then is ready to bounce right back into your nice, new, clean minivan.

- Plastic bags and paper towels (or poop scoop) to clean up after your dog.

- This book! We'd love to join you on your vacation and are glad to serve as a friendly reminder of how to manage your dog in any situation.

- A health certificate, if you're crossing state lines.

Finding dog-friendly lodging

Some people like to plan every aspect of their vacations before they ever step foot out the front door. If this is you, you'll be in a good position to arrange for dog-friendly, on-the-road lodging. If you like to see how far you can get each day and don't like to plan the journey too strictly (if you have small children, for example, you probably know that you can't plan too rigidly), you may find it a challenge to find dog-friendly lodging at the last minute.

It can be very frustrating looking for a motel — any motel — that takes dogs when it is late at night and you're tired and irritable. You can beg, you can plead, you can explain about the doggy den, you can even perform a training demonstration to the hotel management, but some of them won't budge (the old scrooges!).

We have to commend Holiday Inns for almost always taking dogs. While other hotels and motels take dogs, some of them only accept small dogs, and some insist that your dog remain in her doggy den. Be prepared to do a little driving around, and remember to start looking for lodging before it gets too late. Rather than trying to go just two more hours, get up two hours earlier in the morning. You'll all be glad.

When you find a great place that's happy to take well-behaved dogs, make a note of it and file it away in a place you'll be able to find later. If you compile your own list of dog-friendly lodging, you'll find it becomes a great resource both to your own family for future vacations and to your dog-owning friends who happen to mention, "Do you know where we could stay in Atlanta that would take our dog?"

Dog-friendly vacation resources

Over the past few years, more and more books have been written to provide information that makes it easier for you to take your Lab on vacation with you. The Internet is another good source of information for dog-friendly vacations, and several publications exist that keep you apprised of the latest information for successful family vacations with your dog.

If you're going to spend some time in a particular location, contact the local chamber of commerce and ask for any information they have about dog-friendly resources in their area: lodging, parks, and other tourist attractions that allow dogs, for example, as well as a list of local vets. They should be able to provide you with the information you need.

Air travel

Traveling by air? Leave your dog at home unless you can't avoid taking her along. Dogs who are too big to fit in a crate under the passenger seat (that means your Lab) have to ride in the cargo area of the plane. There's no heat and no air conditioning in cargo, and some dogs die during air travel, usually due to overheating when flights are delayed.

If you absolutely must bring your dog, take the following precautions:

- Make a reservation (there will be a fee) and confirm it. Heck, confirm it twice.
- Take direct flights only. Transfers greatly increase the chances of something going wrong.
- Don't put your Lab into her airline-approved crate until absolutely necessary, and be sure to take her for a potty break just before you put her in.
- Make sure your Lab's bedding, food bowl, and water bowls are secured. Freeze one water bowl so that the water doesn't spill and she'll have access to it during the flight.
- Stay with your Lab until the last minute, and then take her to the gate yourself and have her checked through there.

> ✔ Put a big sign on the crate that says "Hi, I'm Buddy" (or whatever your Lab's name is). Not only will airline personnel be more likely to stop and say hello to the dog, but it's a nice (if not very subtle) reminder that the "baggage" in this particular crate is alive and very important.
>
> ✔ Go immediately to the baggage area yourself after the flight to pick her up. Don't be afraid of annoying the airline staff just a little if they won't let you get your dog. Get her as soon as possible!

Chances are, your Lab will be fine, and when you have to fly with your Lab, well, you have to fly. But in general, we recommend that any vacation on which your Lab accompanies you be a driving vacation. If you have to fly, leave your Lab at home and hire someone to stay in your house or drop in a few times a day.

Making Arrangements When Your Lab Absolutely Can't Join You

Yes, we understand. Sometimes your Lab absolutely can't come. Maybe it's a business trip, a ski trip, or a vacation that will be primarily indoors in a place that doesn't allow dogs. Maybe you have to take a long plane trip and don't want to risk stowing your beloved Lab in the cargo hold. Maybe you're going overseas. Whatever the reason, if your Lab can't join you, that's okay. She'll probably miss you and wonder where you went, but you can make her stay at home as comfortable and normal as possible. And boy, will she be glad to see you when you get home! Nothing beats coming home from a vacation to a buddy who is overjoyed to see you. (Watch out for that tail because it'll be wagging like there's no tomorrow!)

If you do leave your Lab, you're responsible for making sure she has proper care in your absence. You can take care of her needs in several ways: by hiring a pet sitter, by boarding her in a kennel, or by leaving her with a friend.

If you will only be gone for a day, a willing neighbor could be a good person to stop in and spend some time with your Lab. For longer periods of time, however, don't expect anyone to care for your Lab who isn't willing to make a significant commitment of time and energy. Don't expect anyone to do it for free, either.

Pet sitters

Hiring a pet sitter is a great solution for when you must leave your Lab at home. She can stay in her familiar environment, and although you'll be gone, everything else will be the same. Pet sitting is a booming business these days, so you probably won't have any problem finding a pet sitter. Although you can always hire a trusted friend or neighbor, a professional pet sitter has a reputation to maintain and a business to run, so he or she can probably be trusted to do a great job. Just in case, however, interview potential pet sitters before you hire them and ask the following questions (based on *Pet Sitter International's Recommended Quality Standards for Excellence in Pet Sitting*):

- **How much experience do you have?** Many pet sitters are also or were previously animal professionals, such as veterinary technicians or trainers. Also ask how long the pet sitter has been pet sitting. Knowledge and skill come with experience.

- **Can you provide references?** Don't just accept the references — check them. You'll be glad you did. Personal referrals from friends who have already used a pet sitter and had a good experience are the best way to find a good pet sitter.

- **Are you bonded and insured?** Pet sitters should be bonded to protect you against theft and insured for liability protection. Insurance is one of the benefits of membership in a professional pet-sitting organization such as Pet Sitters International or the National Association of Professional Pet Sitters. Although membership in a professional organization and being bonded and insured doesn't guarantee quality of service, it does show that your pet sitter is serious about his or her profession.

- **Do you provide written literature describing your services and fees? What about a service contract?** Having everything in writing protects both you and the pet sitter from misunderstandings about fees and duties. Make sure your contract describes everything you expect from the pet sitter.

- **What do you need to know about my Lab?** You probably already know the answer to this question. The pet sitter must have contact information if he or she needs to reach you and phone numbers for your vet, an emergency pet care facility, and a poison control center. The pet sitter also needs to know any medical condition your dog has; how to access the canine first-aid kit (see Chapter 6); your dog's name, age, and routine; what she eats and when; where your dog sleeps; a description of her favorite toys and activities; the location of her leash; and any other personal things about her that would improve her care. Ask this question to reassure yourself that your pet sitter is ready to find the answers to these questions; your pet sitter may even come up with things you wouldn't have considered.

✔ **Do you have a veterinarian on call for emergencies?** Of course you will want to provide your pet sitter with contact information for your own veterinarian, but in the event that your veterinarian can't be reached in an emergency, a good pet sitter should have a reliable backup plan.

✔ **Do you keep regular office hours? Are you easy to find?** Because many pet sitters work at their business full-time, they are often out and about, walking dogs and petting cats. Most pet sitters carry a pager or have an answering machine and return your calls promptly, at least by the end of the day. How easy was it to get a hold of your pet sitter to schedule this interview? You may want to try calling him or her after the interview to confirm the day you'll be leaving. This gives you one more chance to be reassured that your pet sitter is responsible enough to call you back in a timely manner.

✔ **What crime-deterrent precautions do you take?** Part of the benefit of having someone watch your pet is having someone watch your home. Pet sitters are trained to make your house looked lived-in so that would-be thieves won't pick your house as the one that is obviously empty. Careless actions (leaving doors unlocked or windows open) or disclosures (chatting with the neighbors about your fantastic vacation in the Bahamas) by an irresponsible pet sitter could signal that your house is vulnerable. Most pet sitters take in mail and newspapers and turn lights on at dusk and off in the morning.

✔ **Are you aware of federal, state, and local laws pertaining to animal care?** Laws differ depending on where you live. For his or her own protection and yours, your pet sitter should know the relevant laws. (It wouldn't hurt for you to brush up on them, too. Call your local city or county government to find out who legislates the relevant laws in your area or get information on specific state and local laws on the Internet at www.piperinfo.com/state/index.cfm.)

✔ **What's your policy if you get sick or the weather prohibits you from getting to my house?** A good pet sitter has a contingency plan in the event that he or she can't make it to your house for any reason. Many sitters have other good pet sitter contacts they can depend on to step in. If you have neighbors or friends you trust, give the sitter those phone numbers. A friendly neighbor will probably be glad to trudge across the yard in a blizzard to feed your Lab if the pet sitter is snowbound.

Some pet sitters will live in your house while you're away, so getting to your home won't be a problem.

✔ **Will you call to confirm I've arrived home?** You may have every intention of getting home on time, but sometimes the unavoidable occurs. You may end up stranded in an airport where a pet sitter can't return your call to his or her pager. Your pet sitter should confirm that you're home, and if you aren't, should make sure your pets are taken care of until your return.

✓ **Do you provide a service rating form?** Good pet sitters are always trying to improve their service. A service rating form allows them to recognize areas in which they may do better next time. It also helps them to see what aspects of their service are particularly appreciated. (When filling out a service rating form, don't forget to mention the good things as well as the things you think can be improved.)

This process may seem like a lot of work, but would you do any less in hiring someone to watch your children when you leave town? Don't take chances with your Lab. Make sure she has the best of care so you can truly enjoy your vacation.

Boarding kennels

Another option is to take your Lab to a boarding kennel. You can find quite a range in the quality of boarding kennels, so always check out the kennel and ask for a tour well before your date of departure. If your Lab has to be away from her home, make sure she gets a nice little vacation of her own. Some kennels offer extra play time, activities, and walks for your Lab. Some have play areas and offer luxurious grooming services. Some are even called doggy spas and doggy resorts.

Although your dog certainly doesn't need to be in the lap of luxury while you're away, you'll at least want to be confident that the kennel is clean, well-maintained, and that your Lab will be fed well and exercised at least twice each day. Ask your vet for recommendations about good boarding kennels, talk to the staff of the kennel, and don't skimp. This isn't the time to worry about saving a few bucks, and although more expensive doesn't always mean better, in many cases, you get what you pay for.

A friend indeed

No matter how experienced the pet sitter, some people aren't comfortable leaving their pets with someone they don't know. If you have a friend or neighbor you can trust, consider having him stay in your house while you are away. Or have your Lab stay at your friend's house.

If your friend can't stay at your house and your Lab can't stay with him, he could stop in several times a day to spend time with your Lab. Just be sure your friend is responsible and will take the time to keep your Lab company. If you choose someone your Lab already knows and who has a good relationship with your Lab, that's certainly ideal. Your Lab will probably do very well while you're away. Make sure you pay your friend for the service. Your Lab and your friend are both worth it!

Don't have your pet sitter or boarding kennel staff train your Lab while you're away unless you do a thorough job of making sure the person training your dog understands and uses positive training methods. Your Lab doesn't need choke collars, reprimands, or rough handling. You can pick up training when you return. Your Lab won't forget what she has learned.

Preparing your pet

You can prepare your pet for her time away from you by making sure she will be well cared for, comfortably confined, and able to stick as closely as possible to her regular routine. Do lots of positive training and give her an adequate amount of exercise just before you leave, and then let her spend some time in her doggy den resting before you go out the door. This is a good time to get suitcases into the car, which is something that makes many dogs nervous — they know something's up.

If you feel guilty about leaving such that you shower your Lab with excessive attention, it will be an even bigger shock to her when you leave. If you want to spend lots of time with her, do it when you get back. Before you leave, keep things as normal as possible. Don't make a big deal about leaving, or she'll think there must be something to worry about. Act normally, don't disrupt your dog's routine on the day you leave, and tell her good-bye matter-of-factly, as if you're going off to work. Then leave without incident. If you trust the person who will care for your dog and know that you have taken all possible precautions, relax and enjoy your vacation. Your Lab will be fine.

Chapter 14

Keeping Your Lab — and You! — Healthy

- -

In This Chapter

▶ Going hiking, visiting parks, and taking a swim to keep your Lab in great shape

▶ Going to sports events as a fun way to keep moving

- -

*E*veryone wants a healthy Lab, and prevention is the name of the game. Exercise is the best way to keep your Lab healthy and happy (and it will help you, too!). This chapter helps you get off your derriere and get your Lab out and about, improving both of your lives.

If you have both a Lab and kids, lucky kids! And lucky Lab! Labs and kids go great together, as long as the Lab is well-socialized to kids and the kids are old enough to understand how to treat a dog with kindness and respect (although some Labs are great with toddlers, too, and very forgiving of an occasional tug on the ear or game of dress-up).

Hike It Up

If you live near a state or national park that allows dogs (they will probably require your dog to be on a leash), you and your whole family can go hiking together. Hiking is great exercise for people and dogs, and the fresh air and scenery is great for the soul, too. Your Lab will love to go on hikes, and if you come across a safe body of water, your Lab will be thrilled to go for a dip and retrieve a stick or two. Remember, always bring along water and a bowl for long hikes or any hikes on hot days or in warm climates. And don't forget the first-aid kit (see Chapter 6).

Because so many people love to hike with their dogs, manufacturers have come out with all sorts of products to make hiking easier on everyone. Look for collapsible water bowls that fit into a backpack or clip onto your belt. Doggy backpacks allow your Lab to carry his own supplies comfortably. You can even buy doggy shoes, sun visors, sunglasses, and raincoats.

Park It!

If you regularly go to any parks, you already know whether dogs are allowed. If you aren't sure, read the signs or ask the park managers about the rules for dogs. Some parks require you to keep your dog on a leash. A Flexi-lead that can extend up to 25 feet allows your dog to be under control and still run around. Even if the park allows for off-lead dogs (something becoming increasingly rare), make sure that you and your dog have mastered the "Come" request before you find yourself screaming at your dog because he finds the park more interesting than he finds you.

Special *doggy parks* (a safe, fenced-in area, where dogs are encouraged to play together) can be great fun for dogs and dog owners alike, but don't bring a puppy to a doggy park before he has received all his vaccinations. Also, never bring an adolescent or adult dog who hasn't had plenty of experience with groups of other dogs to a doggy park. You don't want your dog involved in a skirmish!

In the Swim

Labs were bred to retrieve fish, fish nets, and birds out of the water. No wonder they love water so much! However, just because Labs love water doesn't mean you can toss your Lab puppy into the pond and expect him to love it. Would you toss your own child into the pond before he knew how to swim? Think about how you were taught to swim. Remember how scary it was at first?

Use gentle, loving care when teaching your Lab puppy to love the water. Find a natural body of water where you can wade in and wade out. Let your puppy follow you at his own pace. Don't get anxious if he doesn't jump right in. The bigger deal you make out of it, the more reluctant your pup may be to follow you. With a little patience, your pup will get his feet wet, so to speak (see Figure 14-1). We like to introduce litters to the water (assuming the weather isn't too cold) when they're about 6 or 7 weeks old, and they all wind up swimming at that age. If your Lab is reluctant, return another day and let your pup see how much fun you're having in the water, or bring along another dog who is a veteran swimmer. Your pup will get the idea.

Make sure the water in which your Lab will swim is clean enough for you to enter. If you wouldn't swim in it, keep your Lab out, too. Also avoid places with heavy currents, where your Lab could be swept out to sea or down a river. If you consider the water safe enough for you or your children, it should be safe enough for your Lab.

Cleanliness is next to dogginess

When people clean up after their dogs, the people who run the parks and national monuments and hiking areas and playgrounds and sports fields have a good impression of dogs. When people don't clean up after their dogs, other people complain and that makes dogs look bad. Too many people have neglected to clean up after their dogs, and that's why dogs are banned from so many areas that would otherwise be wonderful places for you and your Lab to spend time together.

Lots of products exist to make poop scooping easier and more sanitary, but a few paper towels and a big plastic zippered bag also work fine. (Bring along some baby wipes or hand wipes to keep your own hands clean, too.) Set a good example, and if others do the same, perhaps more places will be opened up for you and your dog to spend your leisure time in the future.

LAB TIP Always bring along towels to dry off your pup after a water outing, before he goes back in the car. Don't let him overexert himself or become chilled. Remember, Labs are like children and can't be trusted to use good judgment when doing fun activities. They can get carried away having a good time and trying to please you. It's up to you to say when enough is enough.

Figure 14-1:
Labs are water-loving dogs! Take them to the beach, to a pond, or to a river, or set them up with a baby pool. They'll love you for it.

© Close Encounters of the Furry Kind

The daily groom

Daily grooming from puppyhood on (and we mean every day, even after the novelty has worn off) helps keeps your Lab's skin and coat healthy, shiny, and pest-free. Regular grooming also alerts you to potential health problems and maintains your Lab's good hygiene, from the tip of your Lab's tail to the tip of her canine teeth.

Daily grooming also helps you stay in touch, both physically and emotionally, with your pal. See Chapter 5 for the lowdown on grooming.

Always supervise your Lab when he's in a swimming pool, and be very sure he knows how to get back out. A bad swimming pool experience can traumatize a puppy and make him afraid of all water. If your puppy falls in the pool when you aren't watching and doesn't know how to get back out again, he could drown.

Sporty Labs

Labs love to play, and lots of sporting events that involve humans and dogs have evolved as people look for more fun things to do with their dogs (see the chapters in Part V). If you or your kids are playing in athletic events for humans only, however, your Lab can be a great spectator. Bring him along to Little League games, T-ball, soccer matches, flag football, beach volleyball, or an informal game of basketball on an outdoor court.

Taking your Lab to outdoor events where lots of people are milling around, talking, and cheering is good practice for your Lab's self-control and your management skills (see Chapter 8). Your Lab must know that he can't run onto the field just because his kid is up at bat. You have to know that you're responsible for your Lab's behavior. But if you and your Lab are ready for the challenge, go ahead and bring him along. The more practice he gets socializing, the better behaved he'll be, and any sporting event is more fun when the whole family is included.

Part V
Showing Off and Having Fun

The 5th Wave   By Rich Tennant

"This Lab still needs work. She'll resuscitate, rehabilitate, even return birds to their nests, but <u>dang</u> if I can get her to just retrieve one!"

In this part . . .

Time for some real fun! In this part, we tell you all about the great organizations and events out there providing arenas for dog fun. From working as a rescue dog to participating in organized obedience competition, from hunt tests to flyball and Frisbee, this part has everything you need to know to get started.

And if your Lab is simply gorgeous, we also introduce you to the world of the dog show. Who knows, yours may be the next champion! Of course, official champion or not, we know that your Lab will always be a champion to you, and the more time you spend together, the better life with your Lab will become.

Chapter 15

Having Fun with Agility Trials and Competitive Sports

. . . .

In This Chapter

▶ Training for agility competition

▶ Putting together a flyball team

▶ Dancing with your Lab in freestyle competition

▶ Catching Frisbees for fun and sport

. . . .

Maybe you and your Lab have tackled obedience (see Chapter 11) and think it's fun but are looking for something more. Does your Lab excel at tricks, jumping, and running? Do you think she would be great at maneuvering an obstacle course?

If you're looking for some serious fun, consider training your Lab to compete in the sport of agility or in flyball, freestyle, or Frisbee competitions. This chapter gives you the details.

Excelling at Agility

Agility is one of the latest rages in dog events. Why? Because it's a whole lot of fun! Your Lab gets to perform on a playground of equipment, competing against other dogs to see who can maneuver the courses with the most accuracy, speed, attention to their handlers (that's you!), and grace.

Agility is a great way to keep your Lab in shape; have fun; reinforce and add to basic training; and demonstrate to an appreciative crowd how well-behaved, talented, responsive, and agile your Lab is. Agility trials often draw large crowds because they're almost as fun to watch as they are to do.

The program

All breeds registered with the American Kennel Club (AKC) may participate in agility trials. (Other organizations besides the AKC offer competitions and titles to all dogs, including mixed breeds.) In AKC competition, dogs must be 12 months or older, can be spayed or castrated, and can't be in heat (you can imagine the chaos!). Seeing- and hearing-impaired dogs may not participate, nor may dogs not considered by the judges to be "physically sound" or that are bandaged or have anything attached to them for medical purposes.

Several types of agility trials exist. Member agility trials, held by clubs or associations that are members of the AKC, allow your dog to earn qualifying scores toward titles. Licensed agility trials also allow your dog to earn qualifying scores, but they are held by clubs or associations that aren't AKC members. These organizations are, however, licensed to hold an agility trial by the AKC. Sanctioned agility trials are more informal and don't count toward titles. Clubs or associations holding these trials are sanctioned but not licensed by the AKC. They are practice runs for organizations trying to qualify to hold licensed or member events.

Neither the AKC nor the organization sponsoring an event can be responsible for injuries to a dog during an agility trial. It's your responsibility to be sure your dog stays safe. If your dog is sick, injured, or suffering from a condition such as hip dysplasia that would make jumping or any other agility activity painful or dangerous, retire your dog from competition, at least temporarily.

The course

The fun part of the agility trial is the obstacle course itself. If you're competing in the Novice class, you may walk your dog through the contact obstacles before the competition begins. (*Contact obstacles* are the obstacles in an agility obstacle course that have painted areas with which the dog must make contact while tackling the obstacle. Any part of a dog's foot may touch the contact zone, but the dog will be faulted and lose points if she misses the contact zone. *Contact zones* are often painted bright yellow and are on the A-frame, dog walk, and seesaw obstacles.) Your Lab may do a few warm-up jumps, but these must be done off the course.

The following obstacles are part of an agility trial obstacle course:

✔ **The A-frame:** Dogs must go up one panel of the A-frame and go down the other panel in whatever direction the judge orders. Contact zones are painted on the A-frame, often bright yellow. Your dog must touch the contact zone points with part of her foot on the way down only. The A-frame is about 5 feet to 5½ feet tall, and the top surface is non-slip.

✔ **The dog walk:** This structure has a center section with two ramp sections, all about 1 foot wide and either eight or 12 feet long and about three to four feet off the ground and painted with a non-slip surface. This structure is also painted with contact zones. Your dog must go up one ramp, cross the center section, and go down the other ramp in whatever order the judge specifies, touching each contact zone with part of her foot.

✔ **The seesaw:** This structure is a plank or panel on a center fulcrum, just like a playground seesaw. The plank is about one foot wide and 12 feet long, and the base extends two inches past the sides of the plank so that your dog can see where the center point is. The plank is painted with a non-slip surface, and contact zones that are 42 inches long are painted on each end. Your dog must ascend the plank, cause it to seesaw the other way, and then descend. Your dog must wait for the opposite side of the plank to touch the ground before getting off the seesaw, and she must touch each contact zone with part of her foot.

✔ **The pause table:** This table has about a 36-inch square top painted with a non-slip surface or carpeted. The height of the table depends on your dog's height division. For Labs, it's either 16 inches or 24 inches high. Your Lab must jump onto the table, pause for five seconds in a sit or down position (according to what the judge decrees), and then dismount.

✔ **The open tunnel:** This flexible tube can be formed into different shapes, and the openings are either round or rectangular and are no higher than 26 inches. The tube is 10 to 20 feet long, although the AKC recommends a 15-foot length. It must be positioned so that your dog can't see the end of the tunnel when she enters the tunnel and must also be secured so it doesn't move or roll around when your dog is in it. (Securing the tunnel isn't your responsibility.) Your dog must go in one end of the tunnel (the one the judge indicates), go through the tunnel, and come out the other side.

✔ **The closed tunnel:** This tunnel has a rigid entrance connected to a chute. The opening section is 24 to 36 inches long and about 2 feet in diameter. The bottom inside surface is non-slip. The rest of the tunnel is made of a lightweight, sturdy material such as rip-stop nylon. This chute isn't rigid, so the tunnel looks closed to the dog. It is open, however, flaring to a 96-inch opening at the end. Your dog must enter the tunnel and exit through the chute.

✔ **The weave poles:** This part of the obstacle course consists of 6 to 12 poles mounted on a base or stuck in the ground. Each pole is about an inch in diameter and at least three feet tall, uniformly spaced at about two-foot intervals. The poles must be flexible so that they can bend to make way for very large dogs. Your dog must enter the section of weave poles by going between the first two poles from right to left, then moving from left to right between the second and third poles, right to left between the third and fourth poles, and so on, going through the entire section with this weaving movement.

If your dog makes a mistake when moving through the weave poles by missing an interval or going the wrong way, she must go back to the beginning of the weave poles or back to the place where the error occurred and start again.

- **The single-bar jump:** This portion of the course has bars on supports positioned so the base can be adjusted for different height divisions. Usually, two or more bars are on the supports for the jump. Your dog must jump over the top bar without knocking it off, in the direction the judge specifies.

- **The double-bar jump:** This jump has two parallel bars positioned at the correct height for your dog's height division; it resembles two single-bar jumps placed together. The distance between the two crossbars is one-half the jump height division. For example, if your Lab is in the 20-inch division (22 inches and under at the withers), the distance between the two bars in the double-bar jump would be 10 inches. For the 24-inch division, the distance would be 12 inches. Your dog must jump over both top bars without knocking off either one in whatever direction the judge specifies.

- **The triple-bar jump:** In this jump, the dog must clear three bars of gradually increasing heights. For a dog in the 20-inch height division, the horizontal distance between each bar is 10 inches, but the three bars are 10, 15, and 20 inches in height, respectively. For a dog in the 24-inch division, the bars are 12 inches apart horizontally, and 12, 18, and 24 inches in height. Your Lab must jump over all three bars without knocking off any in whatever direction the judge specifies.

- **The panel jump:** In this jump, six boards are arranged on upright supports to look like a solid wall. Dogs must jump over the top board without knocking it off in the direction that the judge specifies.

- **The tire jump (or circle jump):** This jump consists of a tire or other, similar object suspended from a frame. The inner diameter of the tire must be about two feet, and the frame must allow the tire to be suspended at different heights appropriate for different height divisions. Your Lab must jump through the tire opening in the direction the judge specifies.

- **The window jump:** This jump looks like a wall with a window in it. The window must be about a two-foot square or a circle with a two-foot diameter. The wall must extend for at least one foot around the window, and the frame must allow for the window to be adjusted to different jump heights. Your Lab must jump through the window opening in the direction the judge specifies.

- **The broad jump:** This jump consists of four eight-inch sections or five six-inch sections, each about four to five feet long and of different heights, either arranged in ascending height or in a hogback arrangement (ascending then descending). The length of the entire jump is twice the height of the division. For example, if your Lab is in the 20-inch division, the broad jump length would be 40 inches. If your Lab is in the 24-inch division, the broad jump length would be 48 inches. Your Lab must jump over all the sections without touching them, entering between marker poles placed near the front and exiting between marker poles placed near the back.

Setting up a practice area

Agility courses can be set up indoors or outdoors, but they must be set up on non-slip surfaces such as packed dirt, grass, carpeting, or padded matting. Any course run on concrete must be fully padded to avoid injury to the dogs.

For a list of agility equipment suppliers, check out www.agilityability.com/agility_

equipment.htm. In addition, J&J Dog Supplies at www.jandjdog.com/ and Backyard Agility Equipment at www.goodnet.com/~jliziu/agilitytools.html sell agility, obedience, and flyball equipment online. But be forewarned, the stuff is NOT cheap!

That's it! That's the course. Depending on how advanced your Lab is and what titles she's acquired, the number of obstacles will vary. All courses must clearly show where the beginning and ending are, and each obstacle or jump must be clearly numbered so that you know the order. You'll have at least a half an hour before the start of your competition to see the order and survey the obstacle course layout.

Timing is everything!

In addition to maneuvering through the obstacle course, your dog must also do so in a timely manner. No dawdling and meandering is allowed, even if the obstacles are tackled perfectly. Your dog receives time penalties if she takes longer than the set course time to complete the course. Course times are set by the judges and depend on how big the trial area is. The more advanced the class, the faster your dog must go. Timing starts when your dog crosses the start line and ends when your dog crosses the finish line.

Jumpers With Weaves (JWW)

Jumpers With Weaves (JWW) is a whole separate agility class that further demonstrates how well you and your dog work together. This course is faster because it doesn't include contact zones or a pause table. You and your Lab can just go, go, go! The course is mostly jumps, and your dog is judged primarily on her speed and jumping ability.

The obstacles for the JWW classes are the same as in regular agility, except certain obstacles

such as the pause table, dog walk, A-frame, and seesaw are eliminated.

JWW optional obstacles include the open tunnel (no more than three); the closed tunnel (no more than two); the broad jump (no more than one); and any number of panel jumps, tire jumps, and window jumps. Timing must be slightly quicker in JWW classes, and dogs and handlers are eliminated for taking the wrong course, knocking over a bar, or for any intentional or beneficial handler contact to the dog.

To find out more about agility, write the United States Dog Agility Association at P.O. Box 850955, Richardson, Texas 75085-0955; phone 972-231-9700, send a fax to 214-503-0161, or visit their Web site at www.usdaa.com/.

Flying High with Flyball, Freestyle, and Frisbee

If you and your Lab are born athletes, are looking for some creativity in your activities together, or just want to get into a really good game, look into flyball, freestyle, and Frisbee. These three sports are catching on fast, and if they aren't available in an organized form in your area, they probably will be soon. Fun to participate in, fun to watch, less stringently regulated and formal than many AKC events, and a great way to spend time with your dog, these activities may be just what you're looking for.

Flyball

Flyball is a relay race. Each team consists of four dogs who run a course with four hurdles, spaced ten feet apart, and a spring-loaded box 15 feet from the last hurdle. When stepped on, the box shoots out a tennis ball.

The total length of the course is 51 feet (including a six-foot distance between starting line and the first hurdle). Hurdle heights depend on the height of the dogs and must be four inches lower than the height at the *withers* (the highest points of the shoulder blades — see Chapter 5) of the shortest dog on the team. The minimum possible height is eight inches, and the maximum possible height is 16 inches.

Reading up on flyball

Flyball afficionados may want to get involved in the North American Flyball Association (NAFA). Write to North American Flyball Association, Inc., 1400 W. Devon Ave, #512, Chicago, IL 60660 or visit their Web site at www.flyball.org/.

The flyball newsletter, *Finish Line*, lists all tournament events and results and is available for $20 for a one-year subscription (which includes four issues). Write to Melanie McAvoy, 1002 E. Samuel Avenue, Peoria Heights, IL 61614, 309-682-7617, e-mail: melmcavoy@worldnet.att.net.

The dogs line up at the starting line and then jump all four hurdles, jump onto the box so that the tennis ball shoots out, run to catch the tennis ball, and return over the four hurdles. When the first dog crosses back over the starting line, the next dog takes off. The first team to have all four dogs run the course without making a mistake wins that heat.

You can start training your Lab to learn flyball when he is just a puppy. Whenever practicing retrieving, always run away from the puppy after you throw an object to be retrieved. This will encourage him to chase after you, increasing his speed and his instinct for the relay race.

Freestyle: Gotta dance!

Maybe you're more creatively inclined or want to be out there playing with your dog, not just watching him run relays. Then perhaps canine freestyle is for you! *Canine freestyle,* sometimes called *canine musical freestyle,* is an extension of obedience training that's set to music and choreographed using basic and advanced obedience moves (see Chapter 11). First popular in Canada, it's now becoming increasingly popular in the United States. When your Lab has earned his CD (Companion Dog) obedience title or knows enough that he could earn it if you chose to participate in competition, you and he are probably ready to begin learning canine freestyle. (Where did they get the idea to set obedience training to music? From horses! Equine dressage is a sport in which horses usually perform to music, and if horses can do it, so can dogs.)

Canine freestyle is great fun to watch, so attend a demonstration or competition if you can. Important to a successful performance is creativity and originality, so you'll see some interesting stuff.

The purpose of a canine freestyle performance is to show off — to music — the dog's natural abilities, talent, beauty, and grace in working with his handler. Choice of music and type of choreography should match the dog's breed and individual personality, as well as the dog/handler relationship. Is your Lab feisty and confident? Graceful and feminine? A natural clown? Choose music to match your Lab's style. Keep in mind that your style matters, too. You're out there and as much a part of the performance as your Lab. According to Canine Freestyle Federation (CFF) regulations, "Teamwork is essential."

The technical basis for a canine freestyle performance consists of two basic positions, the heel and front positions. However, a canine freestyle performance shouldn't look like a series of obedience positions. It should be original, artistic, and creative. The choreographed routine will consist of good use of rhythm, movement, space, and direction. You and your dog must both be having fun, and this enjoyment must be apparent in the performance. You even get to wear a costume! (It's like a canine version of figure skating — with some obedience competition thrown in — but neither you nor your Lab have to know how to skate.)

Canine freestyle governing bodies

The Canine Freestyle Federation, Inc., or CFF, was founded in 1995 and incorporated in 1996. It's an international organization that has provided structure, rules, competitions, and demonstrations to organize and promote the sport of canine freestyle. Musical Canine Sports International (MCSI) was also created to regulate canine freestyle, providing competitions, regulations, guidelines, and titles. The MCSI now sanctions competitions throughout the United States.

Canine freestyle competition sponsored by CFF has three competition levels. In Level I, choreography should be interesting and make full use of the space. The routine is performed with the dog on a leash and should last from between one and a half and two and a half minutes. It must also include the following elements:

- ✔ **Heeling, either to the right or left side:** *Heeling* is when your Lab is sitting, standing, lying down, or moving at your left or right side, in line with you and facing in the same direction.

- ✔ **Front work:** *Front work* is when your Lab is sitting, standing, lying down, or moving while facing you with his body centered in front of your feet, without touching them.

- ✔ **Two different paces or speeds of movement**

- ✔ **Backing:** *Backing* is when your dog moves backwards.

- ✔ **Turns and/or pivots:** *Turns* can be to the right, left, or an about-face. Turns are performed while in a heel position. *Pivots* are in-place turns with your dog in a heel position. Either the handler or the dog remains in place.

- ✔ **Movement in circles, serpentine patterns, or spirals**

In Levels II and III, the choreography is more complex, and the dog must demonstrate a greater degree of athleticism, training, and artistry.

 You don't have to be a dancer to be a good handler in a canine freestyle routine, although a sense of rhythm helps. What matters is that you and your dog can move together in harmony and that he enjoys moving to music. Put on some music during a training session and try a few moves. If your dog seems to enjoy it, give freestyle a whirl.

Frisbee: The ultimate retrieve

If you and your Lab like to play Frisbee, and especially if your Lab seems to have a particular skill and love for the game, you may enjoy getting involved in Canine Frisbee events. Labs make excellent Frisbee dogs because they have the retrieve instinct. Some dogs have to be taught to retrieve, but chances are, your Lab will bring that Frisbee back to you without more than a hint of suggestion on your part.

But do you and your Lab have what it takes to compete in serious Canine Frisbee competition? The sport is growing quickly, and Canine Frisbee competitions are held all over the country. Canine Frisbee clubs abound, and other dog clubs and even city recreation centers are holding Canine Frisbee events.

Attend a Canine Frisbee event to see if you think you and your Lab would enjoy competing. One of the main organizations regulating Canine Frisbee is the International Disc Dog Handlers Association (IDDHA). IDDHA sanctions the worldwide Canine Disc trials and competitions and holds tests, gives titles, keeps records, and ranks competitors.

The IDDHA also offers a Retrieval Proficiency Test (RPT). This test measures a dog's proficiency in retrieving any object, including a ball, stick, or a disc — see Figure 15-1. You must stand in one place and throw the object at least as far as a length equal to two body lengths of your dog. You may use verbal requests, hand signals, and praise, but you may not use corrections. Your dog must take no longer to retrieve the object than it would take you to walk to the object, pick it up, and return to where you threw it. After one practice throw, you and your dog get one chance to pass during that test.

Figure 15-1: For a Retrieval Proficiency Test, your Lab must be able to retrieve a ball, stick, or disc and return it to you.

© Ron Kimball Photography, Inc.

If you like the idea of trying canine Frisbee, the first step is to get a Frisbee and try it out with your Lab. Although your Lab may catch the Frisbee on the first throw, don't be disappointed if he doesn't get it. You have to show him what to do. You can start by rolling the Frisbee like a ball. Reward your dog with praise and a piece of food whenever he chases the Frisbee and brings it back to you.

In search of the perfect Frisbee

Although many types of Frisbees will work for competition and training, many Canine Frisbee pros recommend the Fast Back 2000 Freestyle Frisbee by Mattel, weighing 119 grams. This disc is reportedly lightweight and easy to throw.

Never let your Lab use the Frisbee as a chew toy. Plastic can develop sharp areas around chew marks that may injure your dog's mouth and decrease the life of the Frisbee. If your Lab mouths and chews on the Frisbee after catching it, reward him for quick, focused returns. Then, if he's in the mood to chew, give him a chew toy.

If your Lab knows the "take it" request (see Chapter 11), you can use it to teach him to take the Frisbee. Let him take it from your hand as you stand still. Then let him take it from your hand as you run. Next let him take it from the air as you toss it, just a short distance at first. Pretty soon, if you keep the practice fun, your Lab will be chasing that Frisbee with glee and leaping to catch it.

Of course, you need to practice your throwing skills, too. Practice makes perfect! Practice snapping your wrist to produce greater spin. Start with short throws and work up to longer throws, maintaining good control.

Chapter 16

Competing in Hunting Tests and Field Trials

....

....

*L*abs were bred for the hunt. The earliest Labrador Retrievers, way up north in Newfoundland, helped man survive by aiding him in the hunt and retrieving fish and game. Even today, many hunters bring along Labs as their companions and helpers, and Labs are still bred to excel at hunting and retrieving game. If you're a hunter or are interested in the sport of hunting or in pitting your Lab against other Labs to see who demonstrates the most precise and impressive retrieving skills in the field, this chapter is for you.

Hunting Tests

The purpose of hunting tests is to test how well your Labrador Retriever can work with you on the hunt. Hunting tests evaluate the suitability of retrievers as hunting companions in the field, so hunting tests, although structured, simulate actual hunting conditions as closely as possible.

The ability of your Lab to retrieve game birds is tested under many various conditions — including on land and in the water — and all tests and conditions are organized and orchestrated by the judges.

Like obedience, hunting is a sport, and both dogs and handlers are expected to behave with proper sportsmanship. That means no handlers abusing dogs (or judges) and no dogs attacking other dogs.

Although each hunt test is unique because every environment and every judge is different, the basic setup works something like this: When it is your Lab's turn, the judge calls his number. You and your Lab approach the line.

Hunting with the NAHRA

The North American Hunting Retriever Association (NAHRA) is a not-for-profit organization created in 1983 to preserve the hunting instincts of retrievers. The NAHRA believes that retrievers often don't fulfill their hunting potential. The organization, therefore, attempts to provide a structure for the evaluation of hunting and retrieving work, including tests and competitions in which dogs compete against an ideal standard. To find out more about the NAHRA, check out their Web site at `www.starsouth.com/nahra/`.

After your Lab is at the spot where the test begins, he's considered as being tested until the test is over and he moves back out of view of the test area.

Everyone, judges included, is dressed in customary hunting garb. When a bird is shot, your Lab must be able to see it fall. Then, when you instruct your Lab, he should run to where the bird fell, find it, and bring it back to you, gently, without dropping it. Your Lab will be tested on both land and water, having to retrieve birds under all sorts of conditions. Dogs are scored on the following:

✔ **Marking:** *Marking* is the dog's ability to observe and remember where a bird fell so that he can find the bird and retrieve it. A dog who doesn't find a bird that the judges believe he should have found receives a low score in marking. Marking is considered one of the most important qualities in a retriever and a natural ability. Even if your Lab doesn't see exactly where a bird fell, he has good marking if he looks toward the fall, is paying attention to where it went, and goes straight toward the area. Marking scores are lower for dogs that unnecessarily disturb the area looking for or getting to the bird (also called the *fall*).

✔ **Style:** Your Lab's retrieving style is the way he acts, how alert he is, how eager he is, and how quickly he retrieves. Style also includes the manner in which your Lab enters water, picks up birds, and returns them. Dogs who have great style are a pleasure to watch. Style (along with marking) is considered one of the two most important natural abilities of retrievers. According the *Regulations & Guidelines for AKC Hunting Tests for Retrievers*, style includes alertness and obedience in attitude, moving through land and water with speed and determination, searching for the bird aggressively, picking it up quickly, and bringing it back quickly.

✔ **Perseverance/courage/hunting:** This category measures your Lab's determination. How aggressively does he go for the bird? Does he search systematically and without hesitation? When the going gets rough, does he readily enter cold water or mud? Does he look for the bird with interest and come back with the bird? Does he go straight to the bird without looking back to you for directions? Hesitancy, lack of confidence, and lack of drive are all considered faults in the perseverance/courage/hunting area.

✔ **Trainability:** Although considered less important than natural ability, trainability is nonetheless an important consideration in judging a Lab's hunting skill. In other words, you have to do some of the work, too! If you've taught your Lab to be steady on the line without moving around too much (see Figure 16-1), to be under control at all times with good manners, to be responsive to your requests and direction, and to deliver the bird to your hand willingly and easily without dropping it, you've done a good job with your dog, and he's done a good job, too.

Figure 16-1: If your Lab's a natural bird dog, you may want to test his skills in an organized hunt test or field trial.

© Nance Photography/AKC Stock Images

If your dog is so rough on the bird that the bird becomes unfit for people to cook and eat, he can't receive a qualifying score. However, the judges should closely inspect the bird because the dog may not have been responsible for the condition of the bird, which may have been damaged when it was shot or by the fall to the ground. *Hardmouth* is a term applied to a dog who's so rough on birds that he crushes their bones or otherwise severely damages them. This term carries a stigma and marks a retriever as undesirable.

Take your turn according to *The Wall Street Journal!*

Field trials have an unusual way of deciding the order in which dogs will take their turns. Each dog is given a number in a draw. Then the order begins with the dog whose number corresponds with the last two digits of the closing Dow Jones Industrial Average on the Tuesday before the trial or on the most recent day prior to that Tuesday if the New York Stock Exchange wasn't open on the Tuesday. Then the dogs continue in order after the first dog, in sequence from the draw.

Field Trials

If you're in the mood for some stiffer competition than hunting tests, consider field trials. *Field trials* demonstrate the functions for which breeds are bred, so field trials are completely different for different breeds. Retrievers have their own field trials and so do pointing breeds, spaniels, Beagles, Basset Hounds, and Dachshunds. Of course, in this section, we limit our discussion to retriever field trials.

Although hunting tests are a little like Canine Good Citizen tests (see Chapter 11), field trials are more like obedience trials (also discussed in Chapter 11). Also called *non-slip retriever* trials, field trials test a retriever's ability to retrieve game birds under all conditions. (A *non-slip retriever* is a dog who walks at heel, marks the fall [or looks for and remembers where the bird fell], and retrieves game on request. Non-slip retrievers aren't expected to find birds they didn't see fall, nor are they expected to flush out game.) Like hunting tests, field trials are meant to simulate an ordinary shoot. However, field trials are more formal and a lot more competitive than hunting tests.

The best way to find out more about hunting tests and/or field trials is to find people in your area who participate. Go as a spectator at first, talk to people in the know, and get a feel for whether the sport interests you. Does it sound even more interesting or is it not what you imagined when people doing the sport talk about it? If you like what you hear, discover all you can, train your Lab to perform the functions required, and then go out together and have a great time — because having fun is the whole point!

Chapter 17

Doing the Dog Show Scene

In This Chapter

▶ Determining whether your Lab has what it takes to be a show dog

▶ Understanding the structure of dog shows and how they work

▶ Comparing the ideal Lab to the practically perfect Lab

Sure, you like to have just as much fun as the next person. Frisbee, agility, hunting, and runs in the park are just great. But maybe, just maybe, when you look at your Lab you see a true beauty, a rare specimen, the closest thing to Lab perfection you can imagine. Maybe you've known from the start that you wanted a show dog, or maybe you hadn't considered it until your Lab grew into a dog with star quality. In either case, if you're considering showing your Lab, you need to know what's involved, how dog shows work, and most importantly, whether dog shows are something in which both you and your Lab will enjoy participating together.

Knowing When a Star Is Born

How do you know if the dog show circuit is for you? Most people show their dogs in dog shows for one of two reasons:

✔ To earn the Champion of Record title, which will make a dog a more valuable breeder

✔ For fun

No matter what your reason, to do well in competition, you have to have the right kind of dog. What is the right kind? This is a loaded question. The right kind of dog for you may very well not have anything to do with the right kind of dog for a dog show competition.

For Lab dog shows, experts in Labs judge them for how closely they match the breed standard. *A breed standard* is a complete and thorough description of the ideal Labrador Retriever. Standards for all breeds are developed and periodically updated by national breed clubs. The American Kennel Club (AKC) must then approve the standards. After they're approved, that standard becomes the ideal for that breed.

Other breed clubs, such as the United Kennel Club (UKC) and kennel clubs in other countries, have differing standards for each breed and recognize different breeds than does the AKC. The AKC is the largest breed club in the United States and has the most widely accepted standard, but many people choose to join and breed their dogs by the standards of other clubs.

The standard for the Labrador Retriever, for example, states that the eyes of Labs should be brown in black and yellow Labs and either brown or hazel in chocolate Labs, and that the tail should be what is known as an *otter tail,* which means it is covered all the way around in thick, short fur, rather than the long, feathery furred tail you would see on a Golden Retriever. The standard also states that your Lab should weight between 55 and 80 pounds.

Does that mean your 47-pound, yellow-eyed Lab with a long, thin, feathery tail won't be the best pet you ever had? Certainly not. But she may not do very well in a dog show. If, on the other hand, your dog does closely match the standard, loves to perform, thrives on the attention of a crowd, and is proud to strut her stuff, you may have the makings of a champion.

Over the years, priorities for various breeds change, so to see how a breed has changed, you can look at old breed standards. The breed standard for Labs approved in 1957, for example, is far less detailed, has a lower weight limit, and doesn't even mention the Labrador Retriever temperament. The current breed standard, however, is what the judges will use to evaluate Labs in the show ring today.

Understanding the Labrador Breed Standard

Both the AKC and the UKC have developed breed standards for the Labrador Retriever. Of course, no dog meets the ideal in every way, but breed standards provide a standard so that breeds can be continually improved in looks, health, temperament, and skill. Dog show judges use breed standards to give them something by which to judge show dogs.

Breed standards are chock-full of dog-world jargon, so in this book, we translate for you instead of quoting directly. If you want to check out the official standard, flip to the Appendix to find out how to contact the AKC.

The AKC standard

The official breed standard — translated in this section into everyday, simplified language — was last updated in 1994.

General appearance

The Labrador Retriever is a strong and athletic-looking, medium-sized dog with a short, dense coat; a clean-cut look; a broad skull; and warm, friendly eyes. The Lab's size and balanced body make him ideal for retrieving, as well as for a wide variety of other activities. He should be hardy, healthy, and sturdy enough to hunt for long hours under difficult conditions; the character, personality, and looks to do well in dog shows; and the right temperament to be a great family companion.

A *short-coupled* dog, a term mentioned in the official breed standard, is relatively short in length from the shoulder blades to the hips, as opposed to longer-bodied dogs such as German Shepherds.

Size, proportion, and substance

When measured from the ground to the top of the shoulder blade, the ideal Labrador Retriever should be

- Between 22½ to 24½ inches for males
- From 21½ to 23½ inches for females.
- After they are one year old, males in good shape should weigh between 65 and 80 pounds.
- After one year, females should weigh between 55 and 70 pounds.
- Any Lab over ½ inch above or below the standard is disqualified from the show ring.

Proportionally, a Lab should be relatively short from shoulder to hips, but just long and tall enough to make walking and running easy and efficient. Labs in good shape have lots of muscle and no excess fat.

Here's a translation of some of the terms in this portion of the breed standard:

- The *withers* is the top of the shoulder blades and is used to measure the height of dogs.
- The *brisket* may refer to the chest area or to the entire front half of the torso (the thorax).
- When a dog looks *weedy,* he looks light-boned or has an insufficient amount of bone for his size.
- A *cloddy* dog, on the other hand, is low and thickset and looks relatively heavy.

Registering your Lab with the American Kennel Club

If you buy a purebred Labrador Retriever from a breeder and your Lab is eligible for registration with the AKC, you'll want to register him, especially if you want to participate in dog shows or other AKC dog events that require registration.

When you buy your Lab, you should receive an AKC application form that has already been filled out correctly by the breeder or previous owner. When you complete the form, submit it to the AKC along with the specified fee. When the AKC processes your application, you will receive a registration certificate. Keep it in a safe place!

If the breeder or previous owner doesn't have the proper paperwork, but the dog you're purchasing is represented as eligible for registration, the breeder must give you records that provide all the necessary identifying information, and the breeder's signature. This information includes the breed, sex, color, date of birth, registered names of the dog's *sire* (father) and *dam* (mother), and the name of the breeder. If the seller can't provide this information, don't buy the dog.

If you need help filling out the proper information, ask the breeder for help or contact the American Kennel Club (see the Appendix for contact information).

The head

A Labrador Retriever's skull should be wide, but not so wide as to look exaggerated. The top of the skull should be parallel to the top of the muzzle, and both parts should be about the same length. The head should look clean-cut with strong jaws, but without fleshy cheeks or lips. The nose should be wide and black on black and yellow Labs; it should be brown on chocolate Labs. The teeth should be strong and even, with the bottom teeth just behind the top teeth when the mouth is closed.

Ears should hang next to the head, relatively far back and low, and should reach to the inside of the eye when pulled forward. The eyes should show good temperament, intelligence, and alertness because these traits are so representative of the Labrador Retriever. Eyes should be brown with black rims in black and yellow Labs and should be brown or hazel with brown rims in chocolates.

The following is a translation of some of the terms in the official breed standard:

✔ A dog's *foreface* is his muzzle area.

✔ *Scissors bite* refers to a bite in which the outside of the lower six front teeth *(incisors)* touches the inner side of the top six front teeth (also called incisors).

✔ A *level bite* occurs when the upper and lower incisors meet exactly, rather than overlapping one way or the other.

The neck, topline, and body

The neck should be strong without loose skin and long enough to make retrieving easy. The back should be straight and level between the shoulder blade and the hips, and the body should have a nicely tapered rib cage (not too flat or too barrel-chested). (See Figure 17-1.) The Lab tail should be very thick at the base and then taper off. The Lab tail should also be covered in thick, short fur all the way around (called an *otter tail*) rather than long, feathery fur as on a Golden Retriever. The tail shouldn't curve over the back like a Husky tail and should continue the flow of a line from the top of the head to the tail tip.

Figure 17-1:
This Lab demonstrates the suggested neck, topline, and back of the breed standard.

© Close Encounters of the Furry Kind

Here's what some of that breed-standard terminology means:

- The *topline* is the outline of a dog's back (in profile) from just behind the top of the shoulder blade to the base of the tail.

- *Throatiness* refers to excessive loose skin under a dog's throat.

- A *ewe neck* refers to a neck in which the topline has a concave (sunken) curve rather than a convex (protruding) curve.

- The *croup* refers to the pelvic girdle. The *underline* is the outline of the dog's underside (in profile) from the front of the chest to the base of the abdomen.

- The *hock* is the hind-leg joint corresponding to the ankle joint on a human.

- *Docking* refers to the procedure of shortening a dog's tail by cutting it. In America, many breeds have their tails docked, although in many European countries, the procedure will disqualify a dog from the show ring and is frowned upon as unethical.

The forequarters

The front part of the dog should be muscular (but not so much as to restrict movement) and balanced with the back part so that shoulders and hips are in proportion, as are front and back legs. Front legs should be straight with strong bones, and when viewed from the side, the dog's elbows should be directly beneath the top point of the shoulder blade. Feet should be strong and compact with arched toes and well-developed paws.

Check out the following terms from the breed standard:

- *Forequarters* are the front part of the dog, from shoulder blades to paws.

- *Hindquarters* are the back part of the dog, from hips to paws.

- *Pasterns* are the forelegs between the "ankle" and the joint where the toes begin.

- *Dewclaws* are "toes" on the inside of a dog's leg, separated from the other "toes" and comparable to a thumb, except that they aren't used. They are commonly removed because they serve no function.

Must your dog fit the standard?

Must your dog exactly match the AKC or English standard for a Labrador Retriever? Of course not. No Lab will exactly fit every aspect of the standard because no dog is perfect. But your dog may be perfect for you.

If you want a show dog, you have to pay close attention to the published standard because it's used to judge show dogs. But if you want a pet, take more interest in certain aspects of the standard, such as temperament.

If you live in a cold climate, you want a Lab with a good coat in addition to a good temperament. If you would like a hunting companion, you want a Lab who excels in retrieving and has lots of endurance and strength.

You may find it interesting — even helpful — to know what the perfect Lab is like, but your Lab need only meet your personal standard for perfection. And lots of that perfection will come from the way you raise, train, and treat your dog. They don't come pre-perfected!

The hindquarters

The dog's back half, the pelvis, hips, legs, and paws, should be muscular and balanced. From the side, the angle of the rear legs should match the angle of the front legs. Hind legs should have strong bones and defined thighs with steady knees. When standing still, the dog's rear toes should stand just behind the top of the rump. Feet should be strong and compact, with arched toes and well-developed pads.

The following is a translation of some of the terms in the breed standard:

- The *stifle* is the "knee" joint.
- The *patella* is the knee cap.
- The *pasterns* are the knuckle joints.
- *Cow-hocks* refer to turned-in ankles and turned-out toes.
- *Spread hocks* refer to hocks that point outward.
- *Sickle hocks* refer to hocks that can't be straightened.

The coat

Labs have a *double coat,* which means the coat has two layers: a thick, dense, hard, weather-resistant top layer and a soft, downy undercoat for insulation. Labs with woolly, soft, or sparse coats are considered less desirable because they aren't as resistant to inclement weather conditions.

Color

Labs come in black, yellow (from fox red to light cream), and chocolate (light to dark). Other color variations disqualify a dog from the show ring.

Disqualifications

If you want to show your dog in dog shows, pay attention to the following disqualifications from the AKC standard. (Of course, if you don't want to show your Lab, don't give the following a second thought.) If your dog has any of these characteristics, he will be disqualified from show competition:

- Shorter or taller than the height described in the breed standard

- A pink nose or one lacking in color
- Eye rims that don't have any pigment
- Shortening or in any other way altering the tail
- Any other color or a combination of colors other than black, yellow, or chocolate

Brindle, a term mentioned in the breed standard, is a type of coat pattern in which black is layered in areas of light color (often tan), producing a tiger-striped look. This coloring will disqualify a Lab in competition.

Movement

When a Lab moves, he should look free, balanced, and effortless. Elbows shouldn't turn out, the body should move straight without weaving, the legs should remain straight, and all parts of the dog should move in concert.

Temperament

Temperament can make or break a Lab. The ideal Lab is kindly, outgoing, obedient, nonaggressive, gentle, intelligent, adaptable, and above all, eager to please.

The English standard

The standard for the Labrador Retriever in England is much the same as the AKC standard, but it's set by an organization called the FCI *(Fédération Cynologique Internationale),* is a truly international dog registry that's made up of kennel clubs from most major countries in the world except the United States (Russia is the newest member). It's similar to the AKC standard, but it's less detailed and has a few other differences. (For example, the FCI doesn't disqualify dogs if they don't fall within the ideal size guidelines as the AKC does.) All member clubs use FCI breed standards, which are based on the standards set by each breed's country of origin.

If you want to show your Lab for fun, keep in mind that dogs must not be spayed or neutered to participate in AKC dog shows. If you believe in having your dog altered or don't want to deal with the responsibilities having an unaltered dog entails, consider other types of competition — see Chapters 15 and 16.

Visiting a Dog Show

Attending a dog show is a lot of fun, and if you aren't participating, there's no pressure! Whether you're checking out Labs to see whether you would like one or checking out Labs because you've loved them for years and want to see them compete, dog shows can be an interesting way for a dog lover to spend the day.

Getting a feel for how the show works

Dog shows judge a Labrador Retriever's *conformation,* or physical appearance. Three types of conformation dog shows exist:

- *Specialty shows* are for dogs of a specific breed. Each national breed club has a specialty show each year. For example, the Labrador Retriever Club, Inc., has a specialty show in which only purebred, registered Labrador Retrievers may compete.

- *Group shows* are for dogs from one of the seven groups of purebred dogs. Labrador Retrievers belong to the Sporting Group and may participate in Sporting Group shows.

- The AKC recognizes *all-breed shows,* in which different breeds compete, first against their own breeds, then against their own groups (like sporting group or hound group). The best of each group then competes against the other "bests" for the single coveted award of "Best in Show." These are the biggest and usually the most publicized shows, such as the annual Westminster Kennel Club show in New York City.

Other dog clubs, such as the United Kennel Club (UKC), offer conformation shows, as well.

During a dog show, dogs compete to earn points towards the title of champion. A dog can earn anywhere from one to five points during a single show. Fifteen points are required under at least three different judges, plus two *majors* (wins of three, four, or five points, based upon how many dogs are in a competition) earned under two different judges, to earn the title Champion of Record. Also, after your Lab earns this title, you can put the prestigious *Ch.* before her name (for example, Ch. Kellygreens On Target). The best dog in each show wins the Best of Show award, but many other awards and places exist, as well. Males (called *dogs*) and females (called *bitches*) are judged separately.

People who aren't breeders tend to giggle when a female dog is called a bitch, but to breeders and dog show veterans, bitch is the only accurate word for a female dog. Dog usually refers to the male, although it is sometimes used to refer to both sexes.

Understanding the lingo

You may need help deciphering some of the dog show lingo. Like people obsessed with any field of knowledge, dog show people have their own language with lots of terms familiar to them but probably strange to you. Before you attend your first dog show, familiarize yourself with the following terms:

- ✔ **Angulation:** The angle created by bones and joints.

- ✔ **Baiting:** Using a treat to get a dog's attention or have her appear alert.

- ✔ **Bench show:** A dog show during which dogs are kept on benches when not in the ring, making it easier for the people attending the dog shows to see the different breeds.

- ✔ **Exhibitor:** The person who brings the dog to the show and enters her in the appropriate contests.

- ✔ **Fancier:** Someone who is particularly interested in purebred dogs and is usually involved in some aspect of the sport. This could be you!

- ✔ **Gait:** The way a dog moves or walks.

- ✔ **Groom:** To brush, comb, and trim a dog's coat to make her look her best.

- ✔ **Handler:** The person who brings the dog into the show ring and is with the dog during competition. (Also applies to other kinds of events such as obedience [see Chapter 11] and agility trials [see Chapter 15].)

- ✔ **Heel:** The request (what we call "commands") used to keep a dog in control and next to the handler.

- ✔ **Match show:** A more informal dog show in which championship points can't be earned.

- ✔ **Miscellaneous class:** The class for those purebred dogs that haven't yet become fully recognized by the AKC as a part of one of the seven groups (see the "Group of seven" sidebar for more information), yet are still considered purebred and able to participate in some dog show events.

- ✔ **Pedigree:** The written record of a dog's ancestry, dating back at least three generations.

- ✔ **Points:** Credits toward the Champion of Record title or any title.

- ✔ **Soundness:** A dog's mental and physical well-being.

- ✔ **Stacking:** The posing of a dog's legs and body so that he or she looks good.

- ✔ **Winners:** An award given to the best dog and the best bitch in the regular classes.

Group of seven

The AKC recognizes seven different groups of purebred dogs: sporting dogs, bred to hunt game birds on land and in water, including Labrador Retrievers; Hounds, used for hunting by sight or scent; working dogs, used to pull, guard, or search and rescue; Terriers, bred to eliminate vermin; toy dogs, bred to be companions; herding dogs, bred to assist shepherds and ranchers with livestock; and non-sporting dogs, which don't fit into other categories.

Your first time out

If you've never been to a dog show before, you'll want to know more than just the terminology. The following hints will make your experience even more rewarding (these are adapted from the AKC's "Tips for First-Time Spectators" in its *Beginner's Guide to Dog Shows*):

✔ Buy a show catalog and study it. It points you to the rings where the breed(s) in which you're interested will be judged. It also provides the names of breeders and owners of all dogs entered in competition.

✔ To see a particular breed, arrive early. After that breed has been judged, most of those dogs will probably leave.

✔ If you attend with friends, pick out a meeting place. Dog shows get crowded, and you can easily become separated. The superintendent's booth is a good meeting place.

✔ Even if you miss the Labrador Retriever competition, you can still see Labs in the group competition, when the Sporting group is up.

✔ Sometimes grooming areas are open to spectators. Although Labs don't take much grooming, you may be interested to see what professional groomers do to keep Labs looking their best.

✔ Never pet a dog at a dog show without asking permission. If the dog has just been groomed for competition, every hair is in place.

✔ Vendors for pet products and dog clubs set up booths at dog shows. You can find a lot of good (and free!) information at these booths.

✔ Wear comfy shoes. Many dog shows are pretty spread out, so you'll walk a lot. You'll also stand a lot because dog shows are typically crowded and don't usually have enough seats for everyone.

✔ Talk to Lab breeders and handlers if you're considering getting a Lab. They are the experts and can tell you a lot about the reality of owning Labs. Wait until after they've shown their dogs, however, so that they aren't busy.

✔ If you bring your young child to the show in a stroller, be very careful of dog tails and feet, and make sure your child is under control and won't grab or poke at any dogs.

Although dog shows can be fun, they're also highly competitive. Breeders often pay handlers to exhibit their dogs because earning championships can mean a breeder's lines are more valuable. Obedience, agility, or other dog activities (covered in Chapters 15 and 16) may be more fun for you because they're less seriously competitive. Do what's fun for you and you Lab, and when it isn't fun anymore, try something else.

Looking at the Ideal Lab versus the Practically Perfect Lab

Although having a champion is great and is something to be proud of, we'd like to emphasize one more time that your practically perfect Lab needn't ever see the inside of a dog show ring. Many good breeders, while breeding for the ideal, put the health and temperament of their puppies ahead of physical characteristics. Joel breeds first and foremost for excellent family pets, and we both believe that is an excellent priority for a breeder. Using the term *pet quality* to denote inferior specimens misses the point of breeding dogs. Dogs are what they are today because humans wanted companions, helpers, and partners. A dog who looks beautiful but isn't friendly isn't worth much, even if she does have a *Ch.* before her name (which she certainly won't earn if she growls at a judge!).

Puppy or senior dog, perfectly shaped or a little bit crooked, healthy or health-challenged, a Lab who is well-trained and well-loved will repay her owners with loyalty, affection, and the kind of unconditional love you rarely find here on earth. Love like that is worth every ounce of effort and more. It means having a friend, no matter how unsuccessful, how unfashionable, or how poor you are. It means being the object of a Labrador Retriever's devotion — and we can't think of many things we'd rather be.

Part VI
The Part of Tens

The 5th Wave   By Rich Tennant

"My husband would be a perfect match for a Retriever. Everytime I throw something out, he retrieves it from the trash and stores it in the *garage*."

In this part . . .

In lists of ten tips and tricks, this parts tells you how you can train your Lab most effectively; how to choose a trainer or training class (should you choose to go this route); and how Labs can make a difference in the world by working as assistance dogs, volunteer dogs, and emergency dogs.

Chapter 18

Ten Tips for Training Your Lab to Be a Great Pet

*T*his chapter shares ten quick tips for training your Lab.

Avoiding Problems Caused by Lack of Training

A Lab who is not a joy to have around is probably a Lab who hasn't been taught what to do. Just yelling at your Lab to sit or go lie down doesn't work. You must teach your Lab what behaviors are rewarding (the following sections can help). Make sure you do the required training so that you and your Lab have a wonderful life together.

Using Lure-and-Reward Training

Lure-and-reward training is Joel's method of choice for teaching a puppy or dog new requests. Any position or behavior that's easy to lure is easy to teach. You can take a look at Chapter 11 for examples of using this method for teaching the sit, stand, and down requests. You can use this same method to teach a dog to stand up on his hind legs, to roll over, or to bark. The main feature of lure-and-reward training is that you lure the behavior and then you reward it. After you're sure you can lure it, you request the behavior, the puppy/dog does it, and you praise and reward.

Rewarding with a Marker

Reward training with a marker is Joel's method of choice for teaching a puppy or dog new requests that aren't easily lured. (A *marker* is something that associates a sound with a treat.) The most popular form of marker training is *clicker training,* a training method that uses a little hand held device that clicks. In clicker training, you teach your puppy or dog that a click means he will get a food reward. When he does something you like, click and reward.

This is easily done by taking a hungry pup and clicking your clicker, then giving the pup a piece of food. After your pup looks for a piece of food when you click, you can then start grabbing any behavior the pup offers you and click and give a food reward for only that behavior. When he happens to raise his paw, click and treat. When he happens to roll over, click and treat. He'll soon figure out what to do again to get another click and another treat. After the pup is giving you this one behavior over and over again, you can give the behavior a name, request it, and click and reward.

If you don't want to use a clicker, you can use a verbal marker, such as a click of your tongue or a short word like "yes." The point is to associate a sound with the treat. Try using this method to teach your dog to raise a paw, scratch his nose, hide his eyes, or any behavior that he regularly performs and will be easy to click and reward.

Using Pure-Reward Training

Because Joel likes to spend lots of time with his Labs and doesn't want to be working too hard to get the dogs to do what he wants, he is currently doing a lot of pure-reward training. This is very simple and may be something you will find works well for you and your Lab.

Here's how *pure-reward training* works. Take your puppy/dog to a safe area where you can have him off lead and take a walk. Whenever your pup is beside you, reach in your pocket and give the pup a treat as you keep walking. Whenever the pup leaves your side and then returns, give the pup a treat. Your pup will spend more time walking at your side and will start checking in with you more often. Because this is so simple and enjoyable for you and your Lab, you should be able to do this on a routine basis. The result is a dog that finds it very rewarding to be near you but can do a few doggy things (sniffing, checking out something new, and so on), check in for a treat, and continue to do things that are rewarding for him. The only effort on your part is watching your dog and rewarding him when he comes back to you or when he takes a few steps with you.

Avoiding Behavioral Problems

A Lab pup has lots of normal behaviors that can turn out to be problems for you and your family. Pups, however, do what's rewarding for them.

(Some acts are rewarding whether the owner does anything or not. Urinating and defecating are self-rewarding behaviors; the pup feels better after he does them. The way to avoid these problems is to make sure the pup is in the right place at the right time. Chewing is another self-rewarding behavior for pups. Make sure the pup has the right object to chew.)

If your Lab is doing something you don't like, take a close look at what he's doing and what happens right after he does it. If he jumps up on you and you yell at him and he continues to jump up on you, you are somehow rewarding his jumping up. Probably just the fact that he gets your attention is reward enough, even if the attention isn't necessarily positive. Besides training him to sit in front of you instead of jumping up for attention, make sure that you don't react to his jumping up in any manner. Most problem behaviors that persist are somehow being rewarded by the owner, unless the behavior is self-rewarding!

Staying Positive

Sometimes, your Lab won't do what you want him to do. That is usually a sign that he really doesn't know what you want or that he finds something else more rewarding. Here's a way you can handle this in a positive manner: Gently get him under control, prevent him from doing anything that's more rewarding, and make a note to go back and train him some more. Keep him out of situations where he doesn't listen to you until he's better trained. For example, if meeting someone new is more important than coming back to you, set up a situation in which when he comes back to you he not only gets a treat but also gets to meet that new person!

If you get upset and start using a harsh tone of voice, most dogs will be less likely to obey you.

Not Expecting Perfection

Don't expect perfection, but do strive to train your Lab to be as reliable as possible. Remember that you're not perfect. If you do everything 100 percent correctly, you may expect your Lab to also. Improve yourself, improve your Lab.

Not Repeating Your Mistakes

If your Lab runs out the front door because the door didn't latch properly, that's a mistake and may not have been avoidable. If this happens again because you didn't fix the latch, you're setting yourself and your Lab up for a bad outcome. Your Lab will learn that he can go outside by just pushing on the door and he may get hit by a car.

Correct your mistakes at once. If you can't fix the latch right away, lock the door and then get the latch fixed.

Avoiding Physical Punishment!

Many dog trainers and canine behavior consultants having moved away from the old fashioned way of training a dog by praising the dog when he did it right and "correcting" the dog when he doesn't get it right by jerking on a choke collar. Sadly, some trainers have had difficulty giving up using aversive physical punishment. Some of them call themselves *balanced trainers,* with the idea that you have to balance the rewards with physical punishment to have a reliable pet dog. These trainers are probably not evil people who enjoy punishing dogs. Instead, they are trainers who were successful using physical punishment to subdue dogs so that they were easier to have as family pets.

Talented, humane trainers continue to move away from punishment training. Avoid those trainers who choose to continue to use aversive methods. Although aversive physical punishment may work on some dogs, there is always the danger of hurting your relationship and creating big problems, like fear and aggression. This book and the references in the Appendix will help you to train your Lab in a positive manner and stay out of the punishment trap.

Chapter 19

Ten Tips for Choosing the Right Trainer

*T*his chapter gives you ten easy ways to train your dog using professional training services.

Understanding the Different Types of Trainers

You can find several different types of pet dog trainers. Some are just starting out; others have lots of experience. Some trainers are good at teaching owners to train their puppy dogs to do the basic requests; other trainers specialize in problem solving. Most trainers don't deal with aggressive behavior, but some trainers specialize in special types of problem solving.

To decide which trainer is right for you, first list what type of training needs to be done. Want to teach simple requests (what we call "commands")? If you want to learn how to teach your puppy the normal requests that will help him be a good companion, consider a class taught by a lure-and-reward or clicker trainer. Are you looking more for problems with house-training, chewing, play-biting, and jumping up? If these are the major behaviors that need to be worked with, you may want to consider a private trainer who is experienced and successful in managing and altering these behaviors.

Considering puppy and dog classes

Puppy classes and dog classes are inexpensive ways to have a dog trainer help you to train your Lab. The benefit is that the trainer's time is being paid by a group of people. In addition, you and your puppy or dog get to work in a class around other puppies and dogs and other people. The disadvantage is that you don't have training tailored to your individual needs and schedule.

Getting private instruction in your home

Private instruction is nice way to have a dog trainer and/or canine behavior consultant work with you and your dog. The trainer interviews you to find out what your goals are and what behaviors need to be worked on. Then, during the training, your family and Lab are the total focus of the trainer. This option is, of course, more costly than large classes because your family has to pay for 100 percent of the trainer's time.

Sending your dog to boarding school

For busy people with resources, this is an appealing concept. Send your Lab off to boarding school and he will return a trained dog. Wouldn't that be great?

The problem is that dogs tend to work for and listen to only the person who trains them. The real job is training the dog owner, not the dog. So, the idea that you have lots of money and no time and you will be able to pay someone else to transform your puppy dog into the practically perfect Lab is not realistic.

Under special circumstances, however, you may want to consider this option. Joel once had a phone call from a school teacher who wanted to send her Great Dane to boarding school. The dog had injured her and was hard to manage because the dog was much bigger and stronger than she. Because the woman had an arm injury and was unable to work with her Dane, Joel took the dog for a couple of weeks and trained her, then followed up by going to the owner's home, after she had recovered from her injuries, and trained the owner to train the dog. If you already have a canine behavior consultant who has worked with you and your Lab, and you want the Lab to get some training while you go on a non-doggy vacation, having the dog's training continued while you're gone may be a good option.

Distinguishing Humane Trainers and Not-So-Humane Trainers

Some trainers go to seminars and classes and try to master the most effective and humane (non-violent) methods for training owners to train their dogs. They approach each new dog and client as a learning experience. Not only do they train the owner and the dog but they try to learn from them. They try to discover what works, what doesn't work, and what will be easiest for the dog and the owner. On the other hand, some trainers have been training dogs using more traditional (violent) methods for many years and have been successful and haven't found the need to learn anything new.

Asking the trainer what kind of equipment and tools you will need may give you the information you need to decide whether a trainer is humane or not-so-humane. If you're told that a training collar (choke collar), pinch collar, electric training collar (shock collar) or devices of this type are necessary, you can reach a valid conclusion that this trainer may be not-so-humane. If the trainer states that you will not have to use food, you're getting a big clue that the trainer won't be using the most powerful reward for most puppies and dogs.

If the trainer tries to tell you that he can train you and your Lab so he will be perfectly reliable and not disobey or make mistakes by being "balanced" and punishing mistakes and disobedience, be prepared to punish every error and mistake for the life of the dog! Your answer to a "balanced trainer" should be, "I prefer to be unbalanced. Lots of rewards for what's right and no rewards for what's wrong."

Asking Your Trainer to Explain His Methods

Good trainers can explain why they are recommending a certain course of action. If you don't understand why you're supposed to do something, ask the trainer!

Looking for Improvement Over Time

Good trainers make the best recommendations based on their experience and your observations of your dog. Some behaviors take awhile to change — play-biting is the best example. However, if you're following your trainer's recommendations and you don't see any improvement or if the behavior is getting worse, contact your trainer immediately and seek further guidance.

Letting Your Trainer Know When Something Isn't Working

Joel always makes sure that a client knows what she's supposed to be doing with her dog between appointments. He says that it make take a few days to see some improvement, but that if there is no improvement, call right away — don't wait for the next appointment or the next class. Most trainers assume everything is going as planned unless they hear from the client/student. If you go a week and then say "It didn't work," you've wasted a week during which you and your dog could have been making progress.

Getting a Referral from Your Trainer

Good trainers are open to referring you to other professionals for additional help or a second opinion. If your trainer suggests that you take your dog to the vet for a health check because it is possible that there may be a medical or physical reason for a behavior problem, do it! If your trainer suggests that you seek help from someone specializing in fearful or aggressive behavior, do that, too!

Remembering that You Are the Expert with Your Dog

Always remember that you are the expert with your dog. You live with him, whereas the trainer sees him only for an hour or so each week. Make sure you keep good records of what is happening and when (for example, house-training).

If the trainer suggests something that you don't think will work, speak up and explain your misgivings. The trainer may convince you that it is the right course of action or he may change his recommendation based on the added information you give.

Never do anything to your dog that doesn't seem fair or positive. Go with your gut feeling. If it doesn't seem right, don't do it.

Chapter 20

Ten Ways Your Lab Can Make a Difference in the World

- -

In This Chapter

▶ Looking at Labs that help the disabled and seeing how you can get involved

▶ Volunteering your Lab as a therapy dog

▶ Getting inspired by search-and-rescue and law-enforcement Labs

- -

*M*ore Labrador Retrievers serve as guide dogs than any other breed (between 60 and 70 percent of working guide dogs are Labs). Labs also serve as assistance dogs for the hearing-impaired and the physically disabled. Labs make wonderful therapy dogs, brightening the days of hospitalized children and nursing home residents alike. Lost in the mountains? Many Labs are adept at search and rescue, including specializations such as avalanche dogs. Labs are also great at sniffing out explosives and illegal drugs. What would we do without them?

The Americans with Disabilities Act (ADA) in the United States makes it illegal to deny access of a public place, including restaurants, to any disabled person with an assistance dog. Many business people are ignorant of this law and may try to prohibit a guide dog from entering their establishments. People with guide dogs or other service dogs should be aware of their rights and be prepared to educate those who may try to limit those rights.

Labs as Guide Dogs

Guide dogs become the eyes for their sight-impaired owners and must be particularly sensitive to their owners' movements and needs. The rigorous training for these dogs involves practice navigating a wide variety of obstacles, from stairs to busy streets to overhead obstacles that could injure the human half of the team. Guide dogs must also be well-disciplined and not easily distracted from the job.

Raising a guide dog

Many guide dog organizations are in need of volunteer puppy raisers. Puppy raisers are families or individuals who raise, socialize, and love potential guide dog puppies. They also teach basic obedience requests and expose the puppies to a variety of experiences to determine their tendencies. Many organizations work in conjunction with 4-H programs because puppies raised by kids are more likely to make it through guide dog training successfully. At about 12 to 18 months, the puppies enter formal guide dog training. Although puppy raiser and puppy must say good-bye, many keep in touch, and the puppy raiser knows he or she has provided an important service. If you're interested in becoming a volunteer puppy raiser, check out the Appendix for a list of guide-dog training organizations.

Many organizations train and provide guide dogs, and some even have their own breeding programs. And although German Shepherd dogs and Golden Retrievers are other popular choices, no dog is used as often as the Labrador Retriever.

The Lab temperament and intelligence make them ideal guide dogs. Labs are incredibly in tune to their human companions, large enough to direct them with authority, and tractable enough to learn the necessary requests and perform them with pleasure. Many people claim their Labrador Retriever guide dogs are more than guides: They are best friends, confidantes, and companions and are sometimes so in synch with their owners, especially after a few years together, that requests are often not even necessary.

Labs as Hearing Dogs

Labs are also perfectly suited as service dogs for the hearing-impaired and the physically disabled. *Hearing dogs* are trained to alert their owners to important sounds such as doorbells, ringing phones, smoke alarms, and crying babies. Labs aren't the only breed used as hearing dogs but are a great choice because they're friendly, helpful, and in tune with their owner's needs.

Labs as Assistance Dogs

Assistance dogs learn to help their physically disabled (and often wheelchair-bound) human companions to complete many daily tasks that allow for greater independence. Assistance dogs can pick up dropped objects such as eating utensils, remote controls, or keys. They can open and close doors and even help to propel a wheelchair either by pushing or pulling — see Figure 20-1. Many disabled people are able to live on their own because of the independence that their assistance dogs provide. These dogs also serve as companions, friends, and sources of moral support.

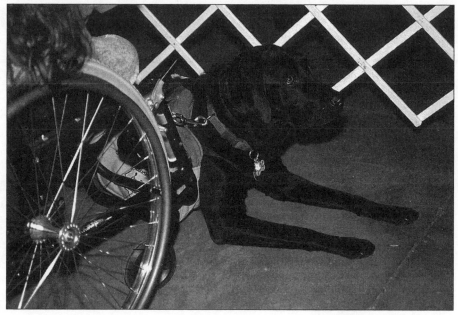

Figure 20-1:
Labs make faithful assistance dogs.

© Kent and Donna Dannen/AKC Stock Images

Although many breeds are used as assistance dogs, Labrador Retrievers are an ideal breed for this job. Their size and strength allow them to help their owners physically in ways a smaller dog couldn't. For example, Labs can reach door handles, help their owners back into a wheelchair, and retrieve relatively heavy objects such as books. These skills, coupled with their friendly faces, gentle natures, and intuition, make Labs one of the most popular choices for hearing and assistance dogs.

Labs as Therapy Dogs

Life in a nursing home can be lonely. Some studies estimate that well over half of nursing home residents never receive visitors. Some caring dog owners and their pets are working to put an end to the loneliness of nursing home residents, as well as hospitalized children, patients in psychiatric wards, and anyone else who is in some way institutionalized and could use a friendly, furry head to pat.

If you have a Labrador Retriever or are considering one, also consider volunteering with your Lab in a *therapy dog program*. Those friendly faces immediately put patients at ease, and although Labs are large, they are far

---

Does your Lab have what it takes?

Is your Lab right for therapy work? Certain characteristics make for more successful therapy dogs. If your Lab knows never to jump on people, is a confirmed "cuddler" who could bask in petting for as long as someone is willing, isn't intimidated by strangers or easily startled, and loves meeting new people, you probably have the perfect therapy dog.

---

less intimidating to many than other large breeds (especially yellow Labs — people can be intimidated by the darker colors).

Organizations such as the Delta Society and Therapy Dogs International have certification programs through which any dog who meets the requirements (which often include passing the AKC Canine Good Citizen Test [see Chapter 11] and/or other temperament tests) can earn the status as a certified therapy dog.

In rare cases, a therapy dog may accidentally injure a patient. One reason to have your therapy dog certified is that many certifying organizations provide therapy dog insurance. With such insurance, you can't be held liable if your dog does injure someone. Of course, this also means therapy dog organizations won't grant certification to a dog who doesn't pass their temperament tests, partially to minimize such an occurrence.

If your dog is suited for the work and passes the appropriate tests, you may find therapy work a great way to spend time with your pet while simultaneously doing a good deed for your fellow human beings. Many cities have organized groups of therapy dogs and their owners who plan trips to facilities. Or consider starting your own! Call, write, or e-mail one of the therapy dog organizations listed in the Appendix for information on how to get started. It may be the most rewarding thing you ever do with your dog.

Labs as Teachers

Think your Lab is smart as a whip? Why not let her be a teacher? Some people take their Labs around to schools and other youth programs to teach children about dogs, demonstrate how to handle dogs, give information on how to approach a strange dog, and educate kids about their furry friends. Because Labs love kids and are gentle, they make the perfect teaching assistants. Contact the American Kennel Club's public education department (Public Education Department, 5580 Centerview Drive, Raleigh, NC 27606-3390, fax: 919-854-0155, email: publiced@akc.org) for information about their many programs for promoting responsible dog ownership and dog safety. They'll even send you some great educational material for kids.

Labs as Search-and-Rescue Dogs

Some Labs that are too active or impatient to be good assistance or therapy dogs may make ideal search-and-rescue dogs. Athletic, well-trained dogs who thrive in the outdoors are perfect for search and rescue, and many people who live in areas such as mountainous regions or the desert (where people frequently become lost) train their dogs to learn this valuable skill. Many of these dogs are Labrador Retrievers. After all, they're great at retrieving game, so why shouldn't they also be great at retrieving a lost hiker?

Search-and-rescue dogs, also called *SAR dogs,* must meet certain standards, and so must their owners or handlers. Search-and-rescue teams must be able to survive on their own in the wild for several days at a time during any season of the year. They must know first aid for humans and dogs and know search-and-rescue procedures and other relevant skills, such as rock or mountain climbing and skiing. SAR dogs must be strong with an all-weather coat and must also be trainable, intelligent, and reliable. They are often sometimes skilled at a specialty, such as avalanche search, disaster search, water search, or evidence search (for instance, at a crime scene).

The easiest time to begin training a dog for search and rescue is in puppyhood, when a dog is more easily socialized and given a good basic training foundation. Older dogs sometimes have to unlearn behaviors. On the other hand, many older dogs have been successfully trained for search-and-rescue work, and you can be more sure of the health of an adult dog.

Many breeds of dogs are successful SAR dogs, but many of the characteristics of Labrador Retrievers make them just right:

- Labs have a double coat, with hair that's short enough to be low-maintenance but warm and water-repellent enough to keep the dog comfortable in any climate, weather, and temperature.

- Labs are big enough to move through difficult terrain and dense brush, but small enough to get into many smaller spaces. Also, Labs aren't too heavy to be lifted by their human companions if necessary (into a helicopter or from a steep ledge, for example).

- Labs were bred to survive, thrive, and navigate the wilderness rather than being bred primarily as lap dogs or herding dogs, for example.

- Labs are highly trainable and ready to learn, so they easily pick up the necessary skills.

- Labs are generally healthy and strong, making them less likely to require first aid themselves.

- Labs have a strong retrieve drive, making them naturals for finding anything.

If you think your Lab may be good at search and rescue, check with your local police department to see if your area has a search-and-rescue organization or search the Web. One site with lots of good information is Avalanche Dogs at www.drizzle.com/~danc/avalanche.html.

Labs with a Nose for the Law

Most people think of police and military dogs as German Shepherd dogs, but Labs are great at these jobs, too. All dogs have a keen sense of smell, and recognizing scents is a big part of retrieving. Dogs can be trained to detect any number of scents. Some work at state or federal borders, sniffing for anything illegal, from drugs to fruits and vegetables. Some work with fish and game departments to sniff out illegal fish catches. Some detect gas leaks, illegal drugs, and explosives. (Dogs have even been trained to detect skin and lung cancer cells by scent.)

Bomb Labs

Explosive- and arson-detection dogs help police or other authorities to find everything from land mines to evidence of arson in a burned-out building.

Drug Dogs

Drug-detection dogs can locate even very small amounts of well-concealed drugs. Many of these dogs are Labrador Retrievers, whose willingness to cooperate, intelligence, and trainability make them perfect for drug detection.

Plain Old Good Citizens

Even if your Lab does nothing more than behave like a good citizen, a good neighbor, and a friend to children, she'll be doing a great service to the community by promoting positive attitudes and experiences with canine friends. Consider her an ambassador of goodwill!

Retriever Resources

• •

*T*his appendix provides information on Lab clubs, sports organizations, discussions, and publications.

Labrador Retriever Clubs

You aren't the only one who loves Labs, which is why so many Labrador Retriever clubs exist — from local clubs to statewide clubs to the American Kennel Club-sanctioned Labrador Retriever Club, Inc.

Joining a Labrador Retriever club puts you in contact with other Lab owners, alerts you to Lab events, and provides you with a way to make a difference in the breed, from getting involved with rescue or fundraising for genetic research to participating in advanced showing, obedience, or other Lab activities.

Labrador Retriever Club, Inc.

Secretary: Christopher G. Wincek
2555 Som Center Rd.
Hunting Valley, OH 44022
Phone: 440-473-5255
E-mail: secretary@thelabradorclub.com
Web site: www.thelabradorclub.com/

Local Labrador Retriever clubs

www.thelabradorclub.com/lrclubs.htm

Labrador Retriever rescues

Labrador Retriever Club, Inc. Rescue Program
Phone: 512-259-3645
Fax: 512-259-5227
E-mail: appyland@texas.net
Web site: www.thelabradorclub.com/rescue.html#net

Canine Organizations

Lab clubs aren't the only dog organizations worth joining. Many other organizations exist for dog or pet owners in general, including organizations that emphasize obedience training, agility and other sports, and hunting.

The American Kennel Club
Public Education Department
5580 Centerview Dr.
Raleigh, NC 27606-3390
Fax: 919-854-0168
Web site: www.akc.org
E-mail: publiced@akc.org

Continental Kennel Club, Inc.
P.O. Box 908
Walker, LA 70785
Phone: 800-952-3376
Web site: www.ckcusa.com/
E-mail: ckc@ckcusa.com

The Kennel Club of Great Britain (KC) or (KCGB)
1–5 Clarges Street
Piccadilly
London W1Y 8AB
Phone: 171-493-6651
Web site: www.the-kennel-club.org.uk/
E-mail: info@the-kennel-club.org.uk

United Kennel Club, Inc.
100 East Kilgore Rd.
Kalamazoo, MI 49002-5584
Phone: 616-343-9020
Web site: www.ukcdogs.com/

Flyball contacts

Labs are great at flyball and they love it, too. If flyball is your Lab's passion, consider getting involved in a club.

British Flyball Association (BFA)
P. O. Box 263
Fareham, Hants PO16 0XB
United Kingdom
Phone: 44-1730-828269
E-mail: email@flyball.org.uk

North American Flyball Association, Inc. (NAFA)
1400 W. Devon Ave., #512
Chicago, IL 60660
Web site: www.flyball.org/

Canine Freestyle Federation

Gotta dance! If that refers to you and your Lab, consider getting serious about canine freestyle by joining a freestyle club.

www.canine-freestyle.org/index.html#Index

Canine Frisbee contacts

If your Lab is born to catch that flying disc, consider joining a Frisbee club.

International Disc Dog Handlers' Association (IDDHA)
1690 Julius Bridge Rd.
Ball Ground, GA 30107
Web site: www.iddha.com/
E-mail: IDDHA@aol.com

For regional clubs and competitions, check out the IDDHA Web site at www.iddha.com/clubs.htm.

Training

We love to see organizations that promote and facilitate positive training methods. If you and your Lab have found success through these methods (and who hasn't?), consider joining a training organization that helps educate people about the kindest and most effective way to train dogs.

American Dog Trainers Network: `www.inch.com/~dogs/`

Association of Pet Dog Trainers: `www.apdt.com/`

Clicker Trainers: `www.wazoo.com/~marge/Clicker_Trainers/Clicker_Trainers.html`

A Dog and Cat Behavior and Training Center by Perfect Paws: `www.perfectpaws.com`

Green Acres Training: `www.greenacreskennel.com/training.html`

Jean Donaldson's Dogs Behaving Badly! Homepage: `www.lasardogs.com`

Karen Pryor's Clicker Training Homepage: `http://dontshootthedog.com/`

Narnia Pet Behavior, Training, and Consulting: `http://users.aol.com/jemyers/narnia.htm`

Walton Family Dog Training LLC: `http://msnhomepages.talkcity.com/DeckDr/wfdt/WFDT.HTM`

On traveling

Where can you and your Lab stay on vacation? What kind of great, dog-friendly places can you go? Are there dog events that travelers may want to attend? Plenty of publications are ready with the answers.

DogGone Newsletter Online: `www.doggonefun.com/`

The Internet's largest pet travel resource: `www.petswelcome.com/`

Lab E-Mail Lists

For a complete listing of dog-related e-mail lists, check out www.k9web.com/ dog-faqs/lists/email-list.html#lab.

Labrador Retrievers

LABRADOR-L is the original mailing list started in 1994 for and about Labradors. Cindy Tittle Moore and Liza Lee Miller co-administrate the list. This is a high volume list.

To: listserv@iupui.edu
Subject: subscribe LABRADOR-L your-name

LABRADOR-H is a Hoflin list moderated by Jake Scott.

To: requests@h19.hoflin.com
Subject: subscribe LABRADOR-H

Training lists

The Aggressive Behaviors in Dogs list (www.egroups.com/group/agbeh) was established by Joel Walton in 1996. This e-mail community is about a serious subject and requires that you read the messages carefully. To subscribe: send a blank e-mail to agbeh-subscribe@egroups.com.

The Start Puppy Training list was established by Joel Walton 1996 and is for breeders, puppy trainers, veterinarians, and puppy owners to talk to one another about puppy training. Topics include: early puppy training by breeders, early puppy training by owners, puppy classes, normal puppy behavior including housetraining, puppy/play-biting, chewing, jumping up and not listening.

The Pre-Puppy Primer List is the e-mail list to join before you get a puppy or a dog. The Pre-Puppy Primer (at www.egroups.com/group/spt) is for breeders, puppy trainers, veterinarians and potential puppy owners to discuss the training required before you acquire a puppy or dog. Topics include: compatible type or breed, puppy socialization, early puppy training by breeders, puppy parties, early puppy training by owners, puppy classes and normal puppy behavior including housetraining, puppy/play-biting, chewing, jumping up and not listening. The Pre-Puppy Primer list is part of the SPT list. To subscribe, send a blank e-mail to spt-subscribe@egroups.com.

One mailing list is dedicated to finding positive solutions to training and behavior problems. Although clicker training is the main focus, non-clicker trainers are welcome. Take a look at www.egroups.com/group/ClickerSolutions to see why ClickerSolutions is considered one of the "Best on the Web." To subscribe: send a blank e-mail to ClickerSolutions-subscribe@egroups.com.

Lab Videos

We can heartily recommend the following video: *Sirius Puppy Training* by Ian Dunbar (New York: Bluford & Toth, 1987).

Labrador CD-ROMs

Jean Donaldson's Dogs Behaving Badly (Montreal: Lasar, 1998) is a fantastic CD-ROM experience.

Lab Magazines

We recommend the following dog magazines:

The Whole Dog Journal
P.O. Box 420234
Palm Coast, FL 32142
Phone: 800-829-9165
E-mail: wholedogjl@palmcoastd.com

Dog Fancy
Fancy Publications
P.O. Box 6050
Mission Viejo, CA 92690

Books about Labs

We're awfully glad you chose to read our book, but we're the first to admit that there are many other great books on Labs, dog training, and other Lab-relevant subjects. This section share a few that we like. (If you have trouble finding these titles, call Dogwise at 800-776-2665 or 509-663-9115. You can also check their Web site at http://dogwise.com or send an e-mail to mail@dogwise.com.)

On Labs

Churchill, Janet I. *The New Labrador Retriever.* New York: Howell, 1995.

Coode, Carole. *Labrador Retrievers Today.* New York: Howell, 1993.

Coykendall, Jr., Ralf W. *You and Your Retriever.* New York: Doubleday & Co., 1963.

Farrington, Selwyn Kip. *Labrador Retriever, Friend and Worker.* New York: Hastings House, 1976.

Hill, Warner F. *Labradors.* New York: Arco, 1966.

Martin, Nancy A. *The Versatile Labrador Retriever.* Wilsonville, OR: Doral, 1994.

Roslin-Williams, Mary. *Advanced Labrador Breeding.* London: H.F.&G. Witherby LTD: 1988.

Roslin-Williams, Mary. *All About the Labrador.* London: Pelham, 1985.

Warwick, Hellen. *The New Complete Labrador Retriever.* New York: Howell, 1986.

Weiss-Agresta, Lisa. *The Labrador Retriever: An Owner's Guide to a Happy Healthy Pet.* New York: Howell, 1995.

Wiles-Fone, Heather and Julia Barnes. *The Ultimate Labrador Retriever.* New York: Howell, 1997.

Wolters, Richard A. *The Labrador Retriever: The History — The People, Revisited.* New York: Dutton, 1992.

On training and behavior

Donaldson, Jean. *The Culture Clash.* Oakland, CA: James & Kenneth, 1995.

Donaldson, Jean. *Dog Are From Neptune.* Montreal: Lasar, 1998.

Dunbar, Ian. *Dog Behavior: An Owner's Guide to a Happy Healthy Pet.* New York: Howell, 1998.

Dunbar, Ian. *How to Teach a New Dog Old Tricks.* Oakland, CA: James & Kenneth, 1996.

Pryor, Karen. *Don't Shoot The Dog.* North Bend, OR: Sunshine Books, 1985.

Pryor, Karen. *On Behavior: Essays and Research.* North Bend, OR: Sunshine Books, 1995.

On health

Giffin, James M., MD, and Delbert G. Carlson, DVM. *Dog Owner's Home Veterinary Handbook.* New York: Howell, 1992.

Siegal, Mordecai (editor). *UC Davis Book of Dogs: The Complete Medical Reference Guide For Dogs and Puppies* by the Faculty and Staff, School of Veterinary Medicine, University of California at Davis. New York: Harper Collins, 1995.

On traveling

Check out Eileen Barish, author of *Vacationing With Your Pet!* (Scottsdale, AZ: Pet-Friendly Pub., 1994.)

General

American Kennel Club. *The Complete Dog Book*, 19th Edition, Revised. New York: Howell, 1998.

Index

Notes

Notes

Notes

FOR DUMMIES®

The easy way to get more done and have more fun

PERSONAL FINANCE & BUSINESS

Investing For Dummies
0-7645-2431-3

Home Buying For Dummies
0-7645-5331-3

Grant Writing For Dummies
0-7645-5307-0

Also available:

Accounting For Dummies
(0-7645-5314-3)

Business Plans Kit For Dummies
(0-7645-5365-8)

Managing For Dummies
(1-5688-4858-7)

Mutual Funds For Dummies
(0-7645-5329-1)

QuickBooks All-in-One Desk Reference For Dummies
(0-7645-1963-8)

Resumes For Dummies
(0-7645-5471-9)

Small Business Kit For Dummies
(0-7645-5093-4)

Starting an eBay Business For Dummies
(0-7645-1547-0)

Taxes For Dummies 2003
(0-7645-5475-1)

HOME, GARDEN, FOOD & WINE

Feng Shui For Dummies
0-7645-5295-3

Gardening For Dummies
0-7645-5130-2

Cooking For Dummies
0-7645-5250-3

Also available:

Bartending For Dummies
(0-7645-5051-9)

Christmas Cooking For Dummies
(0-7645-5407-7)

Cookies For Dummies
(0-7645-5390-9)

Diabetes Cookbook For Dummies
(0-7645-5230-9)

Grilling For Dummies
(0-7645-5076-4)

Home Maintenance For Dummies
(0-7645-5215-5)

Slow Cookers For Dummies
(0-7645-5240-6)

Wine For Dummies
(0-7645-5114-0)

FITNESS, SPORTS, HOBBIES & PETS

Fitness For Dummies
0-7645-5167-1

Golf For Dummies
0-7645-5146-9

Guitar For Dummies
0-7645-5106-X

Also available:

Cats For Dummies
(0-7645-5275-9)

Chess For Dummies
(0-7645-5003-9)

Dog Training For Dummies
(0-7645-5286-4)

Labrador Retrievers For Dummies
(0-7645-5281-3)

Martial Arts For Dummies
(0-7645-5358-5)

Piano For Dummies
(0-7645-5105-1)

Pilates For Dummies
(0-7645-5397-6)

Power Yoga For Dummies
(0-7645-5342-9)

Puppies For Dummies
(0-7645-5255-4)

Quilting For Dummies
(0-7645-5118-3)

Rock Guitar For Dummies
(0-7645-5356-9)

Weight Training For Dummies
(0-7645-5168-X)

Available wherever books are sold.
Go to www.dummies.com or call 1-877-762-2974 to order direct

FOR DUMMIES®

A world of resources to help you grow

TRAVEL

Italy
0-7645-5453-0

Hawaii
0-7645-5438-7

Walt Disney World & Orlando
0-7645-5444-1

EDUCATION & TEST PREPARATION

Spanish
0-7645-5194-9

Algebra
0-7645-5325-9

U.S. History
0-7645-5249-X

HEALTH, SELF-HELP & SPIRITUALITY

Diabetes
0-7645-5154-X

Sex
0-7645-5302-X

Parenting
0-7645-5418-2

FOR DUMMIES®

Plain-English solutions for everyday challenges

HOME & BUSINESS COMPUTER BASICS

0-7645-0838-5

0-7645-1663-9

0-7645-1548-9

Also available:

Excel 2002 All-in-One Desk Reference For Dummies (0-7645-1794-5)

Office XP 9-in-1 Desk Reference For Dummies (0-7645-0819-9)

PCs All-in-One Desk Reference For Dummies (0-7645-0791-5)

Troubleshooting Your PC For Dummies (0-7645-1669-8)

Upgrading & Fixing PCs For Dummies (0-7645-1665-5)

Windows XP For Dummies (0-7645-0893-8)

Windows XP For Dummies Quick Reference (0-7645-0897-0)

Word 2002 For Dummies (0-7645-0839-3)

INTERNET & DIGITAL MEDIA

0-7645-0894-6

0-7645-1642-6

0-7645-1664-7

Also available:

CD and DVD Recording For Dummies (0-7645-1627-2)

Digital Photography All-in-One Desk Reference For Dummies (0-7645-1800-3)

eBay For Dummies (0-7645-1642-6)

Genealogy Online For Dummies (0-7645-0807-5)

Internet All-in-One Desk Reference For Dummies (0-7645-1659-0)

Internet For Dummies Quick Reference (0-7645-1645-0)

Internet Privacy For Dummies (0-7645-0846-6)

Paint Shop Pro For Dummies (0-7645-2440-2)

Photo Retouching & Restoration For Dummies (0-7645-1662-0)

Photoshop Elements For Dummies (0-7645-1675-2)

Scanners For Dummies (0-7645-0783-4)

Get smart! Visit www.dummies.com

- **Find listings of even more Dummies titles**
- **Browse online articles, excerpts, and how-to's**
- **Sign up for daily or weekly e-mail tips**
- **Check out Dummies fitness videos and other products**
- **Order from our online bookstore**

Available wherever books are sold. Go to www.dummies.com or call 1-877-762-2974 to order direct

FOR DUMMIES®

Helping you expand your horizons and realize your potential

GRAPHICS & WEB SITE DEVELOPMENT

0-7645-1651-5

0-7645-1643-4

0-7645-0895-4

Also available:

Adobe Acrobat 5 PDF
For Dummies
(0-7645-1652-3)
ASP.NET For Dummies
(0-7645-0866-0)
ColdFusion MX for Dummies
(0-7645-1672-8)
Dreamweaver MX For
Dummies
(0-7645-1630-2)
FrontPage 2002 For Dummies
(0-7645-0821-0)

HTML 4 For Dummies
(0-7645-0723-0)
Illustrator 10 For Dummies
(0-7645-3636-2)
PowerPoint 2002 For
Dummies
(0-7645-0817-2)
Web Design For Dummies
(0-7645-0823-7)

PROGRAMMING & DATABASES

0-7645-0746-X

0-7645-1626-4

0-7645-1657-4

Also available:

Access 2002 For Dummies
(0-7645-0818-0)
Beginning Programming
For Dummies
(0-7645-0835-0)
Crystal Reports 9 For
Dummies
(0-7645-1641-8)
Java & XML For Dummies
(0-7645-1658-2)
Java 2 For Dummies
(0-7645-0765-6)

JavaScript For Dummies
(0-7645-0633-1)
Oracle9i For Dummies
(0-7645-0880-6)
Perl For Dummies
(0-7645-0776-1)
PHP and MySQL For
Dummies
(0-7645-1650-7)
SQL For Dummies
(0-7645-0737-0)
Visual Basic .NET For
Dummies
(0-7645-0867-9)

LINUX, NETWORKING & CERTIFICATION

0-7645-1545-4

0-7645-1760-0

0-7645-0772-9

Also available:

A+ Certification For Dummies
(0-7645-0812-1)
CCNP All-in-One Certification
For Dummies
(0-7645-1648-5)
Cisco Networking For
Dummies
(0-7645-1668-X)
CISSP For Dummies
(0-7645-1670-1)
CIW Foundations For
Dummies
(0-7645-1635-3)

Firewalls For Dummies
(0-7645-0884-9)
Home Networking For
Dummies
(0-7645-0857-1)
Red Hat Linux All-in-One
Desk Reference For Dummies
(0-7645-2442-9)
UNIX For Dummies
(0-7645-0419-3)

Available wherever books are sold.
Go to www.dummies.com or call 1-877-762-2974 to order direct